Renovating Value

Robert Goldman

Renovating Value

HGTV and the Spectacle of Gentrification

TEMPLE UNIVERSITY PRESS
Philadelphia • Rome • Tokyo

TEMPLE UNIVERSITY PRESS
Philadelphia, Pennsylvania 19122
tupress.temple.edu

Copyright © 2021 by Temple University—Of The Commonwealth System
    of Higher Education
All rights reserved
Published 2021

Library of Congress Cataloging-in-Publication Data

Names: Goldman, Robert, 1949– author.
Title: Renovating value : HGTV and the spectacle of gentrification / Robert Goldman.
Description: Philadelphia : Temple University Press, 2021. | Includes bibliographical
    references and index. | Summary: "HGTV programming poses home renovation as an
    isolated investment, where work and aesthetic taste elevate a housing property. In fact,
    there is a broader world of finance and social meanings that combine in processes of
    gentrification to build a house's value, including history, banking, place, and culture"—
    Provided by publisher.
Identifiers: LCCN 2020045767 (print) | LCCN 2020045768 (ebook) | ISBN 9781439920480
    (cloth) | ISBN 9781439920497 (paperback) | ISBN 9781439920503 (pdf)
Subjects: LCSH: Home & Garden Television. | Gentrification—Social aspects. |
    Gentrification—Economic aspects. | Flipping (Real estate investment)—Social aspects. |
    Flipping (Real estate investment)—Economic aspects. | Dwellings—Maintenance and
    repair—Social aspects. | Dwellings—Maintenance and repair—Economic aspects. |
    Real property—Social aspects. | Real property—Economic aspects.
Classification: LCC HT170 .G65 2021 (print) | LCC HT170 (ebook) | DDC 307.3/416—dc23
LC record available at https://lccn.loc.gov/2020045767
LC ebook record available at https://lccn.loc.gov/2020045768

9 8 7 6 5 4 3 2 1

This book is dedicated to

the principle of housing as a human right.

Contents

	Preface	ix
	Acknowledgments	xiii
	Introduction: Once upon a Time in a Salvage Economy	1
1	A Primer on Value in the Age of HGTV	20
2	Renovation Narratives	40
3	A Moment in the Life of Capital	60
4	Gentrification TV	81
5	Creative Erasure	104
6	A Promised Land of Instant Equity	118
7	HGTV's Value Theories of Labor	137
8	Masking the New Rules of Value	162
	Epilogue: Must-Haves—Four Walls and a Roof	178
	Notes	181
	Bibliography	205
	Index	223

Preface

I finished writing this manuscript on March 1, 2020, just days before the COVID-19 pandemic collided with a wholly unprepared United States. When stay-at-home orders were first issued, the economy and the stock market tanked. I worried that I'd written about the narrative search for value in housing markets during the decade following the 2007–2008 financial crisis just in time for it to be overshadowed by the COVID-19 financial crisis. It seemed that the severity of the 2020 pandemic economic crisis might eclipse the trauma inflicted on housing markets by the 2008 crisis and push my story about the financial crisis and the cultural narratives of restoring order to the world of value to the wayside of history, buried and perhaps forgotten.

But over the ensuing weeks and months, it has become apparent that understanding the 2008 financial crisis and its relationship to housing is far from irrelevant to the crisis that is now unfolding. Perversely, you might even think of the new crisis as a gift from the heavens if you were betting on the home renovation industry to continue outperforming. Indeed, this book shows that a crisis is an excellent opportunity to tell the kind of story about value that HGTV has perfected, even as a more cynical story plays out in housing markets. Foreclosure filings for 2019 showed a decline from a peak of 2.23 percent of total residential units in 2010 to a low of 0.36 percent.[1] Since foreclosures had been the grist that drove the home renovation mill, profits from flipping had begun to slip. However, with the precipitous shock of COVID-19 on unemployment rates, not even a momentary reprieve of mortgage forbearance will be enough to stem new spikes in foreclosure rates, and it's all but impossible to imagine the severity of the housing crisis that will accompany a potential tidal wave of rent evictions when eviction moratoriums expire. By April 2020, Opendoor and Zillow were announcing decisions to resume their technology-driven programs to gain share of the flipping market, recognizing that pent-up demand among millennials for home ownership could make this a very profitable time to restart the engines of corporate flipping. A few weeks later, JPMorgan announced a capital partnership with corporate landlord American Homes 4 Rent to expand its share of the single-family homes-for-rent empires that have been forming since 2012. Billionaires like the head of American Homes 4 Rent recognize that moments of crisis are moments of opportunity that permit private accumulations of capital like his to grab ever larger shares of single-family residences on the cheap. Meanwhile, the severity of unemployment and the accumulation of deferred debt payments basically guarantee that millions of families will never be anything but renters for life. During these major financial crises—the mortgage crisis of 2008 and now the pandemic crisis of 2020—lines of credit and cash rule; when this reality is combined with the disenfranchisement imposed by the insecurity of livelihoods, we will likely see further consolidation of wealth and control over housing stocks as a result of the pandemic crisis.

While the COVID-19 financial crisis has reinforced the effects of structural racism and a widening wealth gap on housing markets, it has also resulted in an array of unanticipated effects that are restructuring real estate markets. Unlike their counterparts in exposed manufacturing and service jobs, office workers have been able to pivot to working remotely from home. As it quickly turned into the new normal, the future of work-from-home positions motivated a move away from overpriced urban areas to suburban and even exurban areas, where home prices have been less elevated, until now. The rush to find more affordable housing in the low-inventory housing markets has driven a feverish residential real estate market with low mortgage rates offsetting, but also propelling, escalating home prices. This interest rate–price spiral has further aggravated a crisis of affordability that has been brewing since the Great Recession. Suburbia beckons because prices seem less unaffordable, and bigger houses with more square feet better accommodate the COVID-19 stay-at-home lifestyle that combines the activities of work at home and domesticity while also promising a measure of domestic peace.

During the first six months of the pandemic, over 36 million unemployment claims were filed. The extreme hardships and vulnerabilities thus imposed on households because of layoffs will likely be compounded by long-term degradation to labor markets. Many jobs just won't be coming back.

When households cannot make their mortgage payments, they risk default; when tenants can't make their rent payments, they risk eviction. And the consequences flow up the financial food chain. Especially vulnerable are small mom-and-pop landlords who are themselves susceptible to default and foreclosure when renters can't pay. But forbearance also puts pressure on the leveraged debt that lies behind the mortgage-backed securities, the rent-backed securities, and the collateralized loan obligations that have grown immensely since 2008. For stakeholders in the lending and structured finance markets, it became immediately apparent that an extended period of suspended rents and mortgage payments has the potential to convulse a financial system of securitized housing investments predicated on the ideal of uninterrupted monthly flow of rents. To ensure investor confidence, the Federal Reserve pushed interest rates as low as possible. Under the CARES Act (the first stimulus package), the Federal Reserve and the Treasury Department poured several trillion dollars into backstopping financial markets, ensuring liquidity and purchasing even high-risk corporate debt to minimize the financial jeopardy that would spill out across markets if the $10 trillion high-risk corporate bond market unraveled. It seems that every financial crisis now drives us deeper into a vortex of dependencies on a financialization system that favors the few and intensifies wealth gaps. The 2008 financial crisis created a road map for maneuvering through future crises by relying on government to inject massive liquidity into markets to guarantee the stability of capital. As with the 2008 crisis, this subsidy approach to managing crises shifts the costs of capital risk to the general public while leaving those in the bottom half of the economy still scrambling to make the rent. The COVID-19 crisis offers a stark reminder that the current system of financialization, built as it is on making debt-leveraged bets about the future, is a risky contract, and as the pandemic demonstrates, there are some catalysts of risk that cannot be anticipated or predicted. In a system built on risk, crisis becomes the new normal.

Meanwhile, even though HGTV halted the production of new shows because of COVID-19's unsafe conditions, its reruns ratings have purred along, as have its advertising revenues. During a pandemic, with viewers confined, who doesn't want some comfort food? For millions trapped at home with kids, kin, or roommates or all alone, doomscrolling through the daily news stream of compound crises (the pandemic health care crises, unemployment, rent crises, racial injustice, the absence of affordable housing, climate change, and so on), HGTV's stories about finding value in home renovations remain compelling as a comforting distraction and a nostalgic fantasy about a form of value that has grown increasingly inaccessible to most.

Acknowledgments

I was late to discover HGTV. I do not follow reality TV, but during the summer of 2014, I happened on the HGTV and DIY channels, binged for several days, and immediately felt that I had found the vehicle I had been seeking for a study that would focus on efforts to culturally salvage the category of value in the years following the 2008 financial crisis. I wrote the first draft of this study that summer. Over the next few years, whenever I had the time, I returned to watching and taking notes. In 2017, thanks to Lewis and Clark College, I had a semester in Italy, which left me time to read about value. I wandered the streets of Siena, notebook in hand, and wrote a second version of this book. I asked Chris Wilkes if he would read it. His encouraging critique proved crucial to keeping me on task. I quit watching HGTV in 2018 and over the next year finished drafting the manuscript. My research into the political economy of flipping made me aware of how difficult it was to find reliable data that were not proprietary, and so I called on Ralph McLaughlin of CoreLogic for assistance. Ralph is the most knowledgeable person I know on the subject of flipping as a subset of real estate markets. Not only did he take the time to speak at length with me about my many questions, but he generously shared with me one of his data sets. I have no doubt that he and I interpret this market differently, but I have not encountered anyone who is more committed to advancing the conversation around these issues. After reading with a keen eye my draft on the political economy of flipping, Kate Smock raised important questions about the differential use of LLCs by individual and corporate investors, which led me to reinterpret anomalies in the data that changed my argument. Michelle Buckley's studies of home renovation labor markets prompted me to contact her. Our ensuing conversation and her substantial critiques of the labor chapter deepened my assessment of the politics of renovation labor. Ryan Mulligan, my editor at Temple University Press, consistently prodded me with deceptively simple queries that compelled me to sharpen my narrative and led me to reexamine questions that I thought I had already closed the book on.

My friend and colleague Bryan Sebok and I have spent countless hours conversing about HGTV as television, as semiotics, and as political economy. Bryan's wide-ranging spirit of inquiry, coupled with his extraordinary familiarity with my trifecta of home renovation, HGTV, and critical theory, has made him an ideal interlocutor for me on this project. Thanks go to Noah Kersey for his practical insights into the semiotics of fonts and what they mean in the world of TV home renovations. As always, Liz Safran's unwavering friendship steadies me. My most enduring thanks go to Johanna Ogden. She has listened and listened and listened, even when she did not really want to, while I went off on one tangent after another about my project. Every new twist, every new discovery, all of it—I couldn't help myself—I ran by her. I am even more indebted to her as a critic for so politely pointing out to me when I am full of crap and when I am not—it is important to know the difference. I am grateful beyond measure for her intellect, humor, love, and support. I dedicate this book to Jo, Emma, and Crash.

Renovating Value

Introduction

Once upon a Time in a Salvage Economy

The "hard law of value," the "law set in stone"—when it abandons us, what sadness, what panic!
—Jean Baudrillard, *Simulacra and Simulation*

In the fall of 2008, the global system of capitalist finance imploded, dragging ten million American households into a nightmare of vulnerability, mortgage default, and foreclosure. Instead of having faith in the promised land of secure home equity, an investment that had been advertised as a perpetual value machine, people felt a mood of uncertainty that clouded hopes of ever again acquiring a source of value that would translate into wealth and stability. This empire-shaking event in the world of valuations prompted a broad social and economic mood of precarity that has since come to inform a politics of protectionist anxiety and fear. But this same crisis has been translated quite differently when filtered through the lens of commodity culture, particularly through the narrative formula of HGTV's popular home renovation programs.

HGTV is the preeminent lifestyle network on television, home to a significant modern fairy tale. It features stories about people who revitalize modern spaces and reinvent property values. A piece of the culture industry often identified with the burgeoning realm of reality TV, HGTV envisions a path for viewers to follow and learn how to find and extract new value from housing properties. Renovation enthusiasts binge-watch these shows. For many it's a guilty pleasure; for others it's insistently seductive: it's easy to become absorbed in this game of adding value to houses. In this, the spectacle of home renovation, the rules of narration and fast-paced video editing crop out the world of relationships that shape and surround our residential lives. HGTV house-flipping programs adhere to a strict formula made familiar by its flagship shows—*Fixer Upper*, *Property Brothers*, and *Flip or Flop*—which invariably accomplish a semiotic transformation from the visually profane (defined by gritty photography that depicts blemished housing) to the visually sacred (defined by fetish photography that epitomizes a promised land of immaculate value). HGTV tracks this visual conversion of interior spaces to the exclusion of housing inequality, real estate and mortgage markets, gentrification, displacement, and dispossession. All of this and more disappears from our screen. What's left is a decorated color palette (if you envision beige and gray) that speaks to emotionally gratifying narratives of familial well-being when you have (and own) the house you love to call home.

Though HGTV already had its foot in the door with programming about house flipping and interior design in the years leading up to the crisis, afterward HGTV ramped up its offerings of flip and renovation shows stamped with an almost hyperbolic reliance on the concepts of value and value added. In fact, following the crisis, the subject of value made its way with intensified frequency into the conversations organized by the channels of commodity culture. Throughout the media, the subject of value keeps cropping up—where to find it; how to recognize it; how to capture and harness it; and how to calculate, measure, and assess it. But nowhere has the conversation about seeking added value been more evident than home renovation TV.[1] Spurred by profitable ratings, the HGTV genre has reproduced exponentially in the decade since the crisis.[2]

Meanwhile, amid flatlining wages, job losses, and a trend toward a part-time gig economy characterized by flexible and uncertain conditions of employment, many found themselves searching for alternative and supplementary sources of income. At the turn of the new millennium, the spigots of credit opened wide in conjunction with a red-hot housing market, and the allure of house flipping as a way to turn a quick buck proved irresistible to many.[3] Many more took advantage of cheap credit to turn second mortgages into an alternative way of funding consumption wants and needs. HGTV quickly capitalized on the flipping mania, turning stories of house flipping into a master narrative about getting ahead in America during an era of otherwise uneasy economic prospects. By 2009, faith in the fairness of the market had further dimmed, as had faith in the conventional tools and strategies for getting ahead, especially among those who had lost jobs and homes. If HGTV could bring itself to use the word "capitalism" (it cannot), it might describe its programming thusly: We have reached a stage of capitalist development in which the best strategies for locating and capturing new value lie in finding dated and tarnished castoffs from past eras of modernity that are undervalued in the current market. By using a little imagination, a bit of elbow grease, and aesthetic know-how, you can turn your found relics into desirable gems, thus restoring the luster of your portfolio and the magic of consumer capitalism.

But why dwell on the seemingly trivial matters of home renovation TV at a time when all around us is going to hell in a Trump basket? I suggest that the apparently insignificant stories of quirky young couples trying to renovate shabby properties into the keystone of the life they'd always imagined (the television discourse of HGTV) are actually addressing, in an attractively fetishized and ostensibly depoliticized way, the underlying anxieties that have motivated the less racist wings of Trump support: those desperate to regain their footing in a value universe, those who have lost their jobs, those who have lost their guarantee of comfort, those who sense that their skills are no longer meaningful in a world of precarious immaterial labor, those who have lost their mortgages, and those who have lost their homes. Even for millennials who may not have voted for Donald Trump, the discourse of barely masked gentrification displayed by HGTV speaks to questions of diminished resources with which to recreate and sustain the good life their parents had but which is ebbing away for the greater number of their generation.

At a system level, 2007–2008 marked a crisis of capital's ability to reproduce itself. At the household level, this was experienced as a crisis of value. The financial crisis and the Great Recession that ensued cemented the end of an economic era already in disarray. While the feeling of crisis may have been acute, the structural backdrop of a systemic crisis of value had been building for decades. The conjoint mortgage and credit default crises simply put a punctuation mark on it. The formation of neoliberal globalization in the late 1980s presents a convenient jumping off point because it's so easy to spot the growing income and wealth gaps that have steadily left a majority of the population with household incomes that lag behind the cost of living. But the story of how the value produced by the capitalist system is distributed and shared begins in the postwar era of the 1950s and the 1960s—precisely the era that HGTV nostalgically imagines being restored in its revered midcentury modern look. In that era characterized by U.S. global business dominance and rising union power, there was roughly a one-to-one correlation between productivity gains and wage gains. By contrast, after the 1980s, in an era marked by declining union power, industrial downsizing, technological automation, and global outsourcing of labor, the correlation between productivity growth and wage growth dipped to one-sixth of what it had been in earlier decades.[4] Relentless technological innovations may have promised increased efficiency and productivity, along with the ability to be more price competitive in the world of commodities, but to working people technological automation meant job loss or deskilling and a paycheck that either shrank or languished. Compounding this, with the ascent of neoliberal politics, there occurred a transfer of benefit costs from the government and the employer to the household. The results were predictable. By the early 2000s, to sustain commodity consumption alongside flat incomes and increased costs for education, day care, and health insurance, negative savings rates became the norm for households. Not surprisingly, total household debt—including mortgage debt, credit card debt, student debt, health care debt, and auto debt—escalated year after year. The mortgage market meltdown and credit default crisis illustrated precisely the vulnerability of that debt when it became the object of high-risk investing.

HGTV is not an innocent observer in the circuitry of consumer credit and debt. A part of a culture industry geared toward continuously reproducing consumer spending, and hence household debt, HGTV is a tributary that feeds a still larger river of debt. Household debt has not diminished, but grown, in the decade since the 2008 crisis. By the third quarter of 2019, total household debt reached an all-time record of $13.95 trillion, $1.3 trillion higher than the peak that marked 2008.[5] Growth and expansion of the U.S. economy requires ever-mounting debt from a population that does not necessarily have the requisite means to afford the price tag of value anymore.

It would be easy to dismiss HGTV as nothing more than escapist fare. True, it is that and has been since its inception. It may offer a space that feels insulated and safe from a world about us that is bewildering and full of peril, but it is more than just entertainment. HGTV renarrates the financial crisis through the discourse and the lens of commodity fetishism, seeking to renormalize the world of value and valuations. In the aftermath of the so-called subprime mortgage market collapse, HGTV's dreamworld of home renovation projected an ideology of hearth and value that speaks to desires to regain a secure place to call home in a neoliberal society. It affirmed the rewards of creativity and risk taking in the new economy. HGTV reconciled the speculative abstractions of value that have characterized our financial system in recent history with the emotional warmth that activates subjective valuation at the level of home and family. It encouraged viewers to hold on to the possibility of realizing their visions of a home life achieved by refining aesthetic judgments like those seen on-screen, thus hoping to seize control of the value of their own properties, real or imagined.

HGTV locates questions about finding value in the master commodity in our lives—the home—a commodity that differs from other commodities because real estate property supposedly appreciates rather than depreciates in value over time. And yet homes did dramatically depreciate in value by 39 percent between late 2007 and the end of 2009.[6] The house makes for an even more contradictory commodity than usual; on the one hand, it comes swathed in cultural and emotional meanings about our primary sites for intimacy and personal meaning making. On the other hand, it also brims with financial anxieties and the precarity of debt obligations. The question of financial gain or loss is a recurring dramatic frame in the stories on HGTV. Will the costs of renovation stay within budget? Miraculously, they always do. Home renovation TV narratives—salvaging, flipping, restoring, repurposing, upcycling, reinventing—capture a cluster of significant cultural aspirations and ambitions of our historical moment. Home renovation TV imagines an entrepreneurial moral economy—enacted as an ethics rather than as a political economy—that optimizes the best interests of consumers and investors in the figure of the same person, you.[7]

In the fall of 2018, journalists seized on the decennial anniversary of the 2008 crisis to revisit what really happened in 2008, to recount the severity of the crisis and the steps taken to counter its effects. My retelling is not about the event itself or about the behind-the-scenes machinations that rescued the big banks. I am interested in a different type of rescue, the ideological rescue of value amid the extinction of affordable housing and the perpetuation of systemic housing inequalities. The focus of my retelling is about a material crisis of value that has left its mark as a crisis of faith about the future of value in America. Anna Tsing recently observed that "precarity once seemed the fate of the less fortunate. Now it seems that all our lives are precarious."[8] On HGTV, we can binge-watch efforts to culturally salvage and distance the neoliberal model from the precarity of financialized capital and its appetite for perpetual indebtedness by recasting the fixer-upper model as a comforting path for the many (not just the few) to thrive in the risk economy.

Remoralizing Value

When a twenty-first-century risk economy rapidly took shape, based on an increasingly common financial practice to leverage risk and hedge it in every possible direction, neither the fiduciary trust nor the morality seemed immediately coherent to observers. Even Ben Bernanke, then the Federal Reserve chair, expressed bewilderment about the "inscrutability" of the financial derivatives and mortgage securities that flooded the market, acknowledging that they were impenetrable to investors, much less to the lay public: "I'd like to know what those damn things are worth."[9] Following the mortgage market meltdown of 2008, pundits lamented the destruction and disappearance of value. Reporters pointed to the eclipse of real value, supplanted by fictitious and virtual capital that apparently defied the banks' accounting practices. Everyone agreed that the economy had been supercharged, running on the fumes of speculative finance. The exposure of the arcane machinations of derivatives, mortgage-backed securities (MBSs), asset-backed securities (ABSs), credit default swaps (CDSs), and collateralized debt obligations (CDOs) all pointed toward the unnerving public conclusion that value had become value-out-of-whack, unmoored from the conditions of the real, from the everyday, and had thus dematerialized and become subject to dizzying sleights of hand. The flip side of this haze of hyperreal financial speculation was the erosion of a long-standing cultural conviction of a bygone capitalist era—that real value gets made materially on farms and in factories, by disciplined people who work hard and with purpose. The moral axis of value seemed to have been flipped around in a world in which the basis of value seemed to hinge less on labor than on the ability to manipulate abstractions, or rather the abstractions of abstractions that operate according to the codes of mathematicized algorithms. And if value could not be counted on materially to stay put, or get measured, then what could we rely on? It all seemed an anomic puzzle.

When regimes of value rapidly morph from one stage of capitalism to the next, so do the rules governing value, about what appropriate economic strategies work best under that system of rules, and about who has a right to share in the rewards of value seeking. But if the rules—and their legibility—aren't clear, there's a problem. Not only were the new rules governing value less immediately identifiable; by contrast to the nostalgia for a prior set of rules, they were variously labeled anarchic, speculative, and fictitious. The crisis of 2008 represented a pretty obvious crack in the neoliberal system of finance capital. While professional investors with access to cash dove in, consumer investors who simply aspired to a house or a nest egg were without a map but were still emotionally invested in a story that seemed to be disintegrating. For them, HGTV crafted a salvation-of-value narrative in response to a legitimation crisis that vibrated around a perceived crisis of value. Whether HGTV producers thought explicitly in terms of legitimation crisis I cannot say. What I can say with certitude is that they were sensitive to the erosion of their viewing audience along with the erosion of housing markets because their bread and butter depended on restoring the luster of home ownership as a vehicle for wealth appreciation.

During the recession that followed 2008, HGTV began expanding its catalog of repetitive programming that spoke to the anomic void that surrounded the crisis of value. Inside the world of HGTV, value could be made tangible, and the rules for finding, measuring, and capturing it were visually reiterated every week. HGTV programming can be read as a series of stories that remoralize and legitimate the political economy of value. Overlaying the recapture of economic value with the emotional satisfaction of the freedom of intimate spaces struck a popular chord. In what follows, I contrast HGTV's narrative of salvaging value to the emergent political economic practices that became the drivers of value production in financial and real estate markets in the decade following the 2008 mortgage crisis.

HGTV actually tells several kinds of stories that hail overlapping audiences. Renovation tales entice consumers who fantasize about customizable yet affordable dream homes that symbolically resurrect the nest-egg imagery of wealth building. Renovation-to-flip shows beckon wannabe flippers with notions of capturing inflated profits by investing in houses. Both of these story types address another audience of already existing homeowners who imagine adding value to their houses by remodeling. This audience is the most profitable for HGTV's advertisers. And a final audience comprises those who don't have the means to do a remodel or a flip, or who don't own a home (perhaps they once did), but can consume the desire. Each of these stories presumes that we have entered a stage of neoliberalism that we may call salvage consumer capitalism, in which value can be sought by making old objects pretty again, or by recombining scraps (via bricolage) that have lost their significance.

This cultural genre devoted to finding and extracting new veins of value in homes carefully sidesteps the web of relations surrounding the mortgage market collapse that imperiled the valuations of so many homes just a few years prior. Millions of foreclosures were still occurring, yet the coordinates of race, class, mortgage markets, and financial institutions never make an appearance on HGTV. Given the particular moment in history, with financial institutions looking outside the framework of labor to devise alternative ways of extracting value from labor, not from labor's productivity, but laser-focused on labor's obligations to pay off its household debts, HGTV's narratives of value sidestep the fundamental contradiction of contemporary housing: the 2008 crisis centered on the consequences of financializing homeowners and their housing, making home ownership vulnerable to default and foreclosure, and making "the 'debt question' . . . the central dilemma of economic citizenship in the United States."[10]

It was no accident that HGTV became fixated on the restoration of economic value following the housing crisis, and it's particularly noteworthy that a key element in its stories about accessing the rebirth of property value is rooted in a heroization of labor—not just any kind of labor but the labor of independent producers who work for themselves. In the wake of a devastating economic crisis driven by the excesses of nonhuman algorithmic models, the HGTV narrative returned to a mythological trope about what made America great. Repurposing nineteenth-century ideologies of free labor, HGTV imagines entrepreneurs as craftsmen independent of capital, free from the will of bosses and the forces of monopoly money.[11] Unlike its nineteenth-century referent, HGTV's entrepreneurial labor can be female as well as male, black as well as white, gay as well as hetero. Willing to take risks, the entrepreneurial labor that takes center stage on HGTV is capable of reaping the value it imagines and produces. By contrast, wage earners, though perhaps necessary ingredients to the realization of value, can expect less in return because they are less worthy as nameless cogs, and not the authors, of the value-producing visions and plans. These allusions to a resurrected nineteenth-century morality of free or independent labor are culturally mirrored in HGTV's favored rustic chic aesthetic—farmhouse modern—that harkens back to farmhouse styles modified by forward-looking modern lines. It taps into a mythology of American populism that nostalgically embraces a hand-built American aesthetic that conjures up an imagery of individual opportunity and economic sanctuary, stick-built from the ground up. Kate Wagner has pointed out that the aesthetic styles of farmhouse modern and industrial chic respectively connote "the idea of labor as a means to living: one embraces the simplicity of rural life, and the other of machine-age optimism" that in the rearview mirror signifies a time of relative prosperity.[12]

Neoliberal Gentrification and the Romance of Creative Labor

Julie Guthman remarks, "In keeping with the idolatry of the market, neoliberal governmentality encourages subjects to make few demands on the state, but rather to act through markets, or like the market, by exercising consumer choice, being entrepreneurial and self-interested, and striving for self-actualization and fulfillment."[13] I am not the first to suggest that HGTV endorses a neoliberal solution to a neoliberal paradigm in crisis.[14] As an expression of neoliberal thinking, HGTV visualizes how individual subjects can choose their dream homes in a social world in which government stays out of sight and personal responsibility for fulfilling housing wants (as opposed to housing needs) lies with individual families. Conversely, HGTV excludes questions of homelessness because the neoliberal worldview frames homelessness as a failure of personal responsibility in the marketplace. According to the HGTV playbook, renovating and flipping houses demonstrates entrepreneurial spunk amid the reverberations of the financial crisis. HGTV's optimistic success stories teach the importance of discipline and vision coupled with old-school shop skills to transform undervalued properties into revitalized pockets of value.

A transition to neoliberal urbanism that began in the 1970s has now become the dominant paradigm governing urban housing policy and development. David Harvey pointed to such a transition when he described a shift "from managerialism to entrepreneurialism" in the mode of urban governance by the late 1980s.[15] A decade later, the transition was sufficiently complete that it had become impossible to disentangle neoliberal urbanism from one of its chief projects—the widespread generalization of gentrification.[16] Within a climate of market deregulation and ebbing enforcement of governmental mandates, decisions about housing now follow the speculative logic of capital investments. Still, the neoliberal dominion of competitive market forces depends on supportive politicians and government programs that steer resources to induce real estate speculators to undertake the risks of building and rebuilding—this includes subsidies in the form of tax credits, low-cost loans, and provision of infrastructure investments via public bond measures. Neoliberal urbanism, salvage accumulation, and generalized gentrification form a kind of unholy trinity that shapes urban housing; each of these formations feeds off the devaluations that flow from disinvestment, recessions, and crises. Such was the mammoth infusion of devalued resources that became available after foreclosure properties flooded housing markets following the damage inflicted by the mortgage crisis. Armed with cash, the same financial interests that had played an outsized role in triggering the crisis also made out like bandits during the crisis, scooping up the skeletons of foreclosed houses while laying the groundwork for a transfer of wealth from the classes below to the classes above.[17]

HGTV's narrative discourse of creative erasure as the prerequisite for stories of home upcycling mirrors the ideological discourse of neoliberal gentrification as creative revival or renaissance.[18] Although the word "gentrification" is never spoken on HGTV, its economic and moral sensibility looms in the shadows as an animating motivation, expressed indirectly via euphemisms such as an "up-and-coming neighborhood." Television ideologically celebrates home renovation and flipping as gentrification opportunities—as a symbolic revitalization of spaces that allows ordinary people to make money, build financial security, and optimize their living conditions. Gentrification as a force reshaping North American cities (and beyond) and aestheticized gentrification as it is imagined on television are not exactly the same thing, though they are rooted in the same forces and have become reciprocally intermeshed with one another in general processes of seeking value.

Broadly situated in a salvage economy, HGTV proposes a generic rent-gap model of gentrification that charts a path to the rehabilitation of value. Rent-gap thinking offers a method for comparing the future values of currently undervalued properties with those of already developed properties. It's the comparison between purchasing a house in a well-established neighborhood at the top of its valuation history with the potential future value of renovating a house in a less popular location for a fraction of the cost. In general, capital investment tends to flow to where it has the potential for a higher rate of return.[19] HGTV's consumer-oriented model of gentrification focuses almost entirely on this economic calculus of gentrification minus its social geography. Its narrative is, oddly, about a gentrification without neighborhoods, because HGTV cuts the coordinates of urban geography out of its visual frames, leaving the focus centered on the remediation of interior spaces dedicated to the narrow confines of family, friends, and consumer desires. After 2008, HGTV's version of the rent-gap formula introduced the category of the entrepreneurial consumer—a consumer who, under the protective wing of an entrepreneurial professional (the HGTV host), is urged to take a modest financial risk as a means of joining the housing privileged.

What Karl Marx designated as exchange value has long since been made synonymous with our culture's convention of expressing value in monetary terms, as price. Coinciding with the early rustlings of capitalism, John Locke put forward an explanation of value and a justification for who has a right to it. Locke's precursor labor theory of value posited the exercise of labor on the object world as the source of value and held that the rights to such value should go to the individuals who have exercised their personhood and made it bountiful. Locke argued that such value, when stored in the form of money, could be accumulated, exchanged, and invested. Marx would later turn Locke on his capitalist head, making a value theory of labor a basis of capitalism's critique—as a principle of justice, a value theory of labor could premise a workers' utopia.[20]

During the decades preceding the 2008 financial crisis, high technology and the elixirs of finance capitalism displaced and eclipsed a decaying industrial infrastructure. From a business perspective, success in globalizing markets depends on a company's ability to price its product competitively. If competitors are doing the same thing, price competition becomes self-defeating as profit margins become thinner and thinner. To stay competitive, manufacturing migrated infrastructure and jobs to low-wage countries; in turn, imports of lower-priced consumer goods pressured remaining domestic producers out of business or prompted them to further squeeze labor's compensation. And, of course, high-tech innovations seek to automate jobs and reduce labor costs. As a result of deindustrialization, outsourcing, transnational commodity chains, and technological automation, over 5.7 million manufacturing jobs disappeared from the United States during the first decade of the twenty-first century. Between 2000 and 2007, manufacturing job losses were largely driven by trade deficits, while the 2008 financial crisis and the ensuing recession drove further factory closures that cost millions more jobs.[21] The diminishing importance of labor dependent on human hands has been long in the making but is still a raw wound.

Systematically substituting technology for labor has proven a seductive, but counterproductive, approach to cost cutting. Eliminating the costs of labor also erodes a traditional capitalist source, and measure, of value. Throughout the history of capitalism, labor's average cost has been a pivotal metric for adducing value. If a machine can now produce a million widgets, but no one is paid a wage, what will a widget be worth? With robotics and now artificial intelligence (AI) muscling aside labor's place, the contemporary model of capitalism still depends on the continuous consumption of goods and services. Reproduction becomes more difficult when wages can't keep up with the cost of living.

Especially after the financial collapse of 2008, value decoupled from labor seemed to have lost its way. Consider the extremely pronounced levels of abstraction built into derivatives; the value they yielded, or simulated, was largely intangible until realized in money form. Even the rating agencies charged with assigning valuations to bonds could not discern the difference between value and its absence. While labor's contribution to the production of material goods declines, the theater of HGTV tells stories about the successful reinvention of value made possible by sweat equity mixed with inventiveness. HGTV settles on personally motivated, individually performed labors to reinvigorate a value theory of labor. Such labor appears to ground and remoralize value. HGTV's reembodiment of value in the figures of the home and personalized labor poses as an encouraging alternative to intangible, illegible value.

Riding as it does on a cultural wave of value fetishism, home renovation TV's preoccupation with adding value returns over and over to the visual aesthetics of modernism. In the commodity world of HGTV, nothing says revitalized like recuperating a midcentury modern look, or the other iterations of modern style ranging from industrial chic to farmhouse modern. The rebirth of a modernist paradise—modernism 2.0—takes symbolic form in the updated single-family dwellings originally built in the mid-twentieth century. Renovation of this sort is said to effectuate both a multiplication of exchange value along with the restoration of an idealized moral center to people's lives. The feel-good popularity of shows like *Fixer Upper* steadies the world around the moral aura of family, friends, and community that spills out of well-lit farmhouse modern renovated homes. In the HGTV universe, housing properties are reinfused with the very spirit that feels as if it has been corroded by an excess of market forces over social life. An amoral system of abstract market value is thus cast as its opposite. Is it a cure to both financial insecurity and moral uncertainty in one stroke? That would be nice.

It helps to keep this narrative sequestered from the subjects of mortgages, debt, defaults, foreclosures, and evictions. TV renovation stories erase racialized urban geographies and working-class poverty as conditions that shape the nature of discounts in real estate markets that favor flipping.

When these forces are kept out of sight, HGTV's narrative manages to reverse the script on affordable housing—turning discounted and renovated properties into affordable homes. In fact, the overall availability of affordable housing opportunities is diminished by pushing the thesis that the principle of generalized gentrification can be effectively distributed to every corner of the housing system. The TV story of value-added flipping requires the erasure of the mortgage crisis and the hemorrhaging of foreclosures and distressed houses it catalyzed.

Creative erasure is a narrative strategy that erases history. It meshes perfectly with the ritualized enactment of creative destruction that premises the television renovation process. The de rigueur tearing down of walls presents a method of opening spaces as well as purging previous ways of life and the contradictions that went with them. All vestiges of former cultural styles and character are cleared away in this process—creating an open visual palette for imagining a new way of life. Reconfiguring the architecture of domestic spaces—the by-now clichéd open-space concept—is the apparent key to realizing affective freedom in a neoliberal world. The key to crafting the appearance of added value falls to the designers and decorators who impose the fashion codes of sign value over these spaces. As the preeminent lifestyle channel, HGTV hinges its revenues to its success in managing this specialized corner of a cultural economy of sign value.

Creative erasure extends to HGTV's representation of race and class. While the mortgage market collapse dashed the hopes of too many black and Hispanic households regarding home ownership, the superficially progressive mythology of color-blind multiculturalism seems to signify an end to the sins of racial segregation and a remedy to the overarching structural racism that daily defines the life chances of those same men and women. HGTV and its advertisers espouse a consumer market-driven ethos of multiculturalism that makes diversity and inclusion the sine qua non of an open palette that welcomes all ethnicities and sexualities, even though HGTV's stories lean toward replicas of a white hetero-patriarchal familial ideal. But the pose of color-blind inclusivity masks a strategic shift that intensified exploitative lending to black and Hispanic households. Keeanga-Yamahtta Taylor documents the history of deregulated racialized capitalism's movement from racial exclusion to "predatory inclusion" into a "dual mortgage market" that proved far more profitable than straight racial exclusion ever had.[22] Laura Gottesdiener observes, "The racial difference in who was allowed to buy what type of mortgage was so stark that the word 'subprime' (the industry's term for predatory loans) became a 'demographic category as much as a financial definition.'"[23]

Insulated from the roiling volatility of financial markets and the visceral political tantrums of our era, home renovation TV envisions utopian domestic spaces that it terms the forever dream home, an interior landscape that nicely conforms to the privatized neoliberal ideal. An ideological counterpart to creative destruction, creative erasure makes plausible narratives of multicultural prosperity and the acquisition of long-lasting value in a neoliberal world, even as it veils the structural racism that made possible the availability of so many distressed properties.

Crisis Narratives

Some HGTV viewers might understandably assume that the sort of housing investment depicted on the network—that of secure families buying property within their means and endeavoring to make it a more valuable home—is not the sort of reckless speculative betting that has come to bear the blame for the financial crisis. But this is a misconception inspired by a pair of narratives. In one narrative, irresponsible securities traders made doomed deals on the backs of hapless borrowers who lacked the wherewithal to navigate their financial future. In another, the one shown on HGTV, middle-class investors make canny investments and turn a profit. The distance between the two narratives leads one to reasonably conclude that the investments celebrated on HGTV are categorically different from those at the root of the financial crisis. As we will see, that distance is illusory, and the extremes of the narratives obscure the common ground connecting them and the commonplace financial machinery that also fed the crisis.

In the decades leading up to 2008, finance capital began chasing higher rates of profit by bypassing production as much as possible and looking to a more immediate route of trading computer-generated securities derived from already existing sources of value—that is, derivatives. When investors finally realized the disconnect between these financial instruments and whatever underlying assets they distantly referenced, an abrupt loss of confidence triggered a bank run. A crisis of hyperreal finance capital saw valuations become so estranged from their underlying referents that the referents could no longer be readily identified. Following the collapse of Lehman Brothers and the subsequent dominoes, an atmosphere of puzzled disorder took hold amid sensational headlines about a vast destruction of value. There ensued criticisms that, left unchecked by regulators, greedy bankers and hedge funds had created trillions in fictitious capital—value that apparently did not exist except in the imagination. Alternatively, the criticism that value had been destroyed implied that it had fully existed in the first place. Both criticisms missed the underlying structural developments—institutions of capitalist finance had adjusted to diminishing rates of profit by amending a system of directly exploiting labor's productivity to focus on the additional value that could be extracted by colonizing labor's household finances. Honing in on household debt and turning its risks into a leveraged asset, finance capital shifted its reliance on extracting value from labor at the point of production (e.g., manufacturing labor) to tapping into laborers' collective capacity for accruing and paying off household debt.[24] Whether the capital in question was fictitious or destroyed, there were still power relations at stake; of course, the haze of immaterial capital flows was symbolic, but that made its implosion no less material. When the house of cards began to fall, jobs, mortgages, and lives were left in shambles. And a crisis of legitimacy—more like a cloud of suspicion—descended over the political economy of value. Dick Bryan, Michael Rafferty, and Chris Jefferis pose the crucial question that goes to the heart of the matter in the twenty-first-century political economy: "How might value be [re]conceived when its two units of measure, labor and money, are undergoing such rapid transformation?"[25]

After the 2008 financial meltdown, the prevailing explanation for what went wrong came to be known as the subprime mortgage crisis. The subprime story wove together grand narratives of greed in the home loan and banking industries, coupled with inadequate regulatory oversight and the victimization of poor households who should never have been approved for mortgage loans to begin with because of deficient credit histories and inadequate incomes. By this account, the outcome could have been easily foretold because those holding subprime loans and adjustable rate mortgages had the deck stacked against them, making it improbable that they would ever be able to keep up with their mortgage payments and so the defaults piled up. It's a believable story because each element had some traction. Greed did run rampant, the credit spigots did open too wide, the working poor did get screwed, and Wall Street's appetite for swallowing unlimited risk in the form of mortgage-backed securities and credit default swaps exceeded even the most jaundiced appraisals. The subprime narrative placed equal weight on predatory lenders and borrowers who foolishly took out more loan than they could afford. Subprime loans and foreclosures rode heavily on the backs of the working poor, especially female-headed households, blacks, and Hispanics. "Among the ranks of the countless so-called irresponsible borrowers, what is especially striking about the subprime borrower is... the experience she represents: highly indebted, underpaid, with flexible (insecure) employment, and carrying an increased individualized responsibility for all kinds of risk."[26]

Whether subprime loans triggered the housing crisis or not, subprime borrowers were left holding the bag for the systemic debt risk that built up and exploded. Leading up to the crisis, borrowers whose credit histories had previously blocked them from joining the wealth-building project of home ownership were turned into fodder by banks and hedge funds that bundled debt into investment bonds. After 2008, HGTV would not touch the subject of the housing crisis with a ten-foot pole, but by routinely including in its stories those demographic categories "formerly excluded from the 'dream' of home ownership, HGTV announced itself as a site for contesting the limits of access to this dream under crisis conditions."[27] In this way, HGTV hailed opportunities for racial and sexual minorities, along with an emphasis on millennials whose lack of financial resources has sharply delimited their access to an inflationary market.

To defenders of the capitalist system, the subprime narrative deflected criticism from the core structure of the financial system, placing blame on rogue capitalists, bad policy decisions by Fannie Mae and Freddie Mac, lax enforcement of credit standards, and the financial illiteracy of the victims. Critics of capitalist financialization also latched on to the subprime narrative because it readily fit with their assessment that subprime loans fed the investment industry's appetite for mortgage-backed securities, yet another instance of class-based exploitation. None of these arguments are wrong so much as they are partial. The focus on subprime loans diverted attention from real estate investors, who had higher incomes and higher credit scores but were also more debt leveraged and took on riskier mortgage contracts than prime borrowers who were not investors.[28] Stefania Albanesi, Giacomo DiForgio, and Jaromir Nosal combed through loan documents and credit files from 2001 to 2007 and found that the expansion of credit was most concentrated among real estate investors and speculators: "The rise in mortgage defaults during the crisis was concentrated in the middle of the credit score distribution, and mostly attributable to real estate investors."[29] These were borrowers who bought multiple homes and held multiple mortgage liens, and often followed already rapidly rising home prices outside their home regions where they were far quicker than locals to bail once the market began to sour. Overrepresented among these real estate investors were "house flippers" whose defaults precipitated the housing market collapse.[30] Whereas subprime mortgage defaults occurred at a relatively constant rate throughout the real estate boom years, sharp spikes in defaults between 2005 and 2008 among real estate flippers triggered the tsunami of defaults that led to the implosion of the big banks.[31] Unlike the conventional narrative that puts the crisis at the feet of subprime borrowers (those with the lowest credit scores), Albanesi and her associates conclude that the crisis hinged to a significant degree on the systemic consequences of entrepreneurial investors who chased the house-flipping wave: "Most of the increase in mortgage debt during the boom, and of mortgage delinquencies during the crisis, is driven by mid to high credit score borrowers, and it is these borrowers who disproportionately default on their mortgages during the crisis."[32] At the epicenter of the red-hot housing markets of California,

Florida, Arizona, and Nevada that collapsed so completely in 2008, the presence of nonlocal investors who carried multiple liens accelerated the crisis: their share of new mortgages purchased in 2006 rose to nearly 45 percent of the total.[33]

Mortgage markets crashed not because poor people were more promiscuous with debt than others, but because real estate investors and middle-class speculators in housing markets aggressively took out loans on multiple properties to chase ballooning housing prices by flipping houses. Nevertheless, HGTV's stories ignore the risks of default on mortgage debt, risks that increase with second mortgages used to finance house flipping. In fact, HGTV thoroughly represses all discourses of debt, sublimating debt's ghostly presence into questions about how to reconcile budgets with fetishized must-haves. Leveraged debt had become essential to the inner workings of a financialized system of capital, but like the housing crisis and the subprime narrative, in the HGTV mythology it falls into a forbidden history. Minus that history, HGTV could construct a plausible narrative about finding a path to a value-added future that hinges on the premise of joining the class of real estate investors while averting our eyes from the financial damage inflicted on those whose property became distressed. While high-risk subprime mortgage loans may not have been the proximate tipping point of the housing crisis, those toxic loans robbed the working poor of what little wealth they had stored in their properties. Concentrated in lower-income neighborhoods, high-risk subprime loans stacked the deck for borrower failure, beginning with higher loan-to-value ratios, a disregard for standards that otherwise checked high debt-to-income ratios, and the inclusion of features that exacerbated default rates, like adjustable interest rates, prepayment penalties, and balloon payments.[34] Subprime foreclosures turned into the distressed (but full-of-potential) assets that HGTV would counsel viewers to look for. HGTV conveniently failed to speak of the housing crisis but knowingly hinted at dislodged housing assets scattered about like so much debris. Between 2009 and 2010, lenders filed six million foreclosure notices in the midst of deep job losses while a vast transfer of wealth from black, Hispanic, and white working-class households to investors armed with cash gathered momentum. In 2010, in the midst of recession, defaults, and foreclosures and the beginnings of a historic wealth transfer, HGTV introduced its new look—renovation programming (starting with *Property Brothers*) devoted to telling stories about renovating and flipping fixer-uppers as a way of addressing the housing woes of individual subjects. This was no conspiracy of interests, but rather a conjuncture of consequences.

Since debt does not exist in the HGTV universe and discounted properties are apparently bloodless, HGTV's discursive exploitation of house-flipping stories as a lucrative route to mining value rests entirely on practicing budgetary restraint (a black box) mixed with creativity and a willingness to take a chance. HGTV's efforts to restore faith in renewed value and wealth-building opportunities for the middle classes draws from the premise that flipping fixer-uppers offers savvy individuals a path to a share of the pie in an economy that has otherwise been stacked against the middle and working classes. To tell this story, it is best for HGTV to keep the subprime theme out of sight: after all, from those subprime home loans came plenty of foreclosures that subsequently formed the stock of flips and fixer-uppers. And every house bought on the cheap, fixed up to look stylish, and sold for top dollar is another residence that is unavailable to the class of former subprime borrowers, who are now subject to a prison of rising rents. HGTV lends itself to the encouragement of another inflationary spiral in housing that works against housing affordability.

The subprime narrative assumed that the market crisis of housing valuations was a result of "personal weakness, speculative excess, and moral corruption."[35] It's a story that distracts from a deeper understanding of the forces that imperiled (and continue to imperil) the reproduction of value in modern-day capitalist society. As Harvey reminds us, Marx thought of capital as "value in motion."[36] In a fully developed capitalist society in which commodity relations have penetrated every corner, when flows of value slow, falter, or are interrupted, the quaking of their deficit can be felt within every part of life organized as a market. There is no better illustration than the MBS crisis. Designed to accelerate market liquidity, MBSs also resulted in the opposite, and in so doing their contradictions arrested flows of capital and froze movement within housing markets. On HGTV and DIY, we are witness to a cultural machinery for reproducing value that aims to reassure TV viewers that faith in the possibilities of value can be salvaged and restored.

The 2008 financial crisis revealed foundational cracks in the neoliberal ground rules that supposedly govern the production and allocation of value in market economies. Further anger and frustration trailed the mortgage crisis in response to the apparent unfairness of government responses to the crisis—particularly bailouts that rewarded the riskiest behaviors that had brought the system to its knees while leaving millions of mortgage holders saddled with defaults and foreclosures. Home ownership was supposed to be a wealth-building activity that ensured personal security. Instead, it exposed uncertainty about how to build and capture value. The 2007–2008 financial crash sparked more than a crisis of value confined to the economic sphere, it also spilled out into perceptions of a breakdown of the market as a system of moral and ethical regulation. My project in this book revolves around how this precarity of value has been culturally mediated in the decade following the 2008 crash. Given its popularity, and its topic of remaking houses into sites of wealth production, HGTV seems to offer an ideal set of cultural frames for thinking about discourses of value. While mortgage markets became entangled in an arcane methodology of extracting wealth defined by financialization and securitization, HGTV told stories of home renovation and house flipping that draw on a nostalgic cultural script for turning houses back into sites of sanctuary and security, all the while restoring the allure of home ownership as a privileged site of wealth building available to all. Even though the twenty-first-century capitalist economy evidences a shrinking reliance on labor in general as the prime generator of profits, on HGTV, certain labors are rewarded, particularly those associated with creativity, inventiveness, performativity, and entrepreneurial risk.

I juxtapose HGTV's guides to value via renovation against the rapidly evolving conditions of a twenty-first-century political economy of housing. My method is to turn the HGTV home renovation shows into a window that allows a light to shine on questions of value following the 2007–2008 financial crisis. Although the crisis centered on the collapse of the home mortgage industry, HGTV's stories avoided the crisis, instead recommending a strategy that looks for beaten-up houses available on the salvage heap to renovate and turn into like-new profit centers. Between the stories of a mortgage debacle that wrecked the lives of millions of families and HGTV's stories about a path to the redemption of value, the contrast is so pronounced that I see in HGTV a unique opportunity to plumb the depths of the ideological and material contradictions of value that surround the single-family residence in an era of finance capitalism. I put HGTV's comfort-food shows to a purpose that their producers never intended, confronting their story lines with the relationships they leave out, and thus leveraging their stories to open up the contradictions of finance capitalism with its penchant for consumer indebtedness and the requirement that each of us is individually responsible for our housing and our financial solvency.

The 2008 financial crisis was more than merely an economic crisis; it effected a breakdown of norms covering the legitimate pursuit of value in the marketplace. The old rules for claiming one's fair share of value through hard work, education, and home ownership no longer inspired confidence. Lauren Berlant expresses this as a "fraying of the fantasy of 'the good life' specifically attached to labor, the family wage, and upward mobility."[37] The financial crisis magnified a dilemma at the scale of individual households—how to secure and display the material signifiers of classier lifestyles while at the same time taking on more and more household debt. This is a double bind that stems from "representing the individual as an autonomous market actor endowed with infinite consumer freedom while also burdening that individual with full responsibility for his own reproduction in an economy fueled by consumer debt."[38]

HGTV resolves this double bind by effacing the question of mortgage debt. Instead, HGTV reroutes the crisis of value through stories of families who appear to transcend the trials and tribulations of the economy as a whole by embracing an already suspect neoliberal narrative that celebrates creative risk taking and the symbolic performance of worth and taste as the path to recapturing home equity in a salvage economy. HGTV's version of this narrative smuggles in the additional premise that suburban gentrification can be made to work as a market strategy that benefits savvy consumers, so long as such consuming subjects are willing to look past their participation in the exploitation of others' misery in difficult times. Fiona Allon summarizes the relationship between this narrative and the position of "the individual as a citizen-speculator required to depend on the home as a site of accumulation and an object of leveraged investment, not only for debt-fueled consumption in the present but also as an asset base for welfare in the future."[39] On HGTV, the fixer-upper home is thus cast as a remedy to a crisis of value, even though this remedy looks suspiciously like what prompted that crisis.

I chose to study HGTV because of its impossibly malleable obsession with value. What happens when we expose that obsession to critique? Chapter 1 begins by thinking about meanings of value in everyday life before turning to how value's meaning has been channeled through the semiotic machinery of television and its structures of commodity representation. HGTV does not simply reflect back at us the conditions of value in the marketplace; it builds and enforces value as a system of signs. A fundamental premise of my study of value as it circulates between HGTV and housing markets after the 2008 mortgage market collapse is that political economy and semiotics do not exist in separate silos. To understand political economies of value today, we cannot divorce them from the interpenetrating contradictions that structure cultural economies of value.

1

A Primer on Value in the Age of HGTV

It is naturally still more convenient to understand by value nothing at all. Then one can without difficulty subsume everything under this category. Thus, e.g., [Jean-Baptiste] Say: "What is value?" Answer: "That which a thing is worth"; and what is "price"? Answer: "The value of a thing expressed in money." And why has agriculture a value? Answer: "Because one sets a price on it." Therefore, value is what a thing is worth, and the land has its "value," because its value is "expressed in money." This is, anyhow, a very simple way of explaining the why and the wherefore of things.
—KARL MARX, *Capital*, vol. 1

Everyday Meanings of Value

David Auerbach rhetorically asks, "What are the abstractions [that] we deal with everyday? More than anything else, they are financial."[1] Though these abstractions preoccupy us, we ordinarily take them for granted because "abstractions of value, as defined and regulated by money, are something we all are forced to deal with, negotiate, share, and be subjected to" every day.[2] Questions of value arise throughout our daily lives in a myriad of ways, from micro evaluations about whether an organic tomato is worth a small money premium to more consequential questions about how to value the installation of solar panels or whether taking on student debt will be worth it. Though we rarely reflect on the category of value as such, in everyday life we dwell incessantly on how to assess, evaluate, and weigh it.

Merriam-Webster defines value as "the monetary worth of something: market price."[3] Price has indeed become a proxy meaning for value. As David Harvey notes, "Money thus enters the picture as a material representation of value. Value cannot exist without its representation."[4] When people speak about adding value, they tend to mean that they can now fetch a greater price. While price considerations dictate thinking about the costs of commodity goods and utilities, another commonsense conception of value persists, as a quality that price cannot capture. When we make assessments of the price being asked for an item, what frequently comes to mind is how a particular price corresponds to a particular intrinsic value. When someone says "that's a good value" or "that's a fair price," she is assessing an exchange value against an underlying judgment of a quality that cannot be fully captured by price. What doesn't get captured by the dictionary definition are the matrixes of fluid cultural, social, and temporal relationships through which this thing called value gets negotiated and enacted. In daily life there is a socially shared recognition that value is fluid, subject to a shifting aggregate of sentiments—a social politics. And yet, in daily life, we often imagine value as a naturally occurring category underneath the social forces that lend it motion.

Price may dictate how we think about exchanges, but the desired result of those exchanges is nevertheless that we hope to get something extra out of it, value—that is, in exchange for our money, we hope to come out ahead. Daniel Miller observes that "in everyday life the word value is commonly used to refer equally to what might be regarded as the incommensurable polarity between value as price, and value as priceless, sometimes portrayed as the contrast between value [economy] and values [culture]."[5] While we may recognize money as an arbitrary measure of worth, our cultural expectation is to seek in exchange for it something of greater consequence. We reserve the concept of "value" for that which is the remainder (what's left over) after the exchange process. We often substitute the word "bargain" for value, as in "I got a bargain—a good value for the money."

Consumers weigh perceived value against asking price. From a consumer perspective, value thus equals a surplus of utility over price. Ironically, the elements of Karl Marx's theory of use and exchange value persist in giving meaning to everyday expectations of value on the consumer side of the coin. From the producer side, as a culture we still harbor romantic fantasies about the Lockean version of a labor theory of value. In this view, value is what gets added when the independent individual mixes his labor with objects, either natural or man-made, and makes it his own. C. B. Macpherson calls this "possessive individualism."[6]

Everyday life in capitalist society finds value bound by a few general principles. Value is always relative—that is, value always represents a comparative measure. As a corollary, no single object possesses value in isolation. Conversely, value is never absolute. Because value is always relational, it is never constant but rather variable. Though we are sometimes apt in daily life to treat value as a thing, it is always a relationship. Value is always a product of symbolic interaction. Though value must have a material referent, value is essentially a negotiated construct of discourse. Put these basic principles together and we confirm what we already know—namely, that value can never be static in a market economy. Not static is, however, a baseline description. In contemporary markets, where discourses over value take the form of electronic signals, value grows increasingly volatile.

Discursive contests about what constitutes value are as old as markets. Markets are fundamentally social in character. Contests between bulls and bears in the investing community consist of a market made by exchanges of discursive opinions and judgments about valuation metrics and strategies. Home renovation TV offers a more stage-managed, and generally prepackaged, discursive effort at constructing and steering value. Taken as a whole, HGTV is nothing less than an organized discourse of value as it pertains to residential real estate—a discourse that presumes that properties do not possess hard, pregiven values but that value can be massaged within a framework of discursive exchange.

Harvey observes that "value is always created in the act of production. But it is realized in the moment of market exchange. . . . Value cannot be produced through market exchange. But it cannot be realized outside of market exchange."[7] More broadly, it is in "the process of circulating as (commodity) capital that value is verified."[8] True enough. But the boundaries of what constitutes the production of value in the age of the spectacle may need some rethinking. The social construction of value may be focused on value hierarchies in the sphere of exchange, but it is also productive of value in the sphere of consumption. While the discursive act of bringing a product to market is necessary to realize a value created in production, the introduction of marketing to frame the social side of the equation also produces value, thus complicating the origins of value in production. HGTV so intermingles the production of value with the discursive articulation of value in exchange that it's difficult to separate these moments. On HGTV, as with the spectacle in general, value is produced, ratified, and recirculated via the "mirror of reproduction."[9]

Contradictions of Value in the Society of the Spectacle

Paraphrasing both Guy Debord and Karl Marx, the spectacle as a form of capital presents itself as an immense accumulation of *discourses* about value.[10] Within the society of the spectacle, a 24/7 cultural preoccupation with the subject of value is proportionate to the speed at which discourses about value circulate. That preoccupation is twofold: HGTV is both a discourse about value and a site for the production, circulation, and reproduction of value. On television, value functions as an iterative preoccupation, and its incessant repetition can grow tiresome, banal, and all too predictable.

Competition within the culture industry creates a permanent interest in commodifying culture. Because the capitalist machinery for reproducing value never rests, value never rests either. Turnover is the game. As a result, chatter *about* the subject of valuation intensifies. Recall Sisyphus and the punishment inflicted on him—sentenced to a never-ending task of rolling a heavy boulder up a mountain, only to have it roll back down just before he reaches the top. As discursive models of value reproduction have taken center stage, entire media industries have arisen to institutionalize these models—home renovation TV is one such site; others include stock market channels, fantasy sports channels, and celebrity news channels, not to mention social media sites such as Pinterest, Instagram, and Facebook. In every instance, we witness the Sisyphus challenge—tackling the same burden every day because the task can never be finished. Immaterial values—symbolic values like that of a stock or a brand name such as HGTV—require continuous effort to keep them elevated. A brand left untended will drift toward entropy, and a stock value is only as robust as the most recent symbolic analyst declares it to be. In the world of immaterial values, the boulder is no longer subject to the terrestrial forces of gravity, but rather to a weightless capitalist psychology of value dependent on quotidian circuits of signification, perception, and comparison.

The culture industry, now overwhelmingly pervasive, has hitched its wagon to this Sisyphean task, the eternal task of reproducing value hierarchies. But this new incarnation of the myth has become structural, not merely the fate of a heroic or tragic individual. Within the capitalist system, the failure to reproduce more value than the year before teases the bankruptcy of the system itself. Indeed, the Sisyphean punishment is no longer a curse visited on one by the gods; it is now the profane means toward keeping a commodity system afloat.

Albert Camus tells us that Sisyphus may have been punished for the sin of desiring too much. Defying the gods, he prolonged his stay amid the pleasures of Earth while refusing death. "His scorn of the gods, his hatred of death, and his passion for life won him that unspeakable penalty in which the whole being is exerted toward accomplishing nothing. This is the price that must be paid for the passions of this earth."[11] If we think of the culture industry being charged today with the Sisyphean task of the eternal reproduction of desire necessary to fueling the fires of value, matters have been reversed. With Sisyphus, the greatest sin was a surfeit of passion and desire, for which there could be "no more dreadful punishment than futile and hopeless labor,"[12] while today the greatest sin is never having enough desire, for which the punishment is to never dwell in satisfaction. For the culture industry, telos and curse are one and the same, perpetually pushing the burden of commodity desire and value up the mountain. Applying the myth to the culture industry, the task of endlessly repeating the exercise of rolling value up the mountain is nothing more or less than an expression of the logic of commodity culture. In the case of HGTV, the viewer who binge-watches episode after episode knows all too well that the satisfaction realized at the end of each episode is at best a fleeting moment that must be revisited with another more or less equivalent moment in the next episode.

This endlessly looping practice of inventing and reinventing value to keep up with the insatiable demands of a capitalist marketplace is not without consequences. Especially within the spectacle, the competitive engines of commodity reproduction tend to flood the field of value to such a degree that it undermines trust in the category of value. Just as money must continuously keep flowing and circulating, so too must images, but with a twist—competing signs try to knock one another off their perches. Because every competitor tries to differentiate his or her sign value, the barrage of imagery intensifies. In advertising and marketing, these signification contests all aim at differentiating the value of a brand vis-à-vis competitors but with the ironic consequence that differentiation becomes harder and harder to sustain in the clouds of advertising noise and clutter thus generated. Jean Baudrillard draws attention to the internal contradictions of the competition in sign values: "All that lives by difference will perish by indifference. All that lives by value will perish by equivalence. All that lives by meaning will perish by insignificance."[13] Too many truth claims about value breed cultures of cynicism, doubt, and suspicion. Value has entered a "fractal stage" in which "properly speaking, there is now no law of value, merely a sort of epidemic of value, a sort of general metastasis of value, a haphazard proliferation and dispersal of value."[14] If everything has the sign of value attached to it, then the category of value itself becomes destabilized and even pointless. Not only does value necessitate a comparison with nonvalue to be meaningful, but the value of any particular commodity requires that it be differentiated from other such branded commodities to stand out. Paradoxically, unending competitions to build and defend differentiated brand values undermine confidence in the category of value itself to the point that "all values have become confused and undecidable."[15]

What can HGTV's fetishized discourses about value teach us about the ways in which our economy and society organize the conditions of value production, exchange, circulation, and realization? Discourses of value are a manifestation of the cultural politics that comprise regimes of value, an always morphing constellation of relations entwined around the conditions and norms of value extraction, exchange, and circulation. In establishing itself as a discursive center of questions about value and home renovation, HGTV does more than merely reflect a current regime of value; its forays into the cultural politics of value have inserted HGTV into that regime of value.

As a commercial entertainment site, HGTV has neither the chops nor the interest in explaining the complicated changes that effect a system of value in motion in capitalist economies of housing investment. Value is an abstraction that can be difficult to conceptually track, especially today when the accumulation of value requires the mastery of flows as well as fixed assets. In a previous era, value was more readily associated with fixed material assets and hence more readily identifiable when it took the form of things, or objects. Notably, HGTV wants nothing to do with the flows of MBSs or cyber currencies: it prefers to embrace a nostalgia for the appearance of past value forms.

HGTV's musings about value are shaped in contradiction. On the one hand, the dynamics of a capitalist political economy has shifted the center of value articulation from the sphere of production to the sphere of circulation and consumption. On the other hand, in the society of the spectacle, the commodity is the organizing principle of culture. Within the spectacle, value tends to be emancipated from its rootedness, such that "signs exchange against each other rather than against the real."[16] Signs of value become self-referential. HGTV is caught in the middle, trying to claim that it is about the real while it is fundamentally entrenched in the project of exchanging signs of value against themselves (the value sign of quartz versus the value sign of granite).

HGTV's Eleven Theses on Value

HGTV stories about home renovation valuations contain a mix of postulates about value, sliding from truisms about scarcity and oversaturation to matters of style, design, prestige, and labor, along with the waves of emotion and desire that prop it up. HGTV's discourses reveal a fog of assumptions rather than a single predominant logic of value at play. I distill HGTV's scattered generalizations about what drives value into a typology and then amplify these tacitly accepted assumptions about how value works by matching them with academic theories of value.

Attempts to define value invariably run into its polysemic character and its multidimensional relationships. Rather than look for some master logic of value, or vainly try to pin down the core thing that defines value, Lawrence Grossberg, Carolyn Hardin, and Michael Palm conceptualize value as "an effect or trace of particular regimes of valuation in which . . . multiple processes . . . are assembled and articulated in different ways."[17] Thinking about value as a set of effects has the virtue of reminding us to treat value as a process and a relationship and not as a thing unto itself. While HGTV visualizes value as a set of outcomes, it shies away from taking account of the very category of value itself, from explaining the why and the wherefore of it. Where does value come from? What animates it? Where are its logics to be found? Are its effects to be discovered or created? Can it be lost, destroyed, dissipated, captured, sustained, or nurtured? What rules, if any, govern value? More often than not, value is the focus of HGTV shows, its pursuit their goal. HGTV's editing practices jumble and scatter the commodity effects of value creation, giving us an ad hoc mix of propositions about things that effect value realization. The assumption of a universal money equivalent is the only thing unifying HGTV's mix-and-match references to value. And yet, while the money equivalent of value is the shiny object that HGTV stories track, the same stories cut out the market forces that shape the pricing of value. Viewers are thus positioned as consumers to see value with price tags in the foreground and a fuzzy marketplace in the background. Fair or unfair, stable or unstable, exploitative or subsidized, the power relations that underlie market forces are simply not visible, so we must take HGTV claims about changes in valuations on faith, or alternatively, subject them to critique.

At first glance, value on HGTV seems to be merely a gloss for what everybody knows, or takes for granted, in everyday life. Hence, value starts with assumptions of exchange value and its expression via the currency of money. The logical conclusion is that value and price represent equivalent expressions of the same thing, anchored in the premise that anything can be made commensurate with money. But even when value is treated superficially as an undifferentiated gloss for what everybody knows, there is considerable referential complexity about what adds up to value on HGTV. To begin thinking about this, consider a real estate agent's seemingly straightforward sales pitch promoting a residential property. She opens with a description of a house as a "gut reno" followed by a reference to its "prime" location in a "trendy" neighborhood on the rise. The home is also said to feature outstanding design and material workmanship. In the current status system of housing choices, phrases like "gut reno" convey a coded shorthand acknowledgment of gentrification. Though the word "gentrification" is *never* spoken on HGTV, it looms behind phrases such as "gut reno," which bespeaks hipness as a signifier. For real estate shoppers who view housing identity as a status, it also implies a basis for a premium value. The mention of a known architect and/or designer further adds to the house's reputational prestige value. The value of trendiness can be seen promoted as well in aesthetic expectations that extrapolate a home's appearance to its value in the market. The promise of high-quality materials and workmanship coupled with appeals to prime locations may also justify appeals to snob-appeal price tags.

HGTV rarely offers hard and fast categories of value, preferring instead the route of allusions and inferences. By matching HGTV's untheorized assertions with corresponding theoretical categories of value, I draw out a typology of value triggers operating within the universe of home renovation TV. Sifting through the references and allusions to value expressed on HGTV, I identify eleven recurring theses about value in the world of residential renovations. Rarely does an HGTV depiction of value turn on just one logic of value; more often, HGTV's narratives of increasing value invoke combinations of these principles. My elevation of HGTV's half-baked propositions about creating value into grander theoretical explanations is meant to draw out the premises that are implicit in HGTV's stories about how to find value in the world of home renovation and flipping.

Exchange relations and perceptual valuation. Reflecting the heartbeat of neoclassical economic theory, perhaps the most generic tacit assumption on HGTV holds that value is generated in the act of exchange itself. Related to assumptions about exchange value is the Hobbesian supposition that exchange value depends on a social psychology of perceptual valuation and its continual social renegotiation. "The difficulty of acquisition, the sacrifice offered in exchange, is the unique constitutive element of value, of which scarcity is only the external manifestation, its objectification in the form of quantity."[18] To Georg Simmel, value is thus constituted in the act of exchange.

Value, in this view, does not strictly inhere in produced objects but instead represents social judgments. Value is neither objective nor subjective but is intersubjective—Simmel sees value as inherently social in nature. If value is constituted by the ratio of perceived sacrifice to perceived gain, then the greater the desire for a particular object or utility, the more willing subjects are to sacrifice to gain its acquisition, while, conversely, the less the sacrifice, the more moderated value becomes. The value of an object is determined by the intensity of a buyer's desire. "Objects," observes Simmel, "are not difficult to acquire because they are valuable, but we call those objects valuable that resist our desire to possess them."[19] In a highly individuated society, turning Marx's value form (use value/exchange value = commodity value) into a personal psychological evaluation resonates with the consumer ideal of free agency in defining value for one's self.

A century after Simmel's observation, a permanent institutional framework has evolved that is daily put to work to steer perceptions of value in a global commodity culture. Modern culture industries like HGTV inscribe on commodities like homes an imagined value that anticipates (and justifies) an exchange valuation. In such a world, perceptions of value—the potential for a sound house to be a dream home—motivate the desire for exchange. This means that value is more than simply the realization of exchange, it also precedes exchange. Theories of marginal utility that have arisen alongside the institutionalization of consumerism conceive value as an effect of consumer preferences, thus inflating the importance of subjective perceptions of value especially among those who have market interests dependent on the manipulation of such perceptions. In practical terms, the sphere of consumer value becomes managed as a province of economic psychology.

Labor and the commodity form. On HGTV, labor is referenced visually as a floating signifier. More often than not, it's the effects of labor, rather than labor itself, that stand testament to the value of investment. Yet just below the surface of home renovation TV lurks a resurrection of a value theory of labor. Like the renovation stories it tells, HGTV's version of a value theory of labor has been repurposed and updated to fit the modern moment in the form of sweat equity. In the TV stories, the voluntary exercise of labor stands opposed to wage labor. The former is situated in the foreground, while the latter speeds across the background. Chapter 7 surveys HGTV's differentiated representations of the performance of labor, from do-it-yourself (DIY) and the crowdsourcing of friends and family to the labor of celebrity hosts to artisans to generic day laborers.

Marx ties the measure of commodity value to the value of the labor that produces it. Under early capitalism, value was measured by the average number of hours required to produce a commodity, or what is the same thing, the exchange value of a commodity reflected the socially necessary labor time for its production. Today, a more individualized value theory of labor suffuses home renovation TV with its focus on how an individual's performance of labor can add value to real estate. This starts with DIY labor, but the home run of value-adding labor on HGTV comes from being the client of celebrity renovators and designers who can deliver the qualities of artisanal imagination and craftsmanship, all at a discount to the market.

In capitalist society, "the commodity law of value is a law of equivalences, and this law operates throughout every sphere."[20] No part of our lives is immune from the logic of commodities. Today, almost no activity or product escapes being structured by commodity frameworks. Historically, the commodity form pushed the general law of equivalency into every sphere of daily life, starting with wage labor. Under the sway of the commodity law of value, exchange value became abstracted from both the performance of labor that produced the value and the specific moment and place in which it was situated. Thus unmoored, commodity values could circulate more widely and more freely in their abstracted form as money exchanges. Exchange value is thus deterritorialized value.[21] In HGTV stories this manifests itself in investments in houses that yield greater valuations independent of neighborhood geographies or historical context.

When the commodity form imposed itself on the social organization of wage labor, it quantitatively indexed its premise of exchange value to the performance of wage labor. The wages thus received became necessary, in turn, to secure the values that consumers need or want, whether that be food, shelter, transportation, entertainments, medicines, tools, clothing, religious artifacts, and so on, with no end in sight. HGTV acknowledges the relationship between value and labor by working backwards from its visual effects. The relationship between value and investment (capital) is made a bit more directly as one of HGTV's recurring punchlines highlights the *instant equity* that may be realized by those who accept the risk of renovation investment. Chapter 6 unravels this construction.

The decade-by-decade replacement of human labor by machine labor has weakened the direct correspondence between labor and value. The capitalist thesis is that technology devalues labor. Machines allow humans to create more value, but because machines make work easier, humans are seen as meriting less through their reduced sweat equity. HGTV sidesteps the fundamental contradiction contained therein. If labor becomes less and less central to the production of value and receives less and less in the value of wages, by what measure will we value commodities?[22] HGTV offers an artisanal answer. From the capitalist side of the coin, mechanization of labor drives productivity, which lowers prices but increases the value equation—getting more for less. From the consumer side, the industrial mechanization of labor prompts a price-quality trade-off that sets up a more nebulous value equation. Coupled with product standardization, the hegemony of the commodity form leaves an opening for a romanticized labor theory of artisanal value as an alternative in which workmanship is closely linked to another axis of value distinction in consumer culture—claims of authenticity. HGTV flirts with both sides of this coin. Flipping shows draw on rigid formulas of product and design standardization joined to a reliance on a faceless division of labor to minimize costs, while the renovation shows promise customized living spaces that contain the distinctions promised by the inclusion of craftsmanship.

Scarcity versus overproduction/oversaturation: supply and demand. Scarcity expresses itself in the characteristics of relative uniqueness and differentiation. In the rule books on value, oversaturation tends to drive down its price. Where demand is high and supply is limited (e.g., Seattle's housing market), price exceeds value. Material scarcity and cultural scarcity intertwine. When something becomes overbought, its socially defined value goes down. Marketing for gentrification tends to work on this premise—when a particular neighborhood gets defined as a prime location, it is by definition special, which means it is in limited supply. Value in contemporary culture is almost always rooted in such comparisons—a property defined as stylish only has meaning relative to a property that is deemed to lack style. In a capitalist society, the tendency is to oversaturate value niches until they violate their scarcity limit. Granite countertops have been highly valued because of their status value, but oversaturation has prompted their devaluation relative to "quartz, the new countertop contender."[23]

Sign value, brand value. When channeled through the television, matters of value are restructured by semiotic codes governed by what Baudrillard calls the "structural law of value."[24] This is the realm of sign value. The marriage of semiotics and the commodity form has become so familiar that it is easy to take for granted our daily practices of reading signs of value. Today, all consumer commodities are swathed in signification practices. Sign value is constituted in the relation of one signifier to another and then attached to commodities. Values assigned to signs do not exist isolated unto themselves but are rooted in a classificatory system (codes) that governs the relationships between signs and the values that they carry.[25] Hence the meaningful values assigned to signs are always mutable and subject to change. Sign values attached to commodities have a shelf life; they may get stale and fall out of circulation, but their signifying components are always available for salvage, recycling, reuse, and recombination. HGTV turns itself into a semiotic factory where signifiers that are visually unhinged from one referent system can be reworked into other meaningful combinations so that fresh sign values may be articulated, reproduced, modified, and recirculated. To illustrate, on *Fixer Upper*, Joanna Gaines is known for a home design style dubbed *farmhouse modernism*, a sign value composed by combining signs that draw on a farmhouse tradition with materials that evoke rustic sensibilities mixed with lines that suggest architectural modernism. Working within her design code, however, Gaines has no difficulty giving it flexibility. Thus, when clients ask for a mix of rustic and coastal or rustic with an Italian flavor, Gaines simply thumbs through her catalog of signifying styles and selects a signifier of coastalness (window shutters associated with the referent system of coastal living) that she then integrates with her usual rustic signifiers (shiplap and exposed wood). Recognition of this sign value gains from placing it along an axis of difference from other such sign values: rustic coastalness is thus differentiated from rustic Italianicity.

HGTV presents itself as an integrator of signs into differentiated assemblages that simulate and fuel the renovation economy by shaping, organizing, and circulating a system of sign values. Whereas exchange value, governed by the logic of the commodity form, depends on the principle of equivalence exchange, the structural law of value that underlies these systems of sign values adds to the mix a value form "governed by a code, and value develops here by reference to a set of models."[26] HGTV can be thought of as a curator of the décor and design codes that administer the expression of value. HGTV's flippers are writers as well as readers of signs and styles, such that the repeated assertion of a style maxim by an HGTV designer can speak the value into existence in the actual marketplace.

Within mass culture, HGTV has itself come to represent an umbrella sign that designates a constellation of sign values. By rearranging sequences of signifiers and signifieds, sign producers propose distinctive sign values that can be associated with commodities. This process occurs in a twofold manner—on both the encoding and decoding sides of the coin. Encoders (producers) set the stage and decoders (consumers) finish or valorize the sign value, or refuse to valorize it. Both encoding and decoding involve sign labor, the consumer side of which is performed as interpretive labor.[27] Even when an HGTV star proposes investing a meaningful value in a visual object, it is still up to the spectator to interpretively digest that investment of meaning. How do viewers enter into and participate in such transactions of sign value? Like almost all commercial television, HGTV positions viewers to mentally try on the look and the value of the house by being interpellated, or hailed. Louis Althusser's theory of ideology begins with this process of being hailed. Suppose you are at a public event, and the speaker says, "Let us pray." You have been hailed if you recognize public prayer as something you are already comfortable with, and you bow your head. If you fidget uncomfortably, then you have not been effectively interpellated by that religious ideology. Ideology works, according to Althusser, by being internalized by the subject, not by imposition from without. HGTV hails the viewing subject, inviting her to identify with the imaginary subject being addressed. Judith Williamson calls this exchange the "trap of alreadyness" because the show addresses us as if we are "already-there-as-subjects" who aspire to be, with the benefit of the commodity being visualized—say, a new kitchen island—even more ourselves.[28]

If use value references utility and exchange value establishes a system of universal equivalence among otherwise incommensurable utilities, sign value operates to maintain an axis of differentiation between commodities. Utility, equivalence, difference—displays of sign value have become closely associated with status hierarchies in such a way that the circulation of sign values governs, and is governed by, cultural capital. A 2019 ad campaign illustrates this concept by turning prestige cultural capital back into its sign: Autograph Collection Hotels—"Because it's what we collect that makes us who we are." Sign values are generally used as social exchange values. When clients on *Property Brothers* abandon the performance of a rational investor for the look they want in a room, it is because they are already envisioning themselves "wearing" their house, already imagining what they want their house to say about themselves. They have invested themselves in a desire to be identified by their choice of design aesthetics. They are pre-trading on those sign values as exchange values.

Design value and aesthetic value. Particularly in the home renovation/real estate markets, design value and its close cousin, aesthetic value, are key material expressions of sign value. Design value is key to the social production of space. Each of these value forms is primarily visual and dependent on perceptual validation. Design value rests on aesthetic codes, and aesthetic values draw on design value. Aesthetics and design are rooted in desire, and they appeal to desire. Of HGTV's interior home designers, Gaines is particularly admired by her female fans because of how she designs spaces to reflect and suit the personalities, tastes, and desires of her client subjects.[29]

The HGTV network stresses a model of value acquisition that accentuates the central importance of signifying labor (discursive labor, design labor) as performed by the celebrity designers and decorators who host the shows. Their practices aim at translating prestige sign values into exchange values. Staging the renovated home for the big reveal represents the penultimate sign value practice on HGTV. Staging fuses aesthetic value with perceptions of desire.

Reputational value. Here, value draws on the recognition of status hierarchies. In Arjun Appadurai's view, reputational value is an expression of the politics of value.[30] The reputation of a craftsperson, a designer, an artist, or a neighborhood functions in roughly the same way to enhance the desirability of a particular commodity. A prominent form of reputational value in the society of the spectacle is celebrity value. Gaines of *Fixer Upper* provides an exemplar. Her show's popularity has solidified her reputation as a design goddess, as well as elevated the valuations of her renovated houses featured on *Fixer Upper*. This narrative extends beyond the show—numerous Gaines-renovated houses have been turned into celebrity Airbnb rentals. The owners of Gaines-renovated properties have been able to convert her reputational prestige value into a rent that exceeds the nominal value of the home because her TV-renovated homes are scarce and in demand. Her reputation is a product of spectatorship. Surplus value has been added because Gaines's fans have made an interpretive investment in the look of the homes she has transformed. Her use of recycled shiplap has made her the darling of those who fantasize about life inside her rendition of farmhouse modernism. Celebrity value cannot catalyze new value without the interpretive labor supplied by fans and consumers. Spectators' interpretive labor is as generative of value as the physical labor that goes into the renovation. This interpretive investment is performative of value. The branding process comes full circle by drawing on Gaines's celebrity value to feed sign value. Joanna has become a signifier of her own brand of paint, which "provides you with 150 of Joanna's hand-selected colors. Within this curated collection, you'll find the perfect shade to tell your family's story."[31] Joanna's reputation, which has been accumulated by virtue of the designs produced for HGTV, is thus transferred into the manufacture of demand for her signature style. Celebrity is a sign value motivator that has the capacity to be a value multiplier. HGTV occupies a sweet spot here—able to draw on its celebrity talent to stylistically produce a signifying value while also promoting its celebrities to generate further demand for the value.

Emotional value. Wherever there is desire, there is an emotional component. On home renovation TV, emotional value must be boosted, steered, and channeled for both client and viewer, requiring the exercise of emotional labor via computer simulations, video editing, and music overlays to choreograph and guide excitement. The commodification of affect has long been a fundamental aspect of contemporary marketing and advertising and has been heightened in the recent marketing buzz about pitching experiences rather than mere things as commodities. Given the increasing centrality of affect in the total value mix, it is also important to recognize the pivotal exercise of emotional labor. The HGTV formula relies heavily on the dramatization of the emotional ups and downs of home renovation. Tracking both the poles of anxiety and affirmation, the HGTV formula amplifies personal emotions surrounding the renovation process, activating cultural narratives about the subject of desire in relation to the subject of its costs. On HGTV, the intersection of emotional desire and sacrifice define the realization of value. The value of a house gets validated by the passionate outpouring of emotion shown by the client. Performative efforts to summon up surplus emotional value figure large in Chapter 2's mapping of HGTV's narrative formula, and Chapter 7 explores the subject of emotional labor. To the extent that viewers are positioned to identify (both empathetically and critically) with the prospective home buyer, emotional highs and lows spill out in both directions.

Comps—market valuations. The opposite of emotional value, comps are generated via a relative valuation model that compares assets to what similarly situated assets have yielded in the marketplace. Experts claim that to be able to assess fair market value depends on a detached, and supposedly rational, accounting of objects as they are constituted in markets. This is the final metric employed on *Flip or Flop* to determine how high a price can go. Like the stock market, value is here forever rolling and tumbling, although HGTV prefers to suppose that comps are always appreciating. So-called value investing in equity markets conjures up an intrinsic value that is measured by discounting projected future earnings against the present calculation of assets. But objective measures of intrinsic value are as entangled with emotionally driven sentiments in the prognostication of value in financial markets as they are in the calculation of value in residential real estate. Instead of quantitative calculations of value standing in direct opposition to emotional judgments, they rather work through one another.[32]

Imagination. Labor consists of both material practice and conceptualization. A consistent subtext of HGTV and DIY programs is that imaginative redesign is the spark plug for adding value to a home renovation. The exercise of imagination as a wellspring of value plays well to the conceits of those who identify with the cult of the creative class. HGTV home renovation shows visualize how design animated by imagination can excite and catalyze new value. Imagination represents the freedom of unalienated labor in these stories. Cast as unbound to convention and decoupled from the routine, the play of imagination is typically linked to another favored trait of our times, entrepreneurial innovation.

Connected to imagination as a source of new value is the continued nod to authenticity as an independent criterion of value. Authenticity is culturally constructed as the absence of overcommodification. If commodification represents standardization, the reorganization of commodity artifacts into unique custom design ideas reflects a desire for authenticity. Commodity culture pairs authenticity as the flip side of alienated consumption. When coupled with creative imagination, the upcycled surfaces of an American past—for example, a feature wall made from recycled barn wood—are said to connote authenticity because the material appears to have an organic relationship with history as opposed to being mass-produced, standardized commodities from a factory. Though specious, this construct of authenticity represents a type of anti-commodity sentiment—a value form rooted in our imagination of a moral economy rather than in an overdetermined corporate political economy. TV land imagines a moral economy guided by an ethic that refuses to allow values (moral and cultural) to be completely eclipsed by value (economic and social).

Real estate value. The real estate truism location, location, location is discursively acknowledged but softened by *Property Brothers* because of the effort to visually repress and conceal geographic location. Houses in the unspecified geography of more distant suburbs require a lengthier commute and are thus cheaper. The message is that you can get more bang for your buck—that is, greater discounts to the market in neighborhoods that are further from city centers. This logic of abstracted geography pushes the principles of rent-gap gentrification into the suburbs. In this way, HGTV supports an impression of generalized, geographically nonspecific gentrification.

Devaluation and creative destruction. In capitalist marketplaces valuation and devaluation work hand in hand, each a prerequisite of the other. As Marx points out, capital always flows to where it might fetch the highest returns. In practice this means that investors look to those areas that appear undervalued or devalued, recognizing that overvalued commodities will fetch a lesser return on investment. A system of capitalist value cannot exist without forces of devaluation. Value implies its absence. In a capitalist system of value, there must also be not value, lesser value, dormant value, and zombie value.

In the *Manifesto*, Marx and Frederick Engels situate the phenomena of creative destruction (though not the term) as a driving force of capitalist development: "The bourgeoisie cannot exist without constantly revolutionizing the instruments of production, and thereby the relations of production."[33] Competition around technological and market innovations has made the history of modern society one in which "all that is solid melts into air, all that holy is profaned."[34] Harvey applies the creative destruction thesis to the urban built environment, arguing that over time the spatial fixity of the built environment becomes a barrier to profitable investment.[35] Large-scale gentrification developments that raze devalued neighborhoods to transform the urban landscape with high-density upscale housing are familiar manifestations of this process. Joseph Schumpeter adapts the Marxian thesis to explain what he sees as the intrinsic growth dynamic of capitalist economies, pitching it as a positive force that draws its energy from the agency of the entrepreneurial innovator.[36] Defenders of the neoliberal faith similarly maintain that this form of erasure is essential to generating a flow of new capitalist opportunities. When HGTV endorses creative destruction as a strategy for transforming the rent-yielding potential of single-family residences, it endorses Schumpeter's version of the thesis but redirects its attention from the general relations of production to the household. HGTV thus dramatizes creative destruction as a cathartic assault on those features of a house that stand in the way of future value. On HGTV, creative destruction focuses on the architecture of interior space, limiting its general scope to the house and not the neighborhood.

HGTV's fundamental premise rests on finding devalued properties to renovate as a necessary precursor to new opportunities for creating value construction. When applied to customized home renovations, HGTV invites us to adopt the thesis of creative destruction as a personal investment strategy rather than as a means of urban policy. HGTV gentrification narratives rest on a tacit dialectic of devaluation and valuation. The idea that opportunities for renewed valuation can be found in a climate of relative devaluation is not new but a classic contrarian strategy that looks for contradictions to leverage in marketplaces that are situated in time, or rather, over time. Valuation is measured against its flawed or featureless past and imagined as it might be in a conditional future space.

Securitization, HGTV's Missing Thesis

Allusions to these eleven theses on value can routinely be found in HGTV's stories of home renovation and flipping. But HGTV is silent about perhaps the most significant contemporary forces shaping value in housing markets. The financialization of housing, which played such a pivotal role in the financial crisis of the last decade, requires our attention. In the 1990s, securitization took off as an investment instrument. Though securitization doesn't even make a cameo appearance in any HGTV story, it has become an essential driver of value in the form of MBSs. As we shall see, the absence of financial securitization in HGTV's accounts turns into a matter of considerable consequence for how one tells the story of value in the early twenty-first century.

Securitization refers to a process of transforming an asset into a more tradable commodity whose key attribute is enhanced liquidity. In practice, the asset most frequently sought for securitization has been debt obligations, particularly mortgage debt. Deregulation of the loan origination industry spurred the evolution of home-mortgage securitization. Traditionally, banks originated loans and held them to maturation. Securitization encouraged banks to move toward an "originate-and-distribute" mortgage model.[37] The originate-and-distribute model meant that loan originators pooled their loans (and the contractual debt obligations these represented) into assets that they sold to other financial institutions. Securitization created a market for selling these pooled assets. Selling debt obligations in this way held several advantages for loan originators: first, it brought in renewed capital so that they could make, and turn over, still more loans; second, it permitted them to remove risk from their accounts. In turn, buyers of these pooled loans sought the cash flows generated by interest payments on the loans, and they converted the loan portfolios into bonds that represented a stake in the assets associated with the portfolio. The goal was to make these MBSs tradable among investors who sought a rate of return based on the aggregated stream of debt payments. "Securitization ... transforms illiquid assets [the home loan] into tradable and liquid financial securities [the MBS], and by so doing, it transforms debt into a commodity that can be traded."[38]

Capital tends to be a more productive return on itself when its flow from owner to owner is neither slowed nor interrupted. Value that is not in motion is stuck (like coins in a piggy bank), can do no work, and actually becomes an impediment to growth. To fully integrate housing into financial markets, a fundamental constraint needed to be overcome. Residential homes tend, with the exception of mobile homes, to be fixed in place; they are stationary and pinned to a foundation. If a homeowner becomes emotionally attached to his house—what HGTV celebrates as one's dream home—this too makes the house less liquid as a commodity. From the perspective of capital markets, the dream home is like an imprisoned resource. That's why it was so important to separate the asset of the house from the house itself. Untethering the mortgage from the house made it possible to bundle with other mortgages, now similarly separated from the geographically and socially located houses they reference. The MBS thus represents a homogeneous commodity that makes it easier to establish a continuously flowing market, permitting the bundle to freely circulate and trade with sufficient speed and volume to promote the perception of uninterrupted liquidity and efficiency.[39] With this maneuver, your debt obligation can circulate in a bond fund traded back and forth between banks across the world while your house remains spatially fixed in place.[40] "By securitizing mortgage debt, finance has given global liquidity to housing. The size of securitized markets [based] on housing as well as household assets and payment streams now dwarf stock markets."[41]

By 2004, investment banks could not concoct MBSs fast enough to satisfy institutional investors, and a market slowdown in the loan origination business stymied their capacity for churning out more product. Loan originators needed to generate more loans and that meant loosening lending standards. The accelerated reliance on nonprime loans elevated the risk profiles of the mortgage bundles, but they were nonetheless attractive to those hawking the securities. Since 2008, these loan origination practices have been subject to scrutiny because too many subprime loans (by definition higher risk loans that carried adjustable interest rates and additional fees) were structured by discriminatory lending practices, especially with regard to loans that went to lower-income blacks and Latinos. These loans were critical, however, to the continued profitability of securitization. "For securitized loans, profits for loan originators depended not so much on long-term home values or the borrower's likelihood of default but on short-term revenues from points, fees, origination charges, and especially the size of the gap between the prevailing interest rate index and the rate paid by borrowers, commonly known as the 'yield spread.'"[42]

When such loans were bundled into risk-delineated tiers (called tranches), the additional fees, points, and yield spreads that added to the profits of loan originators now promised to add to the rate of return that investors might reap from purchasing the riskier tranches of mortgage debt. Competition with other investors and tolerance for risk drove financial institutions to leverage themselves more intensively, seeking ever higher prices on a commodity whose value was open to interpretation.

In this way, household debt feeds capital. Debt and risk have become key value-generating assets of our era.[43] In the run-up to 2008, a prime contributor to this debt stream came from residential mortgages. "At the core of securitization is a process of risk shifting to households."[44] Among the consequences of financial crisis, private equity and hedge funds scooped up portfolios of foreclosed properties and turned them into rentals for many of the households who had been evicted from their homes. Compounding the process of risk shifting to households who lost their homes, the empires of corporate landlords fed the engines of securitization by entrenching the conditions of housing precarity to renters made subject to exorbitant rent hikes and fee-stacking that outpaced wages.[45] The same capital formations that had preyed on MBSs before the crisis have now securitized the revenue streams from rent checks. Securitization is here to stay, a fundamental investment channel that leverages debt and risk into easily tradable securities. Sure enough, by 2016, finance capital had begun to securitize the so-called fix-and-flip loans that have become a feature of a rebounding house-flipping industry.[46]

In the global political economy, the production of value through manufacturing has waned, while the financial generation of value has become a pivotal dynamic. Capital intensive industries have diminished the centrality of labor as a source of value production. Labor's contribution to value formation now comes as much from the consumer side of the coin, or, more precisely, the debt side of the consumer coin. Labor is valued today for its ability to pay off the debt that it is encouraged to incur. Securitization, especially the innovations of synthetic derivatives, creates financial instruments that harness and leverage the stream of interest payments on consumer household debt. Finance capital's ability to capture more than its share of value (think spiraling inequality) in recent decades has a good deal to do with this shift away from employing labor as value producing to leveraging labor's wages to fuel streams of debt repayments.

Though the long shadow of securitization now stretches across the residential real estate markets, HGTV's stories downplay the process of risk shifting to households. Instead, HGTV pictures the risks of betting on a fixer-upper project as a matter of venturous individual fortitude. At its core, HGTV champions a neoliberal ideology that repositions risk management as the task of the entrepreneurial teamwork of renovator and homeowner. There is ultimately a very good reason why HGTV does not include securitization in its procession of value forms. Securitization does not produce value for the homeowner, it preys on homeowners in the service of capital investment firms.

Amplifying HGTV's fragmentary assumptions about what makes renovation value tick disrupts the tacit logic of HGTV's narrative. HGTV's assumptions are simply too unreflexive, as well as historically, sociologically, geographically, and financially dislocated. When critically resituated, HGTV's own words and images can be turned into tools for studying the semiotic practices requisite to constructing a simulacrum of renovation value. But there is little in HGTV's accounts that can prepare us to make sense of a political economy of financial securitization that organizes the extraction of value outside the frame of the television screen. We have seen how the very nature of television's storytelling indelibly imposes its own logic of visual signs into ideas about what constitutes value. The remainder of this book continues to pit HGTV's narratives against those that it leaves absent.

Chapter 2 introduces a cultural analysis of the salvage television genre and its principal subgenres of flipping, renovation, rehab, and restoration shows. I map, annotate, and deconstruct HGTV's narrative formula that governs how renovation programs chronicle the journey to renovation value. This deconstruction reveals how renovation and salvage narratives make a game out of recognizing and creating value where it was not, through canny taste and handwork, to make families' visions of an ideal home possible within the vague limits of their time and finances. My aim is to further illuminate the ideological maneuvers that frame HGTV's pursuit of happiness in a salvage economy, independent of the realities that make its shows possible. Sequenced from frustrated entitlement to imaginative redesign to demolition rituals to managing risk to the performativity of staging and the big reveal, HGTV imagines a cultural blueprint for reinventing value where it has previously been missing.

2

Renovation Narratives

The spectator-buyer is meant to envy herself as she will become if she buys the product. She is meant to imagine herself transformed by the product into an object of envy for others, an envy which will then justify her loving herself.
—JOHN BERGER, *Ways of Seeing*

Following the 2008 collapse of the financial system, Daniel Mrozowski observed that reality TV was producing shows that pulled in opposite directions. From one side, *Hoarders* chronicled cringing morality parables about the perils of collecting too much stuff. From the other side, salvage-oriented shows sifted through the debris of material artifacts to find objects that could be returned to circulation within the commodity system.[1] Home renovation shows may have been the preeminent revaluation genre, but gimmicky small-stakes tests of value conjuring also crowded cable TV.

Hoarder shows reveal the seamy underbelly of commodity desire turned into neurotic obsession. Mary Douglas's study of symbolic systems of purity demonstrates how symbolic rules and classifications define the moral boundaries of our social worlds. As such, we may view the soil in the vegetable garden as a fertility gift from the heavens, while soil on the kitchen floor represents filth and impurity. Hoarder shows thus read like a primer on "matter out of place" prompting audiences to shiver in visual disgust at the unclean accumulations displayed.[2] Witnessing socially isolated souls succumbing to their compulsive desires to hold on to everything that ever came into their lives provokes moral judgments about the hoarders and the chaos surrounding them. Hoarders reveal the perils of indiscriminately accumulating materials that not only are just the hollowed-out shells of former value but become the very antithesis of exchange value. As morality tales, these shows testify to the stagnant accumulation of things disintegrating into the death, indeed, the abomination of use value.

Hoarders' stashes disclose an inability to differentiate what has value from what does not. When everything is assigned value, it becomes unworkable to assign a hierarchy of value. If every object holds significance, the loss of differentiation diminishes the ability to take stock of value as a relationship. While an obsessive fetishism underlies the hoarder's activity, the same root impulse also conditions the treatment of value in the world of capitalist finance, in which the category of value seems to extend in as many directions as possible until there is nothing that stands outside the realm of value.

Hoarders represent an economic disease that threatens the healthy flow of new commodities—the wellspring of capitalist growth throughout the twentieth century requires shedding the used to make room for the new. Hoarders represent the arrest of circulation, while capital demands faster and faster circulatory flows. Following Zygmunt Bauman, hoarding material objects from the past makes for immovability, while finance capital with its hoard of digital currency is unencumbered in its movement: it's not just capitalist elites who are the new nomads; capital itself in its money form is mobile.[3] Yet the crisis of capital was catalyzed by the overaccumulation of investment capital seeking greater liquidity. Securitization aimed to create hyperliquidity or hyperflow, but with the 2008 collapse it spawned its opposite: a system-wide immotility that very nearly brought capitalism to its knees.

Reality TV after 2008 also featured gritty salvage contests such as *Storage Wars* that scoured the landscape of storage bins for objects left behind, forgotten, and covered with dust but still containing the germ of renewed exchange value if properly resituated. Across the post-crash landscape, opportunities for the working class to make a buck were limited, but here one needed only a small roll of bills, a gambler's instinct, and a predatory mentality ready to seize on opportunities. As stories about petty competitions for working-class survival after the 2008 financial crash, *Storage Wars* expresses a cynical realism about making money by preying on the commodities left behind by defaults. The predatory ethos mimics on a microscale the financial services industries. Structured as a competition between salvage players, the show dramatizes how much each player is willing to risk on a bin, guessing whether it contains a buried vein of treasure. To mine that hidden source of value once the bet is placed, players need to supply the savvy to sort out what is fool's gold from what has gained value by virtue of being held out of circulation over time. After trillions of dollars' worth of supposed value in derivatives vanished in a heartbeat from global securities markets, the ability to distinguish between what has real value and what does not seems especially pertinent. In a world of fuzzy value, possessing the special lenses that would allow one to identify value as it lies scattered about in the debris, coupled with the ability to screen the real from the hyperreal, these are empowering skills in the salvage stage of neoliberalism.

On the more masculine-oriented DIY channel, postrecession reality TV has embraced architectural salvage and log repurposing shows. *Salvage Dawgs* and *Barnwood Builders* follow salvage economy professionals. The Black Dog Salvage team picks through structures destined for teardown, disassembling those objects that have value in its architectural salvage business: vintage doors, windows, moldings, railings, stained glass, wrought iron, and industrial hardware—hot items to those renovating with an industrial or rustic aesthetic in mind. *Salvage Dawgs* further demonstrates how salvaged materials can be reassembled into imaginative amalgams of chairs, tables, bars, and gates. Especially focused on the character of handhewn logs used to build the infrastructure of nineteenth-century rural America, *Barnwood Builders* episodes like "Repurposing Every Beam from a Pennsylvania Bank Barn" address the restoration of moral and economic value gained through the recapture of resources while also demonstrating how imaginative and creative skill can repurpose valued materials into reclaimed cabins, furniture, and flooring.

The transition from *Storage Wars* to the renovation genre shifted the narrative from using one's wits to turn forgotten wells of value into cash to the renovation narratives about forging new value through imagination and work (transforming properties of limited but still risky valuations into properties of safe and significantly magnified value). From *Storage Wars* to *Flip or Flop*, one concern prevails: What's that thing worth? In a world overtaken by the hegemony of global supply chains, these shows dwell on what can be salvaged from the afterlife of commodity chains and how such items might be profitably moved back into circulation. Unlike the 1960s' *Price Is Right* fantasies about shiny new consumer goods, salvage TV mined for veins of anthropocentric-modified value in things used up, buried, or locked in a decaying infrastructure.

Another current of television programming dives into the commodity afterlife with value creation contests to unlock value from objects whose value has been all but spent, objects mostly used up and available dirt cheap at flea markets. HGTV's *Flea Market Flip* is a small-stakes contest about who can best maximize their return on investment (ROI) in flea markets. Highest ROI wins. This game of repurposing disassembled junk items into artfully hybridized handmade commodities is quite explicit—making money in the new economy requires a creative bricoleur's eye—spotting the odd bit that can be recombined with another random bit to create a new look commodity (e.g., a cut-up bicycle welded to form a gate). *Flea Market Flips'* version of the salvage economy favors the bricoleur whose semiotic prowess at recombining signifiers opens the door to getting the most value—top dollar.

But it's the house-flipping and renovation shows that represent the highest stakes in salvage economy narratives. Though it might seem that all home renovation shows are pretty much alike, and they are, a closer view can detect a spectrum of differentiation that ranges from rehabilitation and restoration shows to house-flipping shows to home renovation and remodeling shows. The flipping and renovation scripts are readily familiar to viewers as a sequence of prescribed ritual movements that generally include smashing down walls before refacing every visible surface, moving from the outdated or the tasteless to the modern. As it always has, modern mostly means "made to look new" in this discourse. There are microcosm undertones here of Schumpeter's thesis that capitalism renews itself through spasms of creative destruction. Every episode bears witness to enactments of this thesis—creative destruction produces a blank canvas on which to design refurbished, higher-value spaces.

On one end of the spectrum is the salvage genre, which focuses on flippers who faithfully rehabilitate and restore older houses. Unlike the renovation and flip genres, the rehab narrative sets its sights on reclaiming the historical authenticity of the house, alert to the preservation and recycling of materials as opposed to the smash-and-dump style of renovation and flipping shows. *Rehab Addict*, with Nicole Curtis, restores the decaying homes of the early modern bourgeoisie to their glory days before decades of white out-migration followed by disinvestment in Detroit and Minneapolis. Curtis expresses appreciation for homes built between the 1880s and the 1920s and acknowledges their architectural and material histories by repeating her restoration mantra in episode after episode: "Original is always best." She stands philosophically opposed to the renovation shows, all of which consider houses as nothing more than empty shells, fully abstracted from their histories, just as they are fully dislocated from social space. Her voice-over introduction to each episode stresses, "I buy and sell houses, but I'm not your average flipper. I don't just renovate; I restore old homes to their former glory." Her process explicitly endorses a salvage model for restoring value: "I challenge people every day. I really use all salvage materials" because "opportunity comes to those who value what they have."[4]

A second subgenre treats the renovation process as a straight flip and imagines a Wild West economy in which reckless risks prove to be smart money in a fast-paced competitive (and barely regulated) environment. Success at episode's end comes not from meeting the needs of a specific client family but by the metric of the flipper's money pocket. The most prominent flipping show is *Flip or Flop* set in Orange County, California, where Tarek and Christina El Moussa focus on making as much money as possible ("top dollar") by flipping houses. Their show's success has spawned a legion of regional imitators. By 2017, the franchise included spin-offs operating in other metro areas: *Flip or Flop Vegas*, *Desert Flippers*, *Flipping Atlanta*, *Chicago Flippers*, and *Lone Star Flip*. Every decision *Flip or Flop* makes is driven either by how much it hurts or by what aids potential profit margins. The El Moussas bet on houses that have been left in dump-site condition. Because they claim the worst houses present the greatest opportunities for profit, they prefer houses that are "distressed inventory at a discounted price."[5] Introducing an on-screen counter to indicate their mounting total investment in the flip aims at building faux suspense about whether unforeseen costs will overtake the possibility of profit and make the investment a flop. Tarek is the voice of anxiety about money but also quick to take risky wagers, frequently opting for sight-unseen (to amp up the drama) bank foreclosures. Won at auction or bought via direct all-cash offers through a telephone-voice selling agent, the disfigured properties Tarek and Christina take on are by each episode's end neatly morphed into generic showroom houses that appear cosmetically transformed—especially if one subscribes to mainstream middle-class appetites for home décor fashions. Each time they make a sale and record their profits, the El Moussas rush to roll over the profits into their next acquisition. *Flip or Flop* views houses as pure commodities geared toward a speculative housing market, its properties restored according to a paint-by-numbers formula for the market in general, rather than customized for a specific buyer. Following this formula, *Flip or Flop* aggressively seeks its own self-interest in pushing every flip toward a new inflationary real estate bubble.

By contrast, the Waco duo of Joanna and Chip Gaines, who host *Fixer Upper*, revitalize houses for clients who seek them out. They tailor each renovation project, at least nominally, to the aesthetic preferences and social needs of the episode's client family. Joanna is portrayed as an artistic design and decorator savant, while Chip plays a down-to-earth builder, hard working, humorous, self-effacing, skilled in the construction trades, and experienced as a general contractor. Specializing in a farmhouse style leavened with modernist sensibilities, "they've remade many beautiful homes in Waco, all done with a cheery, family-focused energy that springs from deep Christian roots."[6] Portrayed as entrepreneurial heroes embracing a modern-rustic lifestyle, the Gaineses are smart about real estate and keen to help their clients identify and upgrade undervalued pieces of the Waco housing market. Joanna's opening voice-over explains their approach to adding value: "We look for the most decrepit and old falling down places we can find." Where the Orange County stories are indifferent to who the buyer is, *Fixer Upper* and *Property Brothers* claim to make a contribution to the quality of life for each episode's home-buying family. Rhetorically, the show that claims to be most motivated about renovating not simply the house but also the wider neighborhood and community is *Good Bones*, née Two Chicks and a Hammer, a mother-daughter entrepreneurial duo who rebuild houses in older impoverished neighborhoods in Indianapolis because they are "passionate about their mission to improve Indianapolis."[7]

Several other variants of the renovation genre stand out. *Income Property* features Scott McGillivray giving guidance to clients on how to turn renovated properties into income-producing rent machines: how to become part of the rentier class so that you are not just another vulnerable schmuck holding a mortgage that you may or may not be able to cover in the future. The host educates his clients on how to do renovations that yield higher rents, or identify properties likely to appreciate in value for resale. Whereas *Flip or Flop* sees the renovated house as a short-term investment for the flipper, *Income Property* imagines the renovated house as a long-term investment for the homeowner investor. The appeal of the show is made clear in its promos: "I can smell the profits" and "anybody can do it!" When considered in the light of the postcrisis political economy of renovating to rent, *Income Property* has proven to be the most prescient HGTV narrative.

Texas Flip N Move features the North Texas working class, and it is truly home renovation TV for the working class. *Flip N Move* tweaks the flipping renovation formula with the added premise that every house is acquired at auction minus the land on which it sits, thus requiring that it be moved to a redevelopment lot. On the periphery of Fort Worth, run-down working-class shacks occupy property that suburban developers and home builders want to clear away to build new housing projects and developments. Flippers eyeball the aging structures, weathered by decades of deterioration and neglect, before bidding against one another at auction. Were it not for the auctions, these would be teardowns. Bids of $400 to $1,200 win most of the auctions because the houses are damaged, worn, small, and just a shell. Drawing on their knowledge of moving houses, the Snow Sisters, the Lone Wolf, and the Young Guns compete to clear the properties of the houses in exchange for cheap starter boxes for rebuilding inexpensive homes. These working-class flippers bring creative low-cost methods and unconventional materials to accomplish a simulation of the familiar renovation script, going so far as to install discount granite kitchen counters in some cases. By show's end, the renovated houses are reauctioned to a small crowd of bargain-hunting working-class consumers. The renovated houses would appear to be good bargains, and *Texas Flip N Move* comes closer than any other show to producing affordable housing. The homes are relatively cheap providing that the buyer has land on which to site the house. At the very least, *Texas Flip N Move* appears to democratize access to renovated homes.

The show's early popularity may be changing that. By the third season, the flippers were cutting deals prior to auction with investors looking to turn the renovated boxes into rural Airbnbs and hunting lodges (the Texas version of *agriturismo*). *Texas Flip N Move* shows working-class flippers taking advantage of creative destruction aimed at turning economically depressed and undervalued real estate areas into middle-class profit centers. Even on the peri-urban outskirts of Fort Worth, the specter of suburban gentrification looms as an underlying driver of the flipping economy.

Though the history of the real estate bubble's 2007–2008 collapse haunts HGTV shows, that trauma remains thoroughly repressed. With the exception of *Flip or Flop*, the consequences of the subprime mortgage crisis remain resolutely unspoken. Built into the opening voice-over of every *Flip or Flop* episode, Tarek explains, "We're real estate agents. Ever since the market crashed, it's been a rocky road." So, they turned their knowledge of real estate markets into flipping houses and learned to take advantage of the rash of foreclosures that flowed out of the crash.

Narrating the Journey to Added Value

HGTV's home renovation shows are structured by a rigid narrative formula aimed at answering a paramount riddle of our times—how to get more house than you pay for. The repetitive formula produces a narrative that relies heavily on predetermined semiotic binaries and an emotional arc that begins with hopeful anxieties and ends with emotional peaks realized in the triumphant revelation of aesthetic gratification. Renovation shows differ slightly from flipping shows, but all feature tours of beaten-up spaces and worn-out, deteriorating houses that have received no stylistic updates over the years. Renovation shows mediate risk via clients' overdramatized facial expressions, while flipping shows channel the unexpected through the host's anxiety about making less money.

The generic *Property Brothers* HGTV narrative curve mechanically passes through fourteen stations on a predetermined path to a visualized promised land of value. Passing through the obligatory narrative steps prescribed by the formula gives shape and emphasis to the following distilled narrative kernels: (1) a desire for taste on a budget; (2) a TV semiotics of desire; (3) modeling/simulating value; (4) the imperatives of time, speed, and money; (5) demolition rituals and the rebirth of value; (6) risk and its management; (7) staging value; (8) the big reveal, orchestrated fetishism; and (9) tallying the appreciation of value.

Renovation episodes introduce clients with a quick snapshot of their story along with their wish list of must-haves. "We are looking for our forever home, somewhere we can raise a family," a place that embraces "modern design," or better yet, a "midcentury modern" style with "space to entertain." Clients desire open concept or "open sight lines" along with vaulted ceilings, hardwood floors (even if simulated), quartz, granite, marble or concrete countertops, oversized kitchen islands, farmhouse sinks, luxurious en suite spa-like bathrooms, stainless steel appliances, subway tile backsplashes, white cabinets, and upcycled sliding barn doors. Clients follow their wish lists with a declaration of what they are willing to spend—their budget. This establishes a tension between clients' emotional desires for an aesthetics of value versus the limits imposed by their budget. Clients generally want more value than they are able to pay for. Neither clients nor viewers come to HGTV as a tabula rasa. They have been coveting scenes and motifs from interior design and lifestyle magazines, watching HGTV shows, and sharing on Instagram and Pinterest. Their desires have been accumulated and curated from looking at the millions of images circulating throughout the innumerable outlets of real estate porn. Clients thus enter the scene with well-defined conceptions of social class and how they would like to be identified in terms of taste.

Who are the clients? More often than not they're a millennial-ish couple with a starter family. From episode to episode, prospective home-buying clients reflect an HGTV attempt at social diversity—mainly white heterosexual couples but also same-sex couples, interracial couples, African American, Asian, and Hispanic couples, as well as single-parent and blended families, and even an occasional multigenerational household. Yet no matter their demographic variation, every prospective home buyer shares one overarching trait, a profile motivated by an excess (a surplus) of commodity desires—desires that have seemingly become unmoored from rational assessment of prices in the real estate marketplace. All couples who appear on HGTV subscribe to an aesthetics of desire defined by the tastes and styles of white cultural capital.[8] Otherness is thus swallowed and made not just symbolically white but symbolically privileged as well.

How are budgets (already a euphemism for the relationship between income and loan size) calculated? HGTV's producers refuse to permit on-screen considerations of the relationship between budget, income, credit, and loans. What kind of reality television is this—first rule, dramatize the ordinary—that makes no effort to explore conflict- and anxiety-laden stories about credit and loans? Internet memes satirize the absurd mismatch between gig economy jobs, earning capacity, and the budgets required for HGTV renovation projects. A typical meme captions a handsome millennial, white, heterosexual dyad: "HGTV Couples Be Like / I walk iguanas and my wife sells umbrella insurance from home. Our budget is $2.1 million."

Now the refusal to speak about the kind of income necessary to budget a *Property Brothers* renovation makes sense: it would reveal entirely too much about who is excluded from joining this club.

To teach clients their first lesson in the possibilities of renovation gentrification, *Property Brothers* presents a showcase home that checks off all the clients' desires for indulgent beauty but is priced far above their budget. Crafted as they are from the photography of the upscale housing industry, these open-concept spaces speak to pure desire. As the camera takes us through a too-expensive house, the clients can be heard echoing the camera's gaze, expressing exultation and joy at the decorated spaces. A tense moment of sticker shock ensues as the clients realize that their place in the economy will not allow them to live as they had imagined when they oohed and aahed their way through the promise of opulence. Having exposed their client's inflated sense of entitlement, the brothers, Jonathan and Drew Scott, then proceed to chart a way for them to join in the whirl of gentrification-driven inflation, to join the entitled classes. The tease allows the Scotts to set forth an alternative narrative about the relationship between must-haves and possibility. The brothers' tactic translates their client's desire for a refined aesthetic of interior space into the commodity that they are selling—why not consider a fixer-upper? The brothers assure their clients that they can mimic every surface finish the consumer desires in the overpriced bourgeois model home by turning the shell of an undervalued and dated home into a fresh canvas on which to simulate the surfaces of the bourgeoisie.

The brothers' methodology for turning a house into a work of art rests on mimetically installing the codes of modern bourgeois interiors. They exaggerate the rewards and minimize the risks of renovating by offering to take charge with a vision and a plan for turning an ugly duckling into a swan, guaranteeing prospective buyers their dream home, defined by all their aspirational surfaces and spaces, while still keeping it within budget. It's quite a sales pitch: to live in the right neighborhood, but at discounted prices; to live in perfectly controlled and self-contained spaces. The brothers bring the dream of drooling entitlement back to the table by advocating the renovation route, preferably with an experienced guide by your side. Their strategy builds on Georg Simmel's theorem that value is constituted by how much objects "resist our desire to possess them."[9] The *Property Brothers* strategy enforces an initial distance between the object of desire and the couple's resources for realizing it. Thus, *Property Brothers* must make clear the economic gulf that ordinarily stands between desire and its fulfillment while also establishing a narrative assurance that the Scotts can bridge that distance—if the couple and the viewer stay the course through the show's formula to the end. This is another reminder that barriers to the fulfillment of desire are essential to the realization of value.

The quest for a fixer-upper begins with tours of flawed and dated houses. During these tours, clients reject spaces they find off-putting and surfaces they find objectionable. The tours set up binary oppositions including recurring gender stereotypes of wives who want more bling ("I want what I want") and husbands consumed with anxiety about exceeding the budget ("How much does that cost?"). Despite the litany of negative assessments cherry-picked from the edited walk-throughs, the show's flip artists assure their clients that they can turn poorly lit and unglamorous spaces into fantasy visions. After couples express doubts, a lack of vision, and anxiety about the costs and unpredictability of a renovation process, the design partner—the visionary—reveals an on-screen computer simulation that projects a transformative design sketch and photorealistic renderings over the existing spaces to visually imagine how he plans to convert restricted and limited spaces into open and fashionable spaces.

As a representational device, these visualizations of alternative interior spaces project a utopian expectation. Thanks to three-dimensional (3D) digital computer graphics, these renderings of design sketches present hyperreal spaces: "the generation by models of a real" that supersede reality.[10] Such photorealistic representations effectively seduce by stimulating desire and making tangible its satisfactions. As soon as clients see the simulated metamorphosis, we can already feel them salivating because the transformation, though virtual, appears nearly indistinguishable from representations of the real. The simulations are meant not just as a plan for renovating the reality of interior spaces; they also redefine the real, first by erasing the existent real and then replacing that real with coded assemblages of signs that are taken to be a projection of a future reality.

The 3D simulation prompts a dramatic psychological surge in imagined valuation, especially when coupled with a price tag that magically matches up exactly to the clients' maximum budget. How is this accomplished? Partly with sleight of hand, partly with generic aesthetic techniques, and partly with a rigged timeline. Bothersome to fans are behind-the-scenes practices that distort the spectator's calculus of valuation. After the cameras leave, the decorating magic and furnishings that have added so much perceived value to the big reveal may be snatched back.[11] Though this may seem a small detail, it opens up questions about the valuation process and about how much HGTV subsidizes the remodeling process by pitching in for furnishings. The *Property Brothers* website indicates that HGTV sweetens the furnishings pot by up to $25,000 because sponsors like Shaw Industries, Wayfair, and Joss and Main are thrilled to have their furnishing surfaces showcased at the apex of emotional valuation. Even in these staged neoliberal scenarios, the privileged receive subsidies. *Property Brothers* even features on-screen product placements for Wayfair and Joss and Main during the big reveal, and in 2017 the Scott brothers partnered with Lowe's to sell their Aspirational Scott Living Furniture Collections.

> If you're wondering how the Brothers manage to stay within budget while furnishing an entire home, it looks like the two figures that appear in each *Property Brothers* budget—namely, the cost of the house and the cost of the renovation—are actually from two different sources (often a home loan and a renovation loan). . . . Jonathan and Drew also . . . put up $10,000 of their production company's money on each project (mostly for labor), and, of course, receive "certain sponsored products" as they go.[12]

The formula for generating the appearance of spectacular value varies little across the renovation and flipping shows, although both *Fixer Upper* and *Rehab Addict* present their own twists based on repurposing recycled materials (think shiplap). A tried-and-true script concentrates on inexpensive cosmetic transformations including fresh paint on walls and brick, refaced fireplaces, and replacing carpets with engineered or simulated hardwood materials. These are all quick, easy, and relatively inexpensive fixes, especially with wholesale prices on the flooring. Aimed at the lowest common denominator, TV renovations take a safe, generic route, with a color palette limited to neutral shades of beige, gray, whites, and tan covering walls, countertops, tiles, and cabinets mixed with contrasting dark flooring hues.[13] The *Flip or Flop* franchise is a little less disingenuous about when and where to use the cheapest materials available, and about the looks the hosts strive for: they seek the widest possible pool of buyers because it's a spec house. Commenting on his wife's choice of color finishes (cream, tan, and gray for the counters, tiles, and cabinets), the host of *Flip or Flop Fort Worth* explains their preference for neutral signifiers, "What I like about it is that it's general. It will appeal to most everyone."

Property Brothers always stresses a relatively short and inviolable deadline for finishing the renovation (six to seven weeks) ostensibly to meet the convenience needs of impatient buyers. This is much faster than a typical renovation process: the median time to completion ranged from three-hundred days during the precrash flipping frenzy to two hundred days in the years following the foreclosure crisis. Jonathan Scott acknowledges that the shows' timelines are "not realistic. . . . It's a TV show. We haves sub trades lined up, permits ready. We are a top priority for trades and vendors. That helps us do things efficiently. People may not be able to get deals like we do."[14] In the spectacle, time takes many forms. As a narrative form, renovation TV routinely resorts to conventions of time compression, speed-ups coupled with temporal ellipses.[15] A faux dramatic technique, deadlines are imposed mostly by the logic of television production schedules and, to a lesser extent, by concerns for holding down costs. Narrative formulas drive deadlines and deadlines drive narratives—will the project be finished on time? They also provide a device for turning the uncertainty of a renovation into closure.

While the narrative is drawn to fit HGTV's consumer interests, this logic of highly compressed time also fits well with the circulatory logic of capital investment in property renovation projects. Tarek of *Flip or Flop* makes this his cardinal rule: "When you are in the flipping game, speed is of the essence." Speed and the continuous circulation of money as investment capital is an explicit motive force in *Flip or Flop*, in which the signature conclusion of every episode is a reminder that the profits from each flip must keep working: "time to find another house to flip." Squeezing a project into a six-week timeline gives the contractor the possibility of limiting labor costs by organizing labor time more intensively (lining up the trades). Moreover, loans for flips usually come with higher interest rates, so limiting turnaround time for a renovation project and getting it sold quickly drive the thinking of flippers. Manipulations of temporality practiced by HGTV renovation programs contribute to time-compression narrative formulas that are key to understanding the tacit value theories of labor that undergird the genre.

Demolition day pivots the narrative toward creative destruction. This is a mandatory moment of the formula elaborately performed on every renovation and flipping show. Demo day offers the visceral satisfaction of smashing walls, cabinets, countertops, sinks, baths, floors, and ceilings into debris! *Property Brothers* stages this as the ritual bonding engagement of the contractor brother to the client couple. Armed with iconic sledgehammers, the couple take a few ceremonial swings to get the process started before the contractor brother whales away, pent-up emotions directed into beating and tearing down the signifiers of a past that must be eliminated. *Fixer Upper*'s Chip Gaines gives more explicit voice to the boyish pleasure he gets from smashing things on demolition day while also acknowledging its therapeutic expression: "Some guys go to the gym; I beat the crud out of a house." Without exception, demolition focuses on taking out limiting walls to create an alternative social architecture of perceptually enlarged open-space kitchen, dining, and living areas. This is the moment of erasure, the removal of barriers to transcendence—in microcosm, the symbolic rebirth of capitalist society.

This symbolic scene of destruction is necessary to the material expression of a clean and open slate of possibility, and the staged spasm of purposeful violence excites both a psychological and cultural cleansing necessary to actualizing the open concept. To accomplish this, the demolition process focuses on spatially hollowing out the existing house. Ritually removing impurities both materially and symbolically purges the past, a necessary step to turning the shell of a house into an appropriate space for the building of new memories. To make the house to be renovated into an acceptable replica of an upper-middle-class standard, "matter out of place" must be swept out and pollution eliminated to make way for the performance of new value.

> In chasing dirt, papering, decorating, tidying we are not governed by anxiety to escape disease, but are positively re-ordering our environment, making it conform to an idea. There is nothing fearful or unreasoning in our dirt-avoidance: it is a creative movement, an attempt to relate form to function, to make unity of experience.[16]

Demolition scenes represent a recurring motif in the saga of modernization. Just as the traditional needed to be eliminated to create spaces for modernity, so too the reproduction of the modern requires the periodic displacement and demolition of that which stands in the way of progress.[17] As staged performances, demolition scenes reenact a familiar trope of consumer society amid the inexorable force of fashion/technology cycles and the necessity of obsolescence—we must throw away the used to make way for new commodities. Unlike the expenditure of value that characterizes potlatch-like rituals, these camera-ready performances of value-motivated destruction testify to opening up space by destroying that which no longer has enough value.

The rush of excitement that accompanies demolition day opens up the house to reveal new possibilities, but it also reveals the unknowns that lurk inside old walls. Risk rears its fearsome profile as the materialization of problems that threaten the budget. Formerly invisible flaws may include deteriorating electrical wiring or panels that no longer meet code, roof leaks, crumbling sewage lines, termites, rusted-out HVAC systems, disintegrating foundations, or sagging support joists. And, of course, the consequences of tearing out walls now comes due. This is generally framed as a surprise even though one could anticipate that new load-bearing structural beams will be needed to replace the supports that have been destroyed. This dramatic device stretches credulity—one always suspects that inspections have already alerted veteran flippers like the Scott brothers to factor these surprises into their renovation costs. Indeed, behind the scenes, HGTV has planned for these staged crises: prospective show participants report that an up-front "20 percent in-case-of-emergency contingency fee is a non-negotiable requirement for those who appear on 'Property Brothers.'"[18] Thus, though problems invariably appear as unnerving shocks, by show's end what looked like crises are invariably smoothed over without causing significant changes to the overall process, or to the bottom line. Only on *Love It or List It* do these tense revelations translate into disruptions, forcing the designer to adjust her plan, meaning that some items on the clients' must-have list do not get addressed. By contrast, the Scott brothers routinely manage the swelling renovation costs without ultimately sacrificing anything to the budget. The brothers apparently negate momentary hiccups by off-screen maneuvers, perhaps by playing their get-out-of-jail-free card—the remarkably flexible contingency fund to cover unanticipated costs—or by substituting cheaper materials that simulate the desired effect.

Renovation hiccups provide a moment of staged anxiety intended to elicit emotional reaction shots that position clients and viewers to gasp at the possibility that unforeseen costs may steal away the promise of value before it is realized. This is controlled unpredictability. Viewers' familiarity with HGTV's scripted formula allays risk anxiety and turns its management into reassurance. Dramatic recognition of a previously unknown risk is always followed by a pause for a commercial break. Upon returning to the show, viewers learn the problem can be seamlessly managed. Problems are resolved in short order and the new surfaces (floors, cabinets, counters and tile, paint) are then rapidly set in place thanks to video time-compression techniques. This glib neoliberal lesson reminds us that managing risk is a prelude to progress because without risk there can be no reward.

Staging the house represents the decisive final turn in adding value to the home—and, particularly, the arrangement of visual sign value. Home staging involves crafting the interior design aesthetics of the home, transforming open spaces into designed and curated rooms. As Curtis stresses on her show, staging renovated houses is essential "because nobody sees the value in an empty house." *Flip or Flop* brings in professional stagers, drawing explicit attention to the commodified importance of staging the space in preparation for putting the house on the market. On *Fixer Upper*, staging marks the determinant transition to value, when Chip passes the baton to Joanna, moving from construction to the signification practices that will yield the perfected look of value. *Fixer Upper* devotes more screen time to staging the home because Joanna has taken on the status of *virtuoso auteur* who turns houses into works of art. While acknowledging the specialized labor performed by stagers, aside from the deliberative effect of placing cut flowers or fluffing pillows, the value wizardry of decorating is generally veiled in performance, though certainly not in visual outcome.

> A popular trope in shelter TV, staging is an intensely temporal project, operating now, but only temporarily, to provoke an imagination of the future. It makes the possibility of occupancy not only

thinkable but desirable. In this way staging is also a useful metaphor for thinking through the relationship between ownership, finance, and textuality and race, class, and gender. In residential property, staging is a practice intended to facilitate a sale. Its correlates in financial markets, on television, and in representational practices operate similarly.[19]

So thoroughly is staging about an anticipated future utopian space that on their show *Property Brothers: Buying and Selling*, the Scott brothers firmly warn families that they must not muss up the space in any way (i.e., don't live in it) before the open house lest its value be diminished in the eyes of buyers. Turning the polished appearance of value into top dollar is incompatible with the actual lived occupancy of the idealized space.

The camera lovingly fetishizes the decorative expressions of style accomplished via the staging process. The whole of the show, and its adherence to the formula, is based on staging the staging, or a staging of the staging. The most conspicuous staging tool is the signature device of *Fixer Upper*, whereby a billboard-sized picture of the house in its before stage is placed between the client's point of view and the renovated house, thus shielding the spectator's view. The billboard's presence as a tease is a clear reminder that the reveal and all that has led up to it in edited time has been staged, just as the reveal itself is explicitly a product of the show's staging. It's a simulated reveal of a staged simulation.

The design, furnishing, and decoration of the house give the renovation its wow factor, its presentation effect. The culmination of every show is the big reveal and the "Oh, my God" moment of ecstasy. This decisive moment of affirming value realization is framed as an orgasm of value, measured by the intensity and release of the emotional response. The world of value and the world of affect buttress one another here. As Joanna Gaines puts it, "Our reward is the look on our client's faces." The distance between sacrifice and gain has been bridged, and in that moment, spectators are invited to vicariously experience pure unambivalent value as the realization of desire. These money shots are meant to be both inspirational and aspirational.

In contrast to the accelerated video editing that characterizes the labor sequences, in these triumphant moments of consumer desire the camera pans slowly and lovingly across the decorated spaces, allowing viewers to envy and desire the look—validating the commodity fetish. Shifting to slow motion is an essential element to the reproduction of commodity fetishism. The big reveal does in fact disclose that the fixer-upper is a work of art, and its placement within the television formula, with the consumer imperative "Shop the look" superimposed on the screen during the big reveal, is a reminder that it is a work of art that can be semiotically reproduced to fit the

Figure 2.1 Before-and-after images of the shotgun house from *Fixer Upper*. The before-and-after juxtaposition is one of HGTV's preferred money shots for visually establishing the renovation transformation of value. (*Fixer Upper*, season 3, episode 8, "Tiny House, Big Charm" [High Noon Entertainment, HGTV, Discovery, 2016].)

appearances seen in magazines like *Houzz* and *Dwell* or in the catalog of Joss and Main. The art of mechanically reproducing the commodity look is in turn seized on by advertisers, completing the circuitry of commodification. A 2016 Sherwin-Williams television ad for its Designer Color Collections offers the means to realize a comparable ecstatic moment. With the tagline, "Create your own big reveal with HGTV Home [Paint Collection] by Sherwin-Williams," the commercial sells consumers the opportunity to possess the professional eye of the designer whose taste and color acumen has been objectified in the can of paint.[20] This essential deskilling can then be purchased by DIY homeowners who wish to simulate the appearance of HGTV interiors.

The most common video strategy used to frame the big reveal juxtaposes before-and-after photographs to highlight the distance traveled. The stark contrast of "before" photos morphing into "after" photos creates a seemingly objective equation for demonstrating an increase in value. The transformation from before to after bears witness to how value can be crafted, harvested from the debris of the past, and turned into future dream spaces. The way that the big reveal is photographed, edited, and musically scored lends it a spiritual aura. But this visual hymn to the realization of value is not enough; it must be affirmed by adding up the score. The official tally of the costs relative to the budget accompanies updated estimates of the revised value of the property. Assessed value is stated in authoritative terms as if based on an objective methodological measure—now the value of the property can be expressed in objective terms. Shows such as *Income Property, Fixer Upper, Love It or List It*, and *Property Brothers: Buying and Selling* take this opportunity to boast about the equity gain made on the investment in the home renovation. *Fixer Upper* routinely calls it "instant equity."

But the concluding payoff must be more than the sum of its fetish parts. Renovation episodes typically seek narrative closure with client testimonials expressing grateful delight for the "gift" of their affordable dream homes, visually overlaid by emotionally freighted scenes that picture them playing with their children or hosting a gathering of family and friends basking in their freshly renovated open-concept spaces. In this coda, the fetishized payoff of the big reveal gives way to an advertisement for the intimacy of unalienated social belonging. All that effort devoted to the purification of enclosed spaces seems to have paid off in clean commodity finishes that (ironically) seem to enable the possibility of a private life insulated from the morality of commodity valuation measures. For a brief moment, we are allowed to imagine the social life of the commodity, its use values temporarily emancipated from the morality of exchange value. And then it's over, and we start all over again with another episode.

What Formulas Hide

The narrative bias imposed by mechanical adherence to this formula has a flip side, dictating what remains outside the story line. Any information that muddies the story of reaping surplus value or that deviates from the formulaic story line is routinely excluded by HGTV producers. Obedience to unbending formulas prompts logical and temporal inconsistencies that leak out from the way too many sutures required to stitch together the frenetic herky-jerky video editing that jolts viewers back and forth across abstracted time and space. Space and time are terribly abused and warped by the heavily edited video narratives. Though the shows claim a certain verisimilitude, they routinely take shape through the disassembly of time to accommodate the dictates of the television timeline—and, just as much, the dictates of television production schedules.

HGTV screens out its own production practices that reframe perceptions of value. Online discussion sites question HGTV's realness in light of discoveries that HGTV shows require that clients must already have selected and purchased a house prior to being accepted to appear in an episode.[21] To maintain strict adherence to the video formula requires showing two other houses as filler. Not only does this suggest a rigged game, but hiding the fact that houses have been preselected and purchased also conceals all questions having to do with loans and mortgages, since the only clients who will ever appear on HGTV have already been approved for loans. As a result of screening this aspect out, no act or pattern of discriminatory lending practices will ever be seen on HGTV. HGTV can visually suggest a multicultural promised land where home renovation offers a nondiscriminatory opportunity for wealth production, but even in gentrifying neighborhoods that have historically been predominantly African American, people of color are today denied loans at significantly higher rates than whites.[22]

Of all the shows on HGTV, *Flip or Flop* is most apt to include fleeting references to a reality that exists outside the formula when it occasionally acknowledges the constraints and delays imposed by behind-the-scenes considerations such as obtaining permits, passing inspections, scheduling, or homeowner's associations' covenant restrictions. But like all HGTV shows, it suppresses the bruising behind-the-scenes social and economic histories involved in the foreclosures that premise a decade of value-added flipping and renovation. Though *Flip or Flop* may reference externalities as costs that get in the way of profitability, it is loath to allow the politics of housing to intrude into its stories. One *Flip or Flop* episode featured a house vandalized after the flippers purchased it, the camera capturing the damage—floors gouged, windows smashed, feces smeared walls, and concrete poured in toilets. The visual is momentarily disconcerting, but the narrative is anemic and misleading. What might account for the fierce anger that motivated such defacement and property vengeance? For viewers, the scene is narrativized as an incomprehensible act of vandalism that adds unnecessary and unforeseen costs for the flippers, even though insurance covered their damages. A local newspaper filled in the missing context.

> When he started flipping, Tarek El Moussa would often drive around the Inland Empire scouting houses between 10pm and 3am after addresses were announced the night before an auction. In these sales, there are often tenants who have to be evicted. At one house they bought in Anaheim Hills, a mother and son were getting evicted by the police—and poured concrete in toilets, smashed out all the windows and took a hammer to the wood floors before they left, Christina El Moussa said. The damage: $30,000. Insurance covered it.[23]

Potential counternarratives are squashed or rerouted. The central social drama with this flip was the way that a real family's life got tangled up around mortgage default, foreclosure, and eviction. The show erases this conflict and instead tells the story of an angry, now perhaps homeless family, who feel otherwise powerless about being evicted from their home because of a bank foreclosure. Perhaps the "irrational" fury of foreclosure vandalism was aimed at those very banks responsible for what became the credit default crisis and who then evicted the homeowner! Following the foreclosure and eviction crisis, foreclosure vandalism developed into a not-uncommon occurrence. Nationwide in 2009–2010, between 13.9 percent and 19.8 percent of bank-foreclosed homes were so severely vandalized by their former owners that they could not qualify for new mortgage financing.[24]

Of course, even the mere acknowledgment of the Great Recession's human toll following the collapse of subprime mortgage markets raises unsettling questions about the legitimacy of profit margins in the flipping market, so it must be excluded from the narrative. Who knows where this particular instance of mortgage default fit into the broad picture of bank fraud and predatory lending, but Orange County had among the highest rates of mortgage defaults across the nation. The premise of *Flip or Flop* is that distressed housing represents a risky but lucrative way of taking economic advantage of the contradictions of post-crash housing markets. To make stories palatable precludes addressing the circumstances of those forced to abandon homes; to do otherwise might lead to questions about this flipper's predatory strategy for exploiting the misfortune and misery of others.

Repeated often enough, the arc of HGTV's story formula and its one-dimensional outcomes of pitch-perfect interior spaces casts a seductive spell, and its myth can easily be mistaken for some sort of postcrisis common sense. HGTV's preferred spin happens to be a neoliberal homily: individual freedom to choose and risk in the marketplace is rewarded both materially and spiritually. Rather than accept such homilies at face value, I choose to reintroduce some of the historical and structural contexts that HGTV represses so that I may confront HGTV's stories with relationships of debt, foreclosures, institutional racism, gentrification, and financialization that structure America's housing markets.

Chapter 3 shifts gears from cultural criticism to the market economy of flipping as it has evolved from 2000 to 2018. The securitization of housing before and after the 2008 crisis has redefined markets for single-family residences with major implications for the affordability of housing. HGTV likes to picture the business of renovation and flipping as a populist space where mom-and-pop enterprises are free to roam. Though partially true, when put into political economic context, it may be more likely that mom-and-pop operations have become enmeshed within a real estate investment industry that turns house flipping into a lucrative business of securitizing rent checks. Flipping and renovation have become investor driven, whether it's by mom and pop or by a Wall Street bank. Additionally, HGTV itself may be playing a role in shaping the housing market, through its creation of an aesthetic that housing consumers and flippers alike recognize, along with its glamorization of the enterprising flipper as a self-sustaining foot soldier of the new housing economy—yet another pathway that financial institutions with deeper pockets can exploit to defuse risk and package and repackage the asset that has taken the place of real estate as a driver of finance for the wealthiest investors: debt.

3

A Moment in the Life of Capital

When you have mastered numbers, you will in fact no longer be
reading numbers ... you will be reading meanings.
—**W.E.B. Du Bois,** *W.E.B. Du Bois's Data Portraits:*
Visualizing Black America

One cannot study HGTV and its relationship to the flipping industry without wondering about the effects HGTV has had on that market, and vice versa. Though HGTV offers a less than faithful accounting of the forces that condition urban flipping markets, HGTV's imagery of flipping undoubtedly has its source in the buzz surrounding those markets. Prior to the 2008 crash, television's mimicry of flipping referenced the general speculative fever of the day. Afterwards, as the flipping market began rebounding and institutional investors began reshaping the flipping and renovation business, the television version of flipping that appears 24/7 on HGTV beckoned mom-and-pop flippers to imagine themselves making money by renovating and redesigning houses. To understand what has been lost in translation between the flipping economy and its appropriation by HGTV, it's worth considering some big-picture patterns regarding flipping, foreclosures, profitability, affordability, and financing between 2000 and 2018. How did the foreclosure crisis shape house flipping? Who has benefited? How has flipping affected housing markets? Despite a complex superstructure of financialization and professionalization that has reshaped the flipping industry to make it more profitable for investors, a relatively high percentage of individual mom-and-pop investors now constitute the foot soldiers of the industry. Families looking for their first homes, meanwhile, often find themselves priced out of the market.

For millions of viewers, the flipping economy is defined as much by the supposed realism of HGTV as it is by the conditions of the marketplace. I refer to the latter as the political economy of flipping, while the HGTV version is better described as a hyperreal flipping economy. Flipping in both its political economic and hyperreal forms has been about the search for value across the landscape of neoliberal capitalism. The following sketch of recent flipping history presents a moment in the life of real estate capital. Stuart Hall and Doreen Massey refer to such historical moments as conjunctures, periods "during which the different social, political, economic and ideological contradictions that are at work in society come together to give it a specific and distinctive shape."[1] Taken together, the political economy and the simulacra of flipping represent a conjunctural moment of crisis in the life of capital.

HGTV concentrates on visualizing value via stylized flipping and renovation. But what of the relationships—indeed the very thing in itself—that HGTV claims to be about? For the last twenty years, flipping houses has been about finding a crease in the value system in which investors might discover and mine renewed pockets of value. HGTV stories imagine a haven where savvy entrepreneurs and consumer households alike thrive—often they are made to seem one and the same. Outside the realm of television, small investors have scrambled to make money by flipping houses. Some have been successful, some have broken even, and others have not done so well. Their stories and the risks they take make better sense if we consider how housing markets have been restructured by the events of recent decades.

Sketching the history of the flipping economy by the numbers is pretty much the opposite of how HGTV tells its stories. HGTV's way of telling is to lead with personalities and emotions. I propose for a moment to depersonalize flipping, reframing it around foreclosures, devaluations, cash versus loans, empires of rent, and housing affordability during a volatile housing era. Viewing the U.S. housing economy as a national whole reveals the evolving dynamics and contradictions of the flipping economy, but with a caveat. My big picture of flipping relies on national statistics, which neglect the regional and metropolitan unevenness in housing markets that pushes investment opportunities from one locale to another. It's this dynamic relationship between hot and cold markets, between saturated and untouched markets, that drives geographic flows of capital resources from region to region. Cities such as Fort Lauderdale, Las Vegas, Atlanta, and Los Angeles were foreclosure epicenters in 2008, thus magnifying opportunities for profitable flipping after 2008. In other cities, like Pittsburgh, the economics of flipping have unfolded more slowly, hinged to the exhaustion of the most lucrative stocks of distressed properties in former hot spots. When it comes to identifying lucrative investments, geographic differences matter and play a decisive role in shaping investor strategies.[2] And it's not just institutional investors who have been responsive to sharp variations in geographically distinct housing markets. Dramatic differences in market pricing opportunities shape the individual investor's market calculations in ways that could scarcely have been imagined in the abstract. For instance, as access to affordable homes becomes an impossibility for median-income millennial earners working in major cities like San Francisco, those same workers have taken notice of the comparatively modest price tags on unexceptional houses in Texas and thus decided to become absentee landlords. They can't afford to live in San Francisco, but they can invest in multiple houses in Texas and be landlords there.[3]

Flipping, Foreclosure, and Profits, 2000–2018

Since 2010 HGTV has featured a spectrum of approaches to finding value in housing markets, ranging from pure flips to customized renovations and decorations to flipping-to-rent to restoration projects. Across the board, the spectacle glamorizes renovation styles as a potentially lucrative economic practice. These images selectively filter out the nitty-gritty forces that shape the real estate economy and, more broadly, an economy driven by bubbles since the 1990s.

Twice within the opening decade of the twenty-first century the U.S. economy was shaken by crises of valuation. The first shock came when the dot-com bubble burst in 2000. The prospect of quick money to be mined from technology and internet stocks drove a feverish blind faith that high-tech capitalism would spur the creation of new pockets of value open to stock investors. Low-fee online brokerage firms further beckoned to workers that they could share in economic prosperity by focusing not on their wages or their diminishing benefits, but on their stock portfolios.[4] The seductions of the dot-com craze as a path to participation in the riches of neoliberal economics triggered a race to print new valuations via initial public offerings (IPOs), and yet a majority of households remained on the sidelines watching as the wealth gap increased.

After the sharp downturn in tech stock valuations between 2000 and 2002, the surging housing market redirected the search for low-hanging investment returns, and finance capital migrated from technology to real estate.[5] Thwarted in their efforts to strike it rich via the democratization of stock market participation in the late 1990s, many households latched on to easy credit to leverage second mortgages to buy new cars, pay for a college education, and even purchase second homes. Stagnating household incomes combined with negative savings rates and free-flowing credit drew households deeper and deeper into debt. The housing asset bubble enabled households to try offsetting declining incomes by leveraging their "residential investment, made possible by easy credit and rising house prices."[6]

> From 2001 to 2005, rising home values and plummeting interest rates allowed Americans to extract an average $1 trillion per year from their homes, net of closing costs and repayment of other mortgage debt—more than triple the annual "free cash" available over the 1991 to 2000 period and equal to nearly 12 percent of personal disposable income. About half of the money found its way back into the housing market, either by funding new home purchases or home improvements, and a quarter paid for non-home asset purchases like financial securities, stocks and business equity. The remainder went towards personal consumption, including credit card, auto and student loan debt.[7]

Amid the booming housing markets, a rising tide of home prices made house flipping an attractive strategy for cashing in on the home sales gravy train. Flips increased from 103,000 houses in 2000 to a peak of 344,000 in 2005, followed by another 270,000 the following year. During that boom, 1.37 million houses were flipped, financed by loans totaling roughly $180 billion combined with another $95 billion in cash. The inflationary significance of house flipping within the overall housing economy could be seen in the rapidly growing percentage of flips in total home sales: from 4.8 percent in 2000 to 8.3 percent in 2005. Premised on the speculative conviction that generalized price appreciation would guarantee profits across the board, the name of the game in those boom years was to get in and out as rapidly as possible while doing as little as possible to the house. "The housing bubble was inflating so fast, investors could buy, hold—sometimes renting out the properties to make a bit extra, sometimes renting at a loss, sometimes not even bothering to rent—then sell, over and over again."[8] In the most frenzied metropolitan housing markets, flipping rates rose above 20 percent during 2005–2006. Especially during the overheated market of 2001–2006, house flipping turned into little more than arbitrage, the practice of buying a commodity (or currency) at a lower or discounted price and then flipping it to turn a profit.[9] In commodities markets, arbitrage is often considered a riskless investing tactic that takes advantage of price differentials between markets, but in the house-flipping economy of the early 2000s, arbitrage took a particularly risky form that depended less on buying at a discount than on the speculative generalization that all house prices would go up and up. This streamlined approach to flipping was based on applying a minimum of labor and resources to secure a profit through the circulation of houses rather than working to add value.

The allure of easy money to be made flipping houses drew in a dramatic increase of less experienced investors (i.e., rookies and newbies) between the late 1990s and 2006.[10] As long as house prices kept inflating, this game worked, but cracks appeared by the time flips peaked in 2005. Loan defaults piled up and home prices softened. Before the carnage of the mortgage market collapse was complete, some $8 trillion of valuations had disappeared from housing markets. Underwater loans are by now a familiar story—as the value bubble unraveled, some mortgage holders found themselves with a property whose value was now less than the loan that secured it. Between 2004 and 2006, roughly 50 percent of new mortgage originations were made by inexperienced individual investors who owned more than one home. As a group, speculators who chased profits in the flipping market abused the conditions of cheap credit and subsequently played a telling role in the cascade of loan defaults.[11] Indeed, once conditions soured, flipping speculators were more likely to walk away from a bad loan on a house they didn't live in than subprime homeowners who had no place to go if they defaulted on their residences, and so held on as long as possible.

The flipping market collapsed by 2008 with annual flips declining from their peak to 127,000 houses, while the share of flipped houses in the overall market dipped to 3 percent. Losses replaced profits, and in the first quarter of 2009, the flipping market hit its nadir—with housing valuations plunging across the board, flippers lost on average 29 percent of their investments.[12] But within a year, in a market overwhelmed with foreclosed residences, investors ventured back in, sifting through the debris to take advantage of deep discounts on distressed, blighted, and abandoned properties that dotted the worst-hit neighborhoods of the housing market. Heavy concentrations of foreclosures in some neighborhoods drew out the flippers in force.[13]

In this postcrash phase of flipping, investors could no longer assume ever-rising home prices, and the mix of loans and cash that financed acquisition and renovation became inverted from the precrash market. After the crash, flippers relied on cash 80 percent of the time, while the loans available to individual investors shifted to hard-money loans from so-called country club capital.[14] Such loans made flippers more cautious and disciplined in their decisions about which houses to purchase at deep discounts and then how much to put into fixing them up to sell at a premium to the market. After the financial crisis, a shift took place from local "country club capital" toward a more institutionalized and professionalized fix-and-flip loan market—which initially consisted of short-term hard-money loans—with an emphasis on adding value to properties. And what about all that cash floating around? It marked the entry of institutional investors backed by billion-dollar lines of credit.

The mortgage crisis set in motion dual forces that caused long-term restructuring in real estate markets. Widespread loan defaults and foreclosures transformed the demographic landscape of homeowners and renters, swelling the ranks of renters after decades of movement in the opposite direction toward a society of home ownership. It did not take long for financial analysts to declare the end of the "ownership society" and predict its replacement with a "rentership society."[15] Big money quickly recognized the opportunities created by the wholesale evictions that followed the foreclosures—the surge in demand for rental units to house former homeowners pointed capital investments toward the market of foreclosed and bank-owned single-family residences that could be "picked up on the cheap to rent out."[16]

Real estate analysts noticed an anomaly in the housing market in 2012—though home ownership rates were approaching fifty-year lows, home prices were rising. Families were blocked from buying homes partly because investors loaded with cash were outbidding them.[17] Turning houses into impersonal assets effectively cemented widespread housing precarity and rent insecurity. Ousted from home ownership following the foreclosure crisis, many households whose subprime mortgages had forced them into default, foreclosure, and houselessness became renters again and found themselves vulnerable to the pressures of rent insecurity.[18] As they became subject to the regime of corporate rent empires, renters were exposed to sharp rent spikes that exceeded wage gains and hit with eviction rates that exceeded by a long shot the eviction rates imposed by mom-and-pop landlords.[19]

Although the crisis might not have begun with subprime mortgages, the holders of subprime mortgages (concentrated among the working poor, especially blacks and Hispanics because of racially discriminatory lending practices) disproportionately suffered the consequences of the financial havoc.[20] Blacks saw 53 percent of their wealth destroyed as a result of the mortgage crisis, while Hispanics lost 66 percent of their wealth.[21] Their suffering was compounded by the way institutional investors took advantage of the foreclosure crisis. Foreclosures flooded the market, peaking in 2009 and 2010 to the tune of 2,213,000 houses, while foreclosure filings stood at 5,696,000.[22] Foreclosure filings for 2008 represented a 225 percent increase over 2006. One out of every fifty-four households received a foreclosure notice in 2008.[23] The cataclysm that befell subprime mortgage holders proved a boon both to flippers and to the very financial institutions culpable for the derivatives crisis.[24] Well-capitalized real estate funds snapped up thousands and thousands of now bank-owned (i.e., real estate owned [REO]) single-family residence foreclosures on the cheap. The first institutional investors to enter the REO-to-rental business included Blackstone, Colony Homes, and American Homes 4 Rent, between 2010 and 2012. Blackstone led the way, spending $9.6 billion to accumulate almost fifty thousand homes that it then turned into rental properties.[25] Over and over, it outbid working-class families by paying in cash, which it had because of a $3.6 billion line of credit from Deutsche Bank. "You can't compete with a company that's betting on speculative future value when they're playing with cash," observed a realtor whose clients lived in Hispanic and African American neighborhoods. Similar concentrations of wealth bought up over two hundred thousand houses between 2009 and 2012, transferring "$88 billions of wealth accumulation" to Wall Street bankers and investors.[26] By 2019, Invitation Homes had accumulated more than eighty thousand houses.[27]

As postcrash flipping regained momentum, flipping rates revisited highs in 2016, 2017, and 2018 not seen since 2005. In the fourth quarter of 2018, flips comprised a sizzling 10.9 percent of total home sales, even though rates of profit had begun to dip.[28] Figure 3.1 charts flipping profitability from 2002 to 2018, while Figure 3.2 presents flipping rates as a share of overall home sales. As the overall housing market regained its balance, the strategy of relying on deep discounts on distressed housing revived profit margins on flips. "Homes flipped in 2015 were on average purchased at a 26% discount below estimated market value and resold by the flipper at a 5% premium above estimated market value."[29] Loans grew to nearly 40 percent of the financing mix by 2017, in part as a new online financial technology industry (fintech) took shape.[30] One originator of fix-and-flip loans explains that "online lenders like us exist because banks and large lenders don't play in this space, and they aren't using technology to be efficient, nimble and

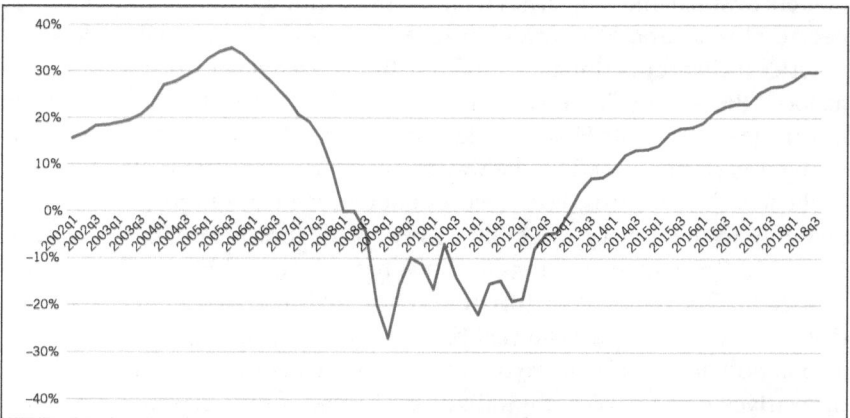

Figure 3.1 Nominal flipping profits, first through third quarters, 2002–2018. (Ralph McLaughlin and Arthur Jobe, "A Wild Flipping Ride: Economic Returns to U.S. House Flipping, 2002–2018," paper presented at 47th American Real Estate and Urban Economics Association National Conference, Washington, DC, May 31, 2019.)

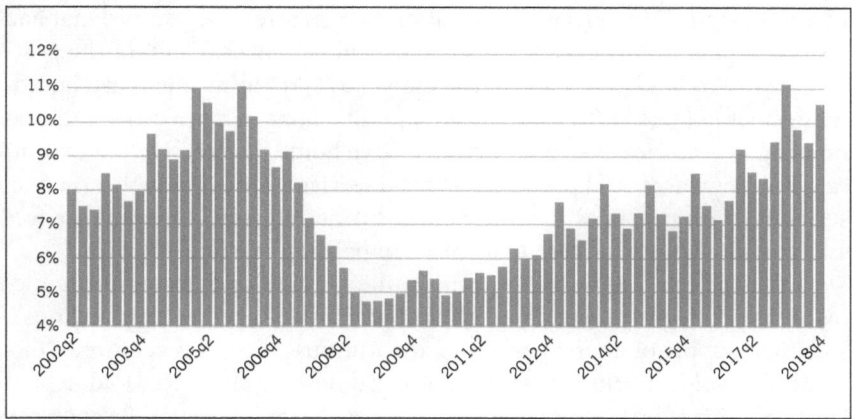

Figure 3.2 U.S. flipping rates, second and fourth quarters, 2002–2018. (McLaughlin and Jobe, "A Wild Flipping Ride.")

fast. Now that investors have digital-native lenders catering to them, financing becomes an attractive alternative to cash."[31] Mortgage originators reported that their fix-and-flip loan business doubled between 2016 and 2017.

Lenders saw opportunities as profitability and ROI in house flipping rose steadily between 2012 and 2017 with gross ROI peaking at over 50 percent. The profitability of flipping was now clearly dependent not on generalized speculation but on the specifics of discounts and premiums that could be found among foreclosures, reinforcing an intertwining relationship between flipping and an evolving form of sprawling gentrification.[32] The more profitable flippers became, the less affordable housing became—a mutually reinforcing circuit. Super profitable flipping benefits a narrow stratum of consumers while punishing the broader spectrum of households that are shut out of those markets and forced into rental markets.

Financiers had stirred the pot that created the first housing bubble with an excess of prime and subprime loans that they overleveraged into the financial instruments of MBSs, but the financial derivatives crisis did not deter the financial behemoths from seeking subsequent paths to securitization. Rather, firms like Blackstone turned their burgeoning single-family residence (SFR) rental empire into the basis for yet another form of securitization rooted in the rent stream paid by tenants. Blackstone made the news in 2014 for selling bonds backed by monthly rent checks just five years after the market collapse surrounding the securitization of home mortgages.[33] Blackstone euphemistically named its house rental empire Invitation Homes and in 2017 merged with Starwood Waypoint Residential Trust to expand its holdings to 82,000 homes with an enterprise value of $20 billion.[34] A rebounding housing market further rewarded these institutional investors with a 114 percent appreciation rate on foreclosed homes that had been scooped up dirt cheap. The chief executive officer (CEO) of the postmerger Invitation Homes touted the merger as "providing enhanced liquidity to stockholders."[35] This enhanced liquidity came at a price as it reduced housing inventories available to prospective home buyers, spurred exorbitant rent increases, and prompted firms like Blackstone to double down on serial eviction practices as a method of extracting (stacking) further fees and penalties as a condition of a tenant remaining in a housing unit.[36]

After the crisis, approximately ten million households exited the homeownership category, creating an obvious demand for rental units. Minus a sufficient supply of apartment units, institutional investors acquired SFRs to fill the void. Blackstone's Invitation Homes simply played old-school landlord with as little maintenance as possible on its properties. By contrast, a second phase of SFR acquisition is dissolving the boundary between the SFR rental business and flipping markets. The corporate rental business has continued to converge with flipping as deep-pocketed tech ventures such as Opendoor, Amherst Holdings, Zillow, and Offerpad attempt to redefine the flipping marketplace. Drawing on computerized models, algorithms and artificial intelligence to analytically calculate the necessary renovation costs and assess the probabilities of profit, these companies aim to eliminate the inefficiencies that plague individual flippers who lack access to the information afforded by massive databases or the capital backing of banks such as BNY Mellon (Amherst) and Softbank (Opendoor).[37] By 2018, Amherst had raked in $300 million in rents that it then turned into investment instruments—residential rent-backed securities, along with a new breed of MBSs based on the development of fix-and-flip loans. Just as the SFR rentals have become securitized, so too the fix-and-flip loan has "become an asset class of its own that is well-financed by banks and highly sought by institutional buyers."[38]

Even after the surge of institutional investors in the SFR market, their acquisitions remain a small fraction of the overall housing market. Institutional investing's impact on the flipping and renovation industry has, however, been transformational, integrating the relationship between home flipping and single-family rentals. Its most immediate impact has been to tighten the inventory pipeline of available homes by diverting blocs of SFRs to the rental market. And organizationally, corporate capital has clear advantages over mom-and-pop businesses in identifying and negotiating discounts on the buy side. During the early stages of the flipping recovery, larger investors were better able to secure discounts in the distressed housing markets—13.6 percent compared to 8.0 percent for small investors.[39]

Flipping statistics around the time of the millennium show a fairly even market division between small, medium, and large investors. Then, large real estate investors represented local and regional sources of capital that bought, at most, hundreds of houses at a time, whereas by 2017, the scale of institutional investors' access to capital had mushroomed, representing national and global financial capital's deeper pockets and purchasing power. As the flipping and renovation industry has grown, it's become a more fully rationalized and organized business with its own specialized division of labor, integrated into the money circuits of capital. The effects have percolated through urban SFR markets, accelerating the search for cost savings. Gross flipping profits reached a record 51.9 percent in 2016,[40] but that number is illusory when factoring in real estate closing costs, taxes, regulatory costs, deferred maintenance and cosmetic renovation, labor and materials, how many days it takes to finish, and property management costs. Taken together, these limits on profits are subject to variable ratios of inefficiency. Individual investors with less experience tend to be more inefficient, and, as a result, their share of flipping profits tends to be lower than corporate counterparts. "The flipping industry has become professionalized.... It used to be contractors buying, fixing and selling one house at a time. Not very efficient. It's now become a very organized business model with companies that have employees looking for deals, securing financing, managing the fix-up. These groups are much more effective and efficient at finding the deals out there and reselling them profitably."[41]

Hastening the professionalization process were the new fintech entrants into the roster of institutional investors. These companies have been designed to streamline the flip-to-rent process via their organization of big data and AI.[42] In 2017, the behemoths of the real estate industry invested more than $12.6 billion into real estate technology start-ups because they believe that using machine learning will reduce inefficiencies—the drag coefficients—that detract from overall profitability. The holy grail of fintech is to cut costs by speeding up the circuitry of real estate loans and investment. Online platforms eliminate the constraints of geography, making it possible to remotely buy, manage, and sell investment properties with the same ease as clicking trades in fantasy football.[43]

The emergence of fintech and the online loan industry has also spurred the rollout of online technology tools and services aimed at mom-and-pop investors who seek to be more efficient in the flip-to-rent marketplace. Even though institutional investors have encountered shrinking profit margins as a result of cap rate compression, smaller investors seem willing to accept a lower rate of return with the help of off-the-shelf software packages and services offered by a new breed of online property management companies. In addition to full-service property management tools, websites such as Roofstock, Mynd, and CrowdStreet offer an investment alternative to Wall Street securitization for smaller investors who are willing to participate in online peer-to-peer crowdsourcing of capital for individual flipping projects in exchange for a specified rate of return on the rent streams thus generated. The individual investor's higher tolerance for smaller profit margins that his institutional counterparts are unwilling to fish for bears closer examination as to the how, the why, and the effects on the macroeconomics of housing.

Since the crisis, corporate investors and professionals have restructured the flipping-to-rent side of the equation. Alongside them, however, individual investors still make up a significant chunk of the fix-and-flip market. The 2015 Rental Housing Finance Survey found that individual investors owned 74.4 percent of the nation's rental properties, while the limited liability entities made up 14.8 percent of the market. But "because the share of rental properties owned by individual investors tends to decrease with the property size, individual investors owned less than half (47.8 percent) of rental units, followed by LLPs, LPs, or LLCs (33.2 percent)."[44]

On one side, "the share of flipped homes . . . sold by a business entity, such as an LLC, INC, or CORP, rather than by an individual" increased dramatically from 11 percent in mid-2005 to 41 percent mid-2018.[45] On the other side, a national property database reported that 69 percent of all flips in 2017 were by mom-and-pop investors.[46] How are these two statistics not contradictory? The answer lies in the adoption of the limited liability corporation (LLC) as a legal form. By definition, an LLC creates a corporate entity, so all LLCs are technically corporations, even though the LLC has grown in popularity among mom-and-pop flippers as an investing strategy. The LLC designation doesn't cost much, and it carries tax benefits while also shielding an owner's personal finances if there are lawsuits against the LLC. This is especially important for those who flip to rent. It's also likely that the growth of corporate flips reflects the entry of professional flippers across the industry. The formation of LLCs by landlords represents a strategic maneuver that has had striking consequences: for landlords of more dilapidated properties that "service" impoverished populations, having limited liability provides an incentive to milk the property, effectively disinvesting in the property.[47]

During the same period, institutional property management companies have made prolific use of LLCs to hide their acquisitions of bank-owned properties (foreclosures) through shell companies. Shrouding the ownership of housing properties behind a veil of anonymity not only makes it difficult for researchers to parse out who is who; it also presents a significant obstacle to urban housing policy.[48] Clouding the magnitude of the impact of LLC acquisitions on housing affordability prevents cities from formulating policies that might protect renters, and it disempowers renters by making it more difficult to identify their landlords when problems arise with rental properties.

A Political Economy of Mom-and-Pop Investors?

In this convergence between LLCs and mom-and-pop investors, institutionalized and well-capitalized investors have gained significant advantages in the size of discounts they are able to negotiate and in their ability to flip homes faster.[49] Furthermore, because of a diminishing volume of discounted foreclosure inventory, rising labor costs, the inflation of land prices, and an inventory of houses that are getting older and more expensive to fix up, flipping profits began dipping from their highs in 2017.

Where then does this political economy of mom-and-pop investors stand in relation to the wider political economy of housing finance? Generally, individual investors "are fix-and-flippers who buy homes cheaply and resell them for a profit (sometimes to owner-occupants, sometimes to out-of-towners who rent the homes out on Airbnb). There are those who buy and hold, generally larger institutional investors who rent the properties out. There are traders who acquire properties and try to resell them once they appreciate, sometimes in weeks, sometimes in years."[50]

While the mom-and-pop tag carries a populist connotation, it bundles together a hierarchy of investors who don't entirely fit the label—some are turning over fifty houses per year while others are lucky to get in one. In 2018, "mom-and-pop landlords push[ed] investor share of home purchases to 19-year high," targeting one-fifth of the inventory of potential starter homes priced toward the lower end of the market.[51] Though institutional investors dominated this market after the crash, more recently some have vacated this space, leaving room for a shift to smaller operators.[52] "Investors who purchased 10 or fewer homes were responsible for 60% of transactions in 2018, up from 48% in 2013. And those mom-and-pop investors are buying entry-level homes: 20.3% of them in 2017 and 2018."[53] Behind these numbers is an evolving industry "that promotes investment in single-family homes: lenders who provide the capital, brokers who handle transactions, wholesalers who buy homes by the dozens and (re)sell them before they even take possession."[54] So, mom-and-pop investors are going to hard-money lenders for fix-and-flip loans, and the hard-money lenders are in turn securitizing the fix-and-flip loans, selling the slices to other investors. Up the capital food chain we go: "KKR, the investing giant, recently announced it would invest $250 million—on top of an earlier commitment of the same size—in such loans."[55]

A key metric for real estate investors is the capitalization rate. Market observers point out that in a compressed cap rate environment, the rate of return on housing properties goes down. Capitalization rates are calculated by dividing the net income a property yields by the market valuation of the property. Operating income references the rent stream minus costs that the property delivers. For the sake of illustration, assume that you paid $200,000 in cash for a house and rent it for $1,000 a month, or $12,000 per year. Your cap rate is thus 6 percent. Compression can occur if the home experiences 10 percent annual price growth, and your property is now valued at $220,000—then the cap rate drops to 5.4 percent. A factor pushing this general price appreciation has been the excess of global cash seeking investment havens in the U.S. real estate market in the years following the crisis. A surplus of global investment capital (in the form of cash) chasing returns has cultivated a very competitive marketplace that drives up property prices and drives down effective cap rates. As a consequence, such investments then tend to become less inviting to institutional investors seeking to put their money to use where it can fetch the highest rate of return. The scenario is complicated by interest rates. Remember that immediately after the crash, the Federal Reserve dropped interest rates as low as possible to restimulate investment flows. But low interest rates carry inflationary risk, and as the economy regained its footing, interest rates pushed back up, making the cost of cash higher. The combination of compressed cap rates and higher interest rates puts a squeeze on rates of return, and if investors borrow to purchase properties in this kind of environment, they must be careful that the spread between interest rates and cap rates is sufficient to justify the loan—in the preceding illustration, if interest rates go back up to 4.5 percent, then the effective rate of return shrinks to 1 percent, not enough to keep institutional investors in the game because they could be getting more than that in the bond market. Hence institutional investors may be inclined to take profits where they can take advantage of price appreciation by selling the property. In sum, compressed cap rates represent opportunity costs to institutional investors, reopening a share of the market to individual investors.

One way of offsetting tendencies toward cap rate compression is to hike rents, fees, and other revenue-yielding penalties. "Wall Street's new rental empire is characterized by aggressive rent hikes, fee gouging, and high rates of eviction. These practices . . . prop up a new asset class known as 'single-family rental securities,' akin to mortgage securities but backed instead by the rent checks of tenants."[56] By their own accounting, firms such as Invitation Homes have been able to boost earnings by 20 percent to 30 percent per year by imposing fees and penalties for a wide variety of sins, including making rent payments with a debit card or being even a minute late with a rent payment.[57]

The first round of corporate acquisitions in the SFR market primarily took the form of cash transactions. Financing then shifted to include leverage through bank lending and securitizations after Blackstone moved into SFR securitization in late 2013. "Leverage becomes a more important component of overall return in an environment with rising house prices."[58] The use of leverage enabled an additional 30 percent ROI for Blackstone's Invitation Homes. By 2017, the notes Blackstone issued in the early rounds of SFR securitization were valued at $19 billion. Again, we must take into account the structural logic of securitization and the impact it has on the housing market.

> At current house prices, the cash flow return is only 4.9 percent. This was higher a few years ago when house prices were lower relative to rents. But as prices have increased faster than rents, the portion of total return generated purely from rental cash income has declined, leading the industry to increase its reliance on leverage. This suggests that demand for SFR financing is likely to grow in the future.[59]

Compressed cap rates thus stimulated an increased reliance on financing, particularly on the loan asset class of single-family rental securities.

Housing Affordability

The rise of the single-family-rental industry reflects profound shifts in the finances and attitudes of America's families. "Homeownership, long a bedrock of financial stability, has become unattainable or undesirable for many middle-income workers—for reasons including tighter lending standards, large college-debt loads, and lagging wage growth and savings."[60] Corporatization of investor acquisitions of local rental markets has contributed to a crisis of affordability. But so too has the surge of middle-class investors into the housing market. Competition for smaller, older starter homes escalates the effects driven by the entry of out-of-town money willing to pay all cash in exchange for fatter discounts. In the most frenzied housing markets, the statistics have been even more stacked in favor of investors and against first-time homeowners. In Atlanta, for example, investors bought up nearly half of the most affordable houses and almost a quarter of all single-family houses. Obviously, removing such a high percentage of potentially affordable homes from the market creates a scarcity effect and puts pressure on affordability. Unlike the pre-2007 climate of zero-down loan financing, qualifying for credit is no longer a slam dunk, and enforcement of the 20 percent down payment requirement followed concerns that a lax regulatory environment precipitated the mortgage crisis. Aggravating the problem has been the fact that so much of flipping aims at the renter market, pushing rents upward. A decade after the mortgage crisis, a crisis of housing affordability continues to unfold, driven foremost by the fact that housing prices have substantially outpaced wage gains. From 2011 to 2017, household incomes grew by almost 17 percent, while housing prices grew by 42 percent. If a household spends more than 30 percent of its income on mortgages or rents, then it is classified as cost burdened. In 2017, 38 million households (31 percent of all households) were cost burdened, and another "18 million households (15 percent) were severely cost-burdened because they spent over half their incomes on housing."[61]

Flipping does play a role in the affordability crisis. The flipper's goal of seeking top dollar means that for an increasing number of potential buyers, 20 percent down payments are that much harder to come up with. High flipping rates and high flip-to-rent rates are antagonistic to the health of the general housing market, "an indication that the housing market is in trouble" because "the problem with a rise in home flipping is that these sales artificially inflate home prices, making housing even less affordable for buyers and increasing the risk of a bubble."[62] Postcrisis, the hottest metropolitan markets have seen flipping rates spiking to 30 percent, with flipping profit rates soaring to the 90 percent range. "Since bottoming out in the first quarter of 2012, U.S. median home prices have risen 69 percent while average weekly wages have risen just 9 percent during the same time period."[63] The chasm between real-estate price inflation and wage inertia has continued to shape a crisis of affordability, so that by the end of 2018, 75 percent of average wage earners were priced out of median-priced homes in U.S. housing markets.[64]

National home sales data from 2002 to 2018 reveal several patterns that further contribute to the crisis of affordability. Before the financial crisis, flippers preferred larger houses, more expensive houses, and newer houses. Kate Wagner has hypothesized that "McMansions" were tailor-made for flippers.[65] They were not just oversized; they tended to be built quickly and often lacked in quality of construction. In other words, they had a reputation for falling apart almost as quickly as they sprouted. Because they were loaded with faux surfaces that had a relatively brief stylistic shelf life, it wasn't long before they could benefit from cosmetic fixes. But in the years following the crisis, investors became more focused on smaller, less expensive, and older houses.[66] This shift has had significant repercussions for affordability because the kinds of houses investors now focus on are precisely that portion of the existing housing stock that might otherwise qualify as starter homes. Moreover, back when institutional investors began targeting the SFR market during the height of the recession—from 2009 to 2012—the distressed housing market was swamped with bank-owned REOs and investors bought in bulk mainly via auctions (e.g., the sales of foreclosed properties by Fannie Mae). Such "bulk purchases by institutional investors for renting reduce the inventory of homes available for purchase by homebuyers."[67] During the next phase of the flipping recovery, newer corporate entries into the market, such as Amherst and Zillow, have come to rely on the multiple listing service (MLS) employed by realtors. This move away from auctions to the MLS puts large investors even more directly into competition with families seeking their first home.[68]

Rising house prices and flipping form a circuit of mutual causation that takes a toll on affordability. On the one side, rising home prices lure in flippers, and in turn flippers by definition seek premiums that push market prices upward.[69]

HGTV in the Political Economy of Housing

HGTV offers representations of home renovation and flipping that take on a materiality in relation to housing affordability. After all, a leading premise of HGTV's discourse is predicated on solving the predicament of affordability by unlocking the value of undervalued properties. This may work for the relatively more affluent couples who appear on HGTV, but when this strategy is replicated too widely across the marketplace, it drives up housing prices. The goal of flipping shows such as *Flip or Flop* is getting top dollar, and getting top dollar is the enemy of affordability.

Prior to the avalanche of mortgage defaults and foreclosures, flipping tended to take the form of speculative arbitrage—buy at the market price and sell higher as the market would surely continue going up. Reality TV's representations of flipping as moneymaking prior to 2008 included dramatizations of this turn-and-burn flipping mentality, the most aggressive of which were not HGTV shows: "'Flip That House' on TLC, 'Flip This House' on A&E and 'Flipping Out' on Bravo played up the idea that with a fresh coat of paint and some stainless steel appliances, practically any home could be resold for a profit."[70] The crisis itself temporarily stilled such representations, and HGTV itself recognized a crisis of direction.

The crisis prompted criticism of HGTV's propensity for heralding excess. A *Wall Street Journal* editorial blamed the housing market bubble on HGTV and its stable of shows that inflated desires and expectations. "HGTV pumped up the housing bubble by parading the most mediocre, unworthy-looking homeowners into our living rooms to watch while they put their tacky, run-of-the-mill tract homes on the market for twice what they paid and then went out and bought houses with price tags too obscene to repeat. You couldn't watch these shows without concluding that you must be an idiot and a loser if you lived in a house you could actually afford."[71]

It's a curious critique. In the society of the spectacle, programming such as HGTV's is obviously more visible than the deep structure of securitization, so it makes sense that pundits would point the finger at HGTV. Notice, however, that the criticism did not extend to the relentless boosterism of

CNBC, Fox, CNN, and Bloomberg that breathlessly reported record highs in the Dow and Nasdaq market indexes, openly enjoining viewers to invest as a way to get ahead. Blaming the market collapse on HGTV programs that encouraged an excess of desires while discounting the overleveraging of debt within capital markets put the onus not on gullible and avaricious investors but on gullible consumers. In fact, the very nature of the commodity system of advertising and marketing via television, print, and internet is meant to cultivate an excess of desires. Prior to the crisis, the home renovation genre lent itself to a panicky race to treat homes as little more than a fungible equivalent of money. In this sense, HGTV probably can be seen as a contextualizing factor in the mortgage meltdown, insofar as it "helped fuel the unfettered consumerism and neoliberal politics that have helped put millions of American homeowners into foreclosure and bankruptcy and that are threatening the economic stability and environmental viability of our society."[72]

Around 2008, HGTV programming actually showcased more interior design shows hosted by celebrity designers than renovation shows. Design experts performed as arbiters of fashionable taste, and their shows emphasized matters of taste over how much value could be added. Designer makeovers of one room at a time celebrated the transformation of tasteless spaces into shiny curated signifiers of cultural capital. Until the mortgage crisis, the audience numbers for HGTV had steadily increased to a high of 43.47 million viewers per week in August 2008.[73] The crisis and recession dampened the fever, and viewership dropped more than 10 percent, so HGTV jettisoned the design shows between 2009 and 2011. Flagging ratings required "a midcourse correction for HGTV, a cable network that fed—and feasted on—the fantasies and delusions of the housing bubble and then, when that collapsed, went into austerity and atonement mode with series like the 2009 'Real Estate Intervention'" that aimed at what to do in a housing market that has collapsed.[74]

Between 2010 and 2014, HGTV reinvented itself, though it never let go of the ever-popular *House Hunters* franchise, even spinning off a renovation-oriented namesake in 2012. HGTV's reinvention remained scattered for several years as it trotted out a potpourri of approaches, looking for a new balance that nodded toward what people were going through during the recession but at the same time continued its mission to encourage consumer desire and spending. If anything, the impulse toward property porn intensified—it is, after all, a television equivalent of comfort food—but frugality also persisted as a theme with shows like *Design on a Dime* doing room makeovers on the cheap.

HGTV is steeped in affect. It embraces affective desires for satisfaction. The bridge between aesthetics and affect has narrowed to such an extent that commodity culture invites us to suspend the distinction. It is no accident that economic decisions on HGTV are coated, as if by confectioner's sugar, with the flavoring of affective desire. HGTV imagines spaces slathered in aesthetic affect that draw in viewers while simultaneously encouraging their engagement by leaving open the space to second-guess the decisions made by the featured participants. This constant two-step of embracing and distancing affective desire and its fetishization gives HGTV its appeal, making "HGTV a favorite go-to destination for affluent, educated viewers, particularly women, unable to resist taking a voyeuristic glimpse into other people's domestic lives and engage in a bit of risk-free real estate speculation."[75]

Two shows in particular signaled the new direction during the 2010–2011 season. *Rehab Addict* with Nicole Curtis as a single entrepreneurial mother who restored deteriorating "historical" homes of the bourgeoisie in Minneapolis and Detroit became popular immediately. At the height of the recession, Curtis possessed just the right qualities for the moment—an independent single mother with a strong work ethic who combined elbow grease with frugal salvage and recycling of materials to restore eyesores into stately beauties. Three months later, *Property Brothers* debuted with the formula that would become HGTV's signature approach. The success of those shows paved the way for a legion of imitations. In 2014, HGTV added *Flip or Flop*, aimed at those who fantasized about flipping grit into glamour, and *Fixer Upper*, which would become the most popular end-user renovation fantasy. By 2014, HGTV programming had fully transitioned to reflect the fix-and-flip approach that relied on finding discounted houses (foreclosures) that could be renovated and fixed up to add value. Thus, for all its misrepresentations of house flipping, HGTV has, in fact, crudely mimicked the broad contours of both the pre- and postcrisis phases of flipping.

Targeting women and millennials, HGTV's ratings surged to an all-time high in 2015, reaching 96 million households. Meanwhile, postcrash flipping markets rebounded to new highs in 2016–2017 while the new asset class we have discussed took shape in the form of a flourishing market for fix-and-flip loans. Investment banks took notice of the fix-and-flip loan market and moved to capture it. Spearheading this movement, Goldman Sachs acquired Genesis Capital, a lending platform focused on professional real estate flippers, and KKR underwrote and made a market for securities generated by Angel Oaks, another corporatized hard-money lender. Genesis Capital had grown from making $50 million in loans in 2013 to over $1 billion in 2017.[76] And just like that, hard-money loans acquired legitimacy within the financial system.

What is the relationship between the cultural phenomenon of HGTV and the solidification of the fix-and-flip loan market? And why do small investors continue to numerically predominate in an industry that has been otherwise restructured by capital since the crisis? Institutional investors armed with surpluses of investment capital and advanced computer technologies have remade the flipping and renovation industries into a system of investors. Investors—both big and small—are purchasing a greater share of homes than they have over the last twenty years. Middlemen have insinuated themselves into this market in the form of wholesalers who have access to cash (usually not entirely their own) to buy houses quickly at discounted prices. In the emerging division of labor within the real estate flipping industry, these wholesalers form one aspect of an intermediation stratum.[77] They then resell these properties at a premium to rookie mom-and-pop entrepreneurs who need to borrow infusions of capital to pull off the renovations and improvements that will increase the value of the home—hence the newfound legitimacy for fix-and-flip loans and short-term bridge loans that start at 8 percent and go higher than 15 percent. Those mom-and-pop operators are fueling the fix-and-flip loan business that has become hefty enough that global investment firms like Goldman Sachs, JPMorgan, Wells Fargo, Nomura, and KKR have taken notice and now seek to take advantage of this new asset class and the securities that can be generated and marketed to other investors.

Since 2016, an accumulation of anecdotal accounts from lenders suggests that a growing number of rookie mom-and-pop investors have been motivated to take the plunge into flipping after watching HGTV. When Goldman Sachs acquired Genesis Capital in 2017 to gain access to the fix-and-flip loan market, the *Wall Street Journal* interviewed a leading Florida flipper who recounted a transition since 2014 when few lenders were willing to finance flips, to a situation three years later when "rising home prices and falling inventories" drew additional lenders because "a lot more new home flippers are coming out of the woodwork. They have seen the [TV] shows."[78] Wholesalers mention familiarity with HGTV as a factor contributing to their markets: "People are watching HGTV and hearing from different gurus about what they should be doing," observed a partner at a New York real estate investment company before adding, "Very often someone who's hungry for their first deal will pay more. If we're averaging $20,000 to $30,000 profit on a house, an extra $10,000 is a big deal."[79] If HGTV has any influence on decisions to enter the flipping market, it's going to be with rookies. When this occurs, we might call it the HGTV premium effect.

And that premium effect continues to reverberate as one of many variables driving contradictions in the housing and lending system. Between 2013 and 2019, the average home valuation rose by 42 percent, while average hourly wages grew by less than 20 percent. In a market defined by tight inventory, this divergence between home prices and wages continues to pressure long-term housing affordability.⁸⁰ A 2019 downturn in home prices did little to remedy the affordability crisis but rather prompted a bind for novice home flippers and lenders alike. "A new crop of flippers, inspired by HGTV reality shows, real estate meetup groups, and get-rich gurus, piled into the market in recent years," and now those mom-and-pop rookies are confronting "losses from houses that take too long to sell."⁸¹ This is the risk of fix-to-flip loans—the hard-money crunch. And it puts loan originators in a difficult spot if they are to keep the machinery of the fix-to-flip loan market from stalling. Before the extraordinary shock of the COVID-19 pandemic, which has further exacerbated affordability concerns, credit-rating analysts expressed concern that the constraints on housing affordability put pressure on "lenders to loosen credit standards to maintain volumes."⁸² Coupled with declining FICO credit scores, this combination of market trends points toward a return to nonprime loans (a reformed version of subprime loans) and the potential for an increasing percentage of defaults. Despite the fact that mortgage interest rates once again stand at historic lows, mom-and-pop fix-to-rent borrowers are especially vulnerable to default under the conditions of the COVID-19 economic crisis.

How then shall we consider the place of HGTV in the flipping economy over the course of the postcrash recovery? It's more than merely a set of representations. HGTV's imprint on the renovations market can certainly be traced in the domain of design and style standards. A slew of home-furnishing companies fronted by Wayfair, Home Depot, and Lowe's have benefited. But there is another, perhaps more significant political-economic effect linking HGTV, the fix-and-flip loan industry, fintech, and finance capital writ large. The persistence and growth of the renovation and flipping markets are responsible for a profitable fix-and-flip loan business, and it is possible that HGTV has given momentum to the formation of this new loan asset class. Let's be clear. Fix-and-flip loans have been a boon for many a home renovator and many a flipper. But they come at a price. Fix-and-flip loans come with double and triple the low-interest conventional home mortgages, and these are short-term hard-money loans. The rapidly evolving fintech and proptech industry has taken aim at this market, and Wall Street banks, including Goldman Sachs, Blackstone, Softbank, and KKR, have invested in them or acquired them as portfolio companies, attracted by the elevated fix-to-flip interest returns, turning the category of hard-money loans from seedy, high-risk usury to a credible high-return asset in corporate loan portfolios.⁸³

HGTV did not create the flipping industry. It did not cause the crisis. But would the flipping industry be as robust minus HGTV and its pump-priming semiotics of consumer desire on the one side, or its imagery of making a living by flipping houses on the investment side? HGTV has morphed into a cultural force that cannot be separated from motivations to flip houses in pursuit of profit or renovate houses to build home equity. Flipping-to-rent has grown dependent on the mom-and-pop flippers to flip the majority of houses. These individual investors have turned into the foot soldiers for the latest turn toward securitization.

It's highly unlikely that HGTV's decision makers ever thought about how they could lend a hand to the forces of financial securitization. They've been focused on a programming strategy that would build up the bottom line by increasing advertising revenues. They achieved the latter so convincingly that the Discovery Channel purchased Scripps Networks Interactive (HGTV's parent) in 2018 for a hefty $15 billion. Though it may never have been its intention, HGTV's approach to flipping and renovation shows has helped shape a climate that furthers the embrace of securitization across the housing industry. From 2012 to 2018, there exists an intriguing correspondence between the remarkable run of popularity enjoyed by HGTV home renovation programming and the upward curves of participation and profitability in the flipping economy. Over that same period, fix-and-flip loans became a legitimate market, and Wall Street securitized those loans as yet another asset class. HGTV is not simply a vehicle for commodity advertising, it is itself one giant advertisement for the value proposition of renovating and flipping houses, and yet the most significant political-economic commodity for which it prompts demand is for a commodity that HGTV tries to keep as invisible as possible in its stories—the fix-to-flip loan and the debt that makes it attractive to finance capital.

4

Gentrification TV

Working class communities are culturally devitalized through gentrification as the new middle class scorns the streets in favour of the dining room and bedroom.
—**Neil Smith,** *The New Urban Frontier*

Coupled with the omission of the political economy of flipping, the formulaic tilt of HGTV's narratives presents stories of individual renovators helping individual families find the housing solutions that fit their needs. Such stories seem contained to their subjects and without a broader politics beyond house and family. Yet within the resolution to these stories, there is a politics—a class politics of gentrification wherein symbols of upper-class belonging become salient consideration in the narratives of value. Housing shapes living; its projected value is bound up with class-tinged ideas about family, identity, and place.

My next question concerns the relationship between representations of house flipping and gentrification on HGTV. House flipping is made to seem deterritorialized on HGTV because the stories withhold the geographic coordinates of houses that are being flipped. The houses might be anywhere; they seem to exist in a geography of nowhere. I call HGTV gentrification TV because of its insistence that the houses most suited to profitable renovations and flipping are those that are discounted to the market as a result of age, neglect, style, changing demographics, neighborhood, or other markers of class. Insofar as HGTV shows interrupt their stories of value in a vacuum to consider markets, obtaining a rent-gap discount and renovating is the method that HGTV pitches as a way of getting more house for the money.

To make its rent-gap sales pitch look appealing, HGTV accents the economic appeal of flipping and renovation while averting viewers' eyes from its social context, its social history, and its social repercussions. Hence

HGTV dwells on remaking upscale-looking interior spaces while erasing the uneven urban development of real estate geographies that seeded rent-gap conditions to begin with (think redlining and white flight). Severed from the institutional forces that shape housing markets, HGTV renovation programs manage to accomplish something that has been otherwise impossible: they visualize the achievement of a *color-blind* open-concept gentrification by diverting attention from histories of racial discrimination, disinvestment, geographies of poverty, predatory lending, and dispossession that so often correlate with gentrification practices. When we bring these subjects back into consideration, it becomes obvious that HGTV shows give voice to a mythological politics of color-blind opportunities for home ownership that presupposes a self-sustaining flipping bubble. But when that bubble pops again, any wealth redistribution effect will be subject again to the structural forces that revert to reproducing wealth inequality.

Making Entitlement Look Affordable

After learning that a previously unnoticed structural problem will eat into his budget for beautifying a fixer-upper, a home renovation TV client laments that "to spend money on something you don't see is frustrating." HGTV clients often strike similar poses, adamantly insisting that "I want what I want." They display an inflated sense of self-entitlement, an expression of self that insists that the world bend to their desires. From this viewpoint, money spent to restore function should be more properly allocated to creating the ensemble of appearances that goes by the name of the forever dream home. They know cosmetic changes are key to adding value in the TV renovation project, while structural amendments to unseen infrastructure barely seem to budge the value needle. The forever dream home may represent the ideal of living in appearances, but forever won't last long if it is structurally unsound. This obvious inconsistency between value as appearance and the goal of durable long-term value gets a bit fuzzy in the HGTV universe, where the fastest way to add the value one wants is through a cosmetic makeover.

HGTV models this promise of neoliberal entitlement on a budget at the same time that the U.S. household wealth gap between the top 10 percent and those below has widened substantially since the financial crisis, mainly "at the expense of households in the 50th to 90th percentiles of the wealth distribution."[1] While the wealthiest households own diversified investments, middle-class households have been overly dependent on home equity as a source of wealth, and thus "were seven times as exposed to the housing bubble and collapse."[2] Within the 40th to 70th percentiles, the average middle-income household lost two-thirds of its home equity between 2005 and 2011 and has still not recovered that wealth despite rising home prices.³ Hence HGTV's mission is to market the dream home in more accessible terms. The Lowe's chief marketing officer said that the appeal of *Property Brothers* to advertisers is its "approachability. A focus on the real American home gives people confidence to go into our stores and say, 'You know what? I can change a home or a room with a reasonable budget.'"⁴

The commodity look of entitlement belongs not just to the rich anymore! Stories about clients seeking their dream homes at prices they can afford envision a quest for amplified value in which "'aesthetics' envelopes 'structure' and celebrates the definitive wedding of the object to your 'personality.'"⁵ Episodes invariably conclude with clients feeling themselves more fully expressed in the transformed spaces they come to occupy. In this way, HGTV can be viewed as attempting to symbolically remediate the wealth gap.

HGTV shows reproduce a currency of sign-value appearances framed by a visual code of aesthetic finishes. The designers, the realtors, and the buyers all speak in what amounts to a semiotic language of interior design aesthetics. Quartz, we are told, signifies modernity, whereas granite says traditional refined elegance and good taste. Granite was once a preferred countertop on home renovation shows because it signified "a pursuit. An ambition. A glossy, reflective surface that allows us to gaze at ourselves and know where we stand."⁶ Reiterated across its many shows, HGTV's aesthetic code is unified and tightly branded, offering aspirational but democratized kitchen surfaces. "HGTV is the land that viewers visit when they are trying to cultivate a personal design aesthetic by spying on what everyone else is doing."⁷

This home remodeling simulacrum turns the home's interior into a curated sanctuary. Clients state preferences for living in special neighborhoods, but without an impulse towards neighbors or community. They seek respect and recognition, not so much in the realm of the immediately social, but by bathing in the reflection of semiotically coded design spaces. Given that the search for value in the real-world housing market had become clouded by risk, uncertainty, and strangling debt loads, it is not surprising that HGTV's guided tours in search of value now reference a hyperreal world, a simulacrum of home renovation. TV renovation stories thus appear to resolve the tension between unchecked commodity desires and pocketbooks that have not kept pace with the price of their satisfaction.

Fiona Allon notes that, before the housing bubble burst, "with assets appreciating much faster than incomes, consumers eagerly embraced asset accumulation" in the form of houses "as a primary substitute for employment security and the social wage."⁸ Inflated asset values collapsed and incomes continued to lag during the Great Recession that followed. "In 2013, the median income of U.S. households was $51,939, down substantially from $55,562 in 2001."[9] But there were also millions of foreclosed properties on the market. HGTV revisited the promise of asset accumulation via the renovated house—this time by playing rent gaps between housing stocks that were worn down or foreclosed off against the envied showcase homes in special neighborhoods with great schools and amenities. Following *Property Brothers*' lead, HGTV shows make a clear pitch for gentrifying urban and suburban houses as an investment-worthy path to building home equity and becoming enviable yourself. The ideal of atomized, private, and detached households that buttressed the heyday of modernist suburbanization gets a nostalgic revival in the HGTV rendition of home renovation. But on HGTV, the yearning to live encased in midcentury modern styles can be sited anywhere that the rent-gap logic pencils out. In short, the "privatized geography of suburbanization" is not just for suburbia anymore.[10]

Gentrification, Rent Gaps, and HGTV

One long-standing political-economic explanation of gentrification focuses on rent gaps. In 1979, Neil Smith defined the rent gap as "the disparity between the potential ground rent level and the actual ground rent capitalized under the present land use."[11] Back then, the greater the gap between higher suburban land rents and land rents in older inner cities, the more attuned investors became to the disparity between potential and actual ground rent in the undervalued regions of housing markets. An early stage of gentrification began when investors/property owners sought out the comparative economic advantage of renovating properties left behind by prior generations of the bourgeoisie, the value of which had been depreciated by decades of racially motivated disinvestment. Public revenues declined as manufacturing industries moved offshore and the geographic movement of the service sector and consumer businesses followed the path of suburban housing. Portrayed as the consumer ideal during the postwar decades, suburbanization represented the full development of modernity. But the cultural alienation it fed over the years prompted dissatisfactions with suburban lifestyles that propelled a portion of an educated upper middle class to take advantage of rent gaps. Urban planners, eager to find ways to bring business back into cities but strapped for public sector resources, embraced the entrepreneurial capital that developers and bankers were willing to invest when they realized how much money could be made by taking advantage of then-prevailing rent gaps. Eventually, those suburban homes that once seemed the epitome of consumer modernity became, in turn, dated and worn down. As opportunities for gentrification in inner-city neighborhoods exhausted themselves, the logic of the rent gap moved back toward middle-ring suburbs where relatively discounted prices became more attractive as opportunities for the gentrifying touch.

By the time HGTV took up the rent-gap sales pitch, the movement to remodel rent capital in the central-city neighborhoods had long since displaced the economically disadvantaged who lived there. HGTV's endorsement of rent-gap strategies divorces itself from both the preconditions and the consequences of gentrification as urban policy. By treating each episode's flip as a unique and isolated occurrence unrelated to the history of unequal geographies, HGTV resolutely keeps all social and economic externalities out of sight. The outside world simply disappears, and with it the general preconditions of a flipping economy that has been taking shape over decades of gentrification history. Early stages of gentrification from the late 1970s through the 1990s hollowed out inner-city neighborhoods, displacing and pushing poverty outward into inner- and middle-ring suburbs. Those decaying suburban neighborhoods were also being reshaped by the demographics of aging, retirement, and the death of decades-old white-flight occupants. When the mortgage crisis hit, it hit these already devalued suburban housing stocks particularly hard, flooding the market with heavily discounted foreclosures that investors aggressively targeted and turning a competition to flip the discounts into a new wave of collateral gentrification.

Though gentrification is pictured neither spatially or socially, taking advantage of rent gaps is the fundamental element of the sales pitch that all HGTV renovation shows present. When *Property Brothers* encourages clients to seek customized open-concept dream scenes in fixer-uppers, it unveils a strategy that boils down to taking advantage of prevailing rent gaps between upscale houses and those that have fallen out of favor but can be aesthetically renovated according to current tastes. By focusing entirely on the aesthetic and budgetary advantages of pursuing the rent-gap strategy, gentrification as the renovation of interior spaces ignores the surrounding streets and neighborhoods, and HGTV renders the wider landscape of gentrification invisible. Thus, whereas Smith wrote about gentrification as the movement of capital obeying the logic of rent gaps, HGTV now packages and sells the logic of the rent gap as a consumer lifestyle choice.

The visual ontology of private space—what we might call interior design porn—is a chief accomplishment of HGTV. A tight camera focus on cloistered interiors frames the value-added home as a self-contained and perfected set of spatial appearances insulated from its immediate surroundings. So doggedly does *Property Brothers* abstract the ideal of the secluded home from all that surrounds it that its location disappears and with it the dynamic contradictions of urban social life. Private spaces, not city spaces, form the contours of TV gentrification.

Television gentrification molds itself around a neoliberal revision of an embourgeoisement fantasy. Joanna Gaines summarizes this in her voice-over that introduces *Fixer Upper*: "Every town has that neighborhood, the one with the perfect commute, great schools, and amazing homes. It's the one everyone wants to live in but few can afford.... We are Chip and Joanna Gaines, and we've made those out-of-reach neighborhoods reachable." When the sociology of embourgeoisement surfaced in the late 1950s, it examined a premise that working-class individuals could be absorbed into middle-class life by virtue of access to education, independence of one's work, and home ownership. By contrast, in current home renovation stories of embourgeoisement, the postrecession vision of becoming middle class dwells primarily on HGTV's maps of the status and value encoded in the interiorized landscapes of home ownership. HGTV dedicates its renovation shows to reproducing, modeling, and validating a system of commodity aesthetics that simulate the coded lifestyle of the magazine bourgeoisie. It's a Pollyannaish script that continues to exert remarkable hegemonic influence during an era when there is considerable public wailing about the economic erosion of the middle class.

As a corollary to this inward-looking fixation on taste, when prospective buyers tour houses they express a strong preference to *not* be able to see neighbors or, worse, be seen by neighbors. Not only is their preference to be isolated at home, but they never inquire about who the immediate neighbors are. While neighbors might be a no-no, buyers do have preconceived ideas about neighborhoods that appeal to them because of schools or proximity to amenities and the built environment for gentrified consumption—cafés, bakeries, brewpubs, and restaurants. Neighborhoods may be hot, but neighbors are not and should remain out of sight. This fits with the extraordinary social privatism that spills out from these shows—satisfactions are sought from an internally insulated world mediated by the commodification of all possible gratifications. The questions about value that dot the housescapes of these shows are answered with scenes and narratives of value fetishism coupled with testimonials about bringing family together. A recent study of relationships between neighbors concludes that "Americans are left with a sense of isolation from neighbors nearby: we keep 'inner-ring' relationships with family and close friends plus 'outer-ring' with Facebook friends we see infrequently, but we have lost middle-ring relationships with families down the street and a barber around the corner."[12] Avoiding the social part of everyday life—the unexpected encounters with neighbors and others who exist in social proximity—means interacting only with those whom one voluntarily chooses. Translated by the women and men who speak on home renovation shows, this is expressed as a desire for connected isolation.

Each family, tucked away to its own devices, wishes to avoid engaging neighbors, keeping neighbors as strangers if possible. For all the rhetoric about wanting to live in the midcentury retro modern style, gone is the emphasis on the picture window and what it signified, a desire to play out the social status of one's living space for the benefit of others: to be seen. In postwar suburbia, the picture window aimed at simulating the conditions of a *petite aristocratie*—able to look *out* at an undisturbed picture of nature and desirous of having others gaze *in* with envy at the scene of domestic comfort inside. Critics of conspicuous consumption took aim at the "overexposure of the domestic interior" as part of the vulgar commercialism spreading across the 1950s' social landscape.[13] By contrast, if we take seriously contemporary desires to screen off the gaze into domestic space, we see a steady deterioration of the social in validating our domestic identities and well-being. Just as the social-from-without is kept at arm's length and out of sight, so too renovated spaces tend to be devoid of art—particularly painting and sculpture—but decorated instead with disconnected signifiers pulled from flea markets or ready-made mass-produced kitsch purchased via Wayfair. Such décor is selected to signify a stylish simplicity; far from the status and wealth pretensions of higher art, they supposedly connote "homespun." In TV real estate land, the desire is to avoid being seen, as if being seen diminishes one's control over personal space. Given revelations in recent years about the inclination of governments (National Security Agency) and corporations (Facebook) to cyber-electronically gather information on individuals, this obsessive desire to avoid being seen by neighbors seems at first glance a little hysterical, and perhaps misplaced.

From a sociological point of view, it seems implausible to tell a story about the gentrification of housing markets without acknowledging income inequality, the history of redlining, and white supremacy. Visually and ideologically, HGTV's representation of rent gaps as opportunities for middle-class wealth building requires cordoning off the collateral damage of the financial crisis inflicted on vulnerable populations who have been dispossessed and displaced. HGTV weaves a dialectic of sumptuary vision and blindness—each is necessary to achieving the dream that the generalized rent-gap approach represents a reopening to middle-class wealth accumulation. Structuring the scene by excluding all that surrounds it invites clients and viewers alike to share in the pretense that we can "create a new world with clean hands."[14]

Ideological Traces of Social Life

Beyond the obvious that everyone wants to retire from society to a secluded sanctuary, a few recurring social accents from these shows deserve mention.

With the exception of the metrosexual Scotts on *Property Brothers*, who choose to bond on-screen with the children of client families by performing as playful uncles, other flipping and renovation shows routinely devote video time to scenes of the hosts' kids. Renovation and flipping shows typically star a married couple with young children, frequently infants. HGTV envisions mom-and-pop flipping businesses as a dual commitment to entrepreneurialism and the hearth and home of the middle-class nuclear family. The symbolic symmetry of renovation and rebirth marks both the economy and personal life. On flipper shows, transition scenes often include an adorable baby as little more than a prop—held for a moment before dashing off to inspect a house—to buffer the appearance of flippers as cold and calculating. On *Rehab Addict*, Nicole Curtis routinely dispenses her philosophy for raising her son, teaching him to appreciate the virtue of hard work and how to navigate markets. In Waco, where renovation is the game, *Fixer Upper* draws its charm from the Gaineses' young family—two boys and two girls—on their budding farmstead complete with baby goats and gardens. Their *Fixer Upper* brand embraces the organic incorporation of children into their hectic lives, teaching their children to respect heritage while learning the basics of being little entrepreneurs. In a video trailer for *Fixer Upper*, Chip and Joanna explain why they choose to raise their family in Waco: "We really feel like our hearts connect with the concept of growing what you eat, you know, making what you sell. I mean, it's a beautiful place and we hope it rubs off on our family a little."

Whereas *Property Brothers* assumes a landscape of insulated home spaces abstracted from geography and social life, and Orange County's *Flip or Flop* sees houses as merely fungible commodities devoid of subjective significance, *Fixer Upper* proposes a vision of a world in which families can make choices that reground themselves—either in imagined communities or place. Linking the conditions for raising a family to ideals of growing what you eat and making what you sell references a modest critique of a global economy that functions as an overwhelming system of impersonal commodity circulation and exchange. The Gaines family claims to imagine a place (not a space) where families can participate in shaping the conditions of producing a living, a family, and a faith. As their business empire grows, Joanna reflects on the paramount goal of their home renovation business: "What we do is for the sake of family."

A recurring theme in HGTV shows presents the home as a site not only for family but also for work. A disproportionate number of clients (especially millennials) claim to need a home office to work from. The home is narrativized as a site for independent work minus the overbearing presence of bosses. Self-motivated work joins itself to an emphasis on the enclosure of nuclear-style family units. HGTV home renovations aim to unify the conditions of work and family. Client fixations on open-concept interior spaces are not just about aesthetic tastes; they also reveal clients' social conceptions of living space. Separate formal dining rooms can be folded into living rooms because after-dinner conversation has been supplanted by big-screen TVs. The open concept stresses the kitchen as a set of appearances—hence the outsized desire for factory-new stainless-steel appliances—rather than mere functionality. Moreover, clients routinely express a desire to monitor or surveil young children from the kitchen space via unimpeded sightlines. Because open-concept designs create illusions of spaciousness and freedom, open-concept interior space is the currently preferred architecture of value creation.

When we consider television history's marginalization of nonwhites and nonheterosexuals, the depiction of social diversity on HGTV might initially seem breathtaking. Long-term migrations from Latin America, East Asia, and South Asia to North America have prompted consumer-oriented corporate marketing to steer toward an imagery of greater consumer diversity, and HGTV's programmers and advertisers have jumped on board lest they become less competitive in garnering market share. Originally owned by Scripps Networks Interactive, which defined itself as a lifestyle media platform, HGTV's potential global market is not strictly white or heterosexual or Christian. Its programming includes interracial couples, same-sex couples, African American and Asian couples, and Spanish-speaking families. This nod toward diversity is intentional according to HGTV's general manager: "We absolutely seek it out. Our goal is to represent our viewing base, and our viewing base is very diverse, so one of the things that we make sure that we do is to have as diverse of a homeowner population as we can. And I'm glad that you notice, because we work hard to do it, and it really is reflective of the American population."[15] HGTV depicts racial, sexual, and ethnic differences becoming integrated into a commodified set of panethnic cultural expressions defined by open-concept demographics. HGTV's advertisers visualize a color-blind world of commodified home ownership and interior design, tweaked to fit the cosmopolitan tone of commodified tolerance and acceptance of a global society.

HGTV shows come across as unabashed libertarian supporters of the family as a domestic unit independent of the particular liaison that forms it. Socially, this permits an agnostic stance on questions of sexual preference, permitting HGTV to endorse an open-concept approach to the family that can accommodate a range of sociation from same-sex couples to extended kin arrangements. In the renovation narrative model, it is the expert host (an entrepreneur) who guides clients safely through the turbulence of the marketplace and who ensures the negation of former modes of discrimination. According to these stories, equal treatment before the law no longer requires intrusive, coercive government regulation. Instead, the realtor/designer personalities function as paternalistic, caring, and moral souls able to navigate the market without the heavy hand of the state and who are thus able to serve (at least ideologically) the best interests of her/his/their client.

HGTV sponsors a social universe where signs of diversity and inclusion define the landscape—where home buyers express desires to live freely inside open interior spaces located in unspecifiable communities where they can be as closed off as possible from prying eyes. Perhaps it is easier to tolerate otherness if it stays tightly enclosed and separate in its own privatized spaces? In HGTV's stories, admission to this universe of home ownership is not dependent on the state—no state presence is required in these stories—and it is not bound up in the extension of traditional conceptions of citizenship. It takes place instead within what appears to be a consensual and nonjudgmental marketplace where the integrity and expertise of entrepreneurial heroes steers renovations to their just conclusions. Even though gentrification patterns frequently have deleterious effects on housing affordability for the urban working poor, in the world of TV gentrification nothing happens external to the home.

Michelle Alexander has drawn attention to a supposed era of color blindness surrounding the law.[16] On HGTV, the long-awaited color-blind society is part of the script. In its selection and representations of both clients and entrepreneurial flippers, HGTV signals a prejudice-free home renovation market. But this color blindness is mostly an appearance that renders discrimination invisible. On HGTV, color blindness does less to remedy past racialized inequities than continue to shroud the many ways that the post-2008 housing economy remains structured by the racialized antecedents and consequences of the housing crisis.

The TV version of home renovation offers an inviting vision of neoliberal multiculturalism that substitutes consumer rights over citizenship. In this postcitizenship model, rights appear to materialize through access to an enlightened and responsive entrepreneurial marketplace where discrimination is a thing of the past. The difficulty with this postcitizenship ideology is that just as it excludes the state, it also imagines a world that naturalizes the power of finance capital to ethically pick and choose which demographic categories get to participate in the benefits of home ownership.

At first blush it would seem that the home renovation TV phenomenon seems to run counter to the nationalist politics of Trumpism and the racist populism that it thrives on. The global expansion of commodity lifestyle markets requires an expanding demographic, not a more limited one. While the network must seek to encourage diversity as part of its globalizing market strategy, ideologically its shows feed the base dream that Trumpism proclaims: get government out of the way to allow the power of the free market to serve the dream.

Gentrification in Nowhere Land

HGTV shrouds geography's relation to value in the home by concealing housing geographies in the cities where stories take place. Without location information, we have no sense of variations in specific housing markets. Chip Gaines summarizes the *Fixer Upper* approach to the housing market in a voice-over that frames each episode: "We look for the worst home on the best streets and turn them into our clients' dream homes." Location, as we all know, is a crucial ingredient in real estate pricing. While home renovation shows allude to this mantra, actual information about geographic location generally remains unspoken and off-camera. Speaking in the vaguest of generalities, TV realtors mention differences between "close in" and "farther out" to denote trade-offs in price versus distance from trendy amenities and longer work commutes. Bigger houses farther out cost less money. Relationships between social status, culture, geography, and valuation are so shallow they are not worth mentioning. Only *Income Property*'s didactic host offers speculative projections about the appreciation of properties based on how established a (once again unidentified) neighborhood is, or where there may be profits in reselling the property to developers.

Neighborhood is a key variable in the subjective calculation of value because, as the real estate agent on *Property Brothers* points out, trendy neighborhoods offer "a world of amenities at your fingertips," but still *Property Brothers* does everything it can to conceal the particular city or neighborhood where the shows are being filmed. This repression of geographic and market specificity seems puzzling until we read *Property Brothers'* website explanation: "We don't emphasize the geographic location of the houses, as we want to focus on the informative aspects that could be applicable to a house in any city," to encourage viewers to think generically about a house for themselves.[17] HGTV is selling the concept of the renovated house *in abstracto*, where place becomes a space "that is homogeneous yet at the same time broken up into fragments."[18]

If we are to believe *Property Brothers'* Jonathan and Drew Scott that they intentionally suppress the geography of housing, their effort to abstract the house from its coordinates in place invites viewers to occupy a disembedded housing landscape. In sociology, disembeddedness refers to the way that modern institutions, primarily the market and the state, develop by lifting social relations from their specificity in daily life. For markets to advance and expand requires a uniform canvas rather than a multitude of specificities. To rebuild the modern demands that the old-fashioned, the antiquated, even the culturally idiosyncratic be pushed aside to accommodate the greater efficiencies of the universal market. Notice the parallel between this sociohistorical dynamic of modernity and the desire for open-concept canvases that break down partitions to create empty space for home renovation—in each case, the past needs to be purged as much as possible to achieve new value.[19]

Property Brothers uses only the briefest establishing shots of the house exteriors the brothers visit. For the Scotts, the visual style of the exterior was largely irrelevant to the articulation of an enhanced home value in their early Canadian shows. By contrast, in Waco the exterior appearance—its curb appeal—receives significant attention in the before-and-after contrast that is the first measure of added value. Still, even in Waco the value of the renovated house must be evaluated entirely against itself, as it remains photographically isolated from that which surrounds it. The pivotal narrative is about reshaping interior spaces, not the surrounding geographic landscape, to excite new value.

Paramount to HGTV's production of space is the open-concept architecture of lived space that eliminates as many partitions as possible. So knee jerk is HGTV's pursuit of taking out walls to create the open-concept appearance that Chip Gaines pokes fun at his designer wife about it: "If we could open up a couple of those big rooms into a couple of those other big rooms, you'd have one big, big room. And that's what everyone's looking for, you know. I mean that." A key ideological trope as well as a spatial figuration that holds special appeal for consumers, open-concept architecture speaks to a dialectical dance between homogeneity and customization. The story goes that within this fully hollowed-out space, each individual household can find, with the aid of HGTV's designers, its own true identity—its own special look. This is the social promise of value that HGTV makes.

Distributed Gentrification

The Scotts are sometimes wont to remind clients whose taste for bling exceeds their checkbooks that if they are willing to go a little farther out, a fixer-upper in the suburbs will get them more square footage and the renovated look-alike they covet in already gentrified neighborhoods. When put into practice, their pitch to renovate discounted (by age, neglect, or foreclosure) properties in inner- and middle-ring suburbs endorses a spatially diffused gentrification that spiders outward from the center of cities. This corresponds to what Smith and Jason Hackworth observed in the early 2000s about a "generalization of gentrification" spreading across the "urban landscape."[20] The vectors of distributed flipping patterns are no longer faithful to neighborhood-centric gentrification, instead leapfrogging unevenly across the urban map, seeking opportunity wherever it presents itself. If we could superimpose a map of the geography of flips and home renovations over a map of gentrification from the 2007 crisis till now, what might it show? Has the geography of gentrification morphed since the mortgage crisis of 2007? Has the stage of gentrification that Hackworth and Smith identified as "diffused gentrification" in the early 2000s changed in the wake of the financial crisis? Smith observed in 2002 that the "impulse behind gentrification is now generalized; its incidence is global, and it is densely connected into the circuits of global capital and cultural circulation."[21]

To encourage viewers/consumers to consider renovations as commodity abstractions, *Property Brothers* shrewdly abstracts home renovations from their fixity in urban landscapes. On HGTV, the house being renovated could exist anywhere, its geographic location defined by the coordinates of absence. Abstracted from place, instead, the houses meaningfully exist in a geography of nowhere defined by TV space. Is this television's mimicry of the stage of diffused gentrification as it has become structured by the entry of financialization that provoked the 2007 financial crisis? In this warped fashion, HGTV unintentionally gives expression to the deterritorialization of housing finance in the age of securitization.[22] The crisis consolidated a shift in gentrification "characterized by the emergence of corporate landlords, highly leveraged housing, platform capitalism (e.g. Airbnb), transnational wealth elites using cities as 'safe deposit boxes', and a further 'naturalization' of state-sponsored gentrification."[23] With distributed gentrification, the patterns of rent-gap opportunities have become further scattered, generalized, and disengaged from the clusters of fashionable commodification that identify gentrification hubs as hubs.

On HGTV, picking the worst house and recalculating its post-renovation value invariably seems to bear positive returns on investment. On *Flip or Flop*, Tarek El Moussa pushes the rent-gap envelope as far as he can. His methodology for evaluating potential profits relies on measuring the difference between the list price for a deteriorated or neglected property and recent comps (comparative sales) for similarly sized and featured properties in the surrounding geographic area. Hence he prefers properties that look the worst because these kinds of properties generate the greatest leverage in realizing the potential of rent gaps and because visually on television the before-and-after contrast is that much more vivid as an indicator of swollen value. *Flip or Flop*'s strategy is indifferent to neighborhoods, except insofar as the real estate neighborhood designations that Tarek consults carry with them a quantitative multiplier for valuation purposes, meaning that real-estate defined geographic areas carry variable multiples of value. In these kinds of TV calculations, neighborhoods are stripped of social and cultural relationships, their value compressed into the abstraction of the comp. The house is not judged by the houses situated to the left or the right, instead its value is judged in comparison with other houses that home shoppers have visited, and, of course, the asking price is set by the abstracted measure of comps for the area, which are geographically absent.

In a monologue that opened the second season of *Flip or Flop* in the fall of 2014, Tarek shared his philosophy of flipping in response to the diminishing availability of foreclosed properties in the Los Angeles real estate market:

> In my opinion, real estate is real estate, and values are there just based on the numbers. Foreclosures are getting harder to come by, so expanding our search into new areas is necessary to stay competitive. Real estate is a numbers game; a good buy is a good buy no matter where the house is.

This geography-indifferent methodology of flipping suggests a significant historical transition in the relationship between flipping and gentrification. Tarek's approach to flipping contributes to a geographically distributed gentrification pattern that relies less directly on neighborhood locations than on a radically abstracted, property-by-property, model of rent-gap opportunities.

Smith's thesis about gentrification and rent gaps points to a purely economic logic that motivates the movement of capital investment to take advantage of uneven development patterns.

> Gentrification occurs when the gap is wide enough that developers can purchase shells cheaply, can pay the builders' costs and profit for rehabilitation, can pay interest on mortgage and construction loans, and can then sell the end product for a sale price that leaves a satisfactory return to the developer. The entire ground rent, or a large portion of it, is now capitalized; the neighborhood has been "recycled" and begins a new cycle of use.[24]

Smith's definition of gentrification as rent-gap economics fits HGTV too well. HGTV's exaggerated rent-gap sales pitch leaves no room to consider gentrification's sometimes messy social consequences. Of course, it's the social definition of gentrification that rightly concerns those with a public policy focus—especially when a crisis of affordable housing follows the displacement of lower-income, disproportionately minority populations from neighborhoods characterized by long-standing discrimination practices of disinvestment. Gentrification has been visible to the lay public since the

1970s as a pattern of economically forcing out low-income residents from central-city districts to make way for a social invasion of higher-income residents. After decades of these processes, poverty has been pushed into decaying inner- and middle-ring suburbs.

What is the relationship between gentrification, rehabbing, upscaling, and flipping? Each historical moment of gentrification has consequences for successive moments of gentrification that follow. Earlier waves of gentrification drove rising rents and population displacement that put upward pricing pressures on real estate in adjoining neighborhoods. As the attractiveness of urban amenities goes up, the restless search for lower rents draws other neighborhoods into the logic of gentrification and upscaling. So when Chip Gaines talks about transforming the worst house on the best street, he is addressing upscaling rather than gentrification per se. Upscaling occurs typically in middle-class neighborhoods where the housing stock may have been rehabbed in prior decades and the median income of the area is too high to consider the area eligible for gentrification. Upscaling means rehabbing homes in those neighborhoods to bring them equal to or above the existing median home valuations there.

While flipping and home renovation strategies are not necessarily the same as gentrification, for obvious reasons flippers look for overlaps where neighborhoods are gentrifying. In HGTV's narratives, flipping and home renovation depend heavily on constricted applications of rent-gap thinking, with one significant qualification: HGTV performs rent-gap calculations exclusively at the level of the single-family residence, as opposed to the form of "corporatized gentrification" that dominates core cities.[25] Tunnel vision on the home steers viewers away from the geography of neighborhoods, away from the upscaling of tastes and amenities in reinvented neighborhoods. Once again, HGTV's visual strategy is oddly indifferent to the trajectory of neighborhoods as a source of value.

There are two exceptions to this rule on the HGTV and DIY channels, each featuring women who renovate and flip distressed older properties in core urban areas. *Good Bones* stars a mother and daughter team, Karen Laine and Mina Starsiak, who renovate houses in transitional districts in Indianapolis. They frequently repeat their motivation to restore the vitality of not just the houses but the neighborhoods as a whole, though there are no wide-angle shots of the neighborhoods. So too *Rehab Addict*'s Curtis focuses on restoring the still older, and once elegant, homes of the early modern Minneapolis bourgeoisie, working in areas that are undergoing early-stage gentrifying processes. These hosts voice concern about the future of neighborhoods in which they have chosen to work while their definition of neighborhood revitalization screens out questions regarding the displacement of poor populations. *Good Bones* buys profoundly distressed homes in central-city districts that have suffered decades of disinvestment and performs minor miracles on the bones of these structures. Hipsters brought an energy to neighborhoods such as Fountain Square, and then more upscale cafés and boutiques displaced the artist pioneers and became a draw to the next wave of gentrifiers. Once renovated, the transformed homes court a multiracial clientele of more educated and relatively more affluent millennials that include lesbian and gay couples, racially mixed couples, and African American singles; the poor white Appalachian renters who previously inhabited these homes have already been eased out of the picture before the show even starts filming. Though the initial condition of these houses screams poverty, *Good Bones* manages to screen out the historical antecedents of anonymous urban poverty rooted in race and class relations, just as it screens out the poor themselves. *Good Bones* stories inadvertently remind us that gentrification of housing is fundamentally about spatial relations of class inequality. It often involves the displacement and erasure of African American communities, but here poor whites are also vulnerable to dispossession and loss.[26] We see only one side of the value proposition, the salvage of material artifacts, while the human costs are left blank in the concluding tally of value. For all the good feeling that *Good Bones* tries to engender in these now less-blemished districts, there is no mention of the structural crisis of affordability that even well-intentioned flippers contribute to.

Bubble Pushers across the Hidden Geography of Dispossession

Good Bones seems to represent HGTV's conscience of gentrification. The mother-daughter team renovates and flips, but without seeking outsized returns on their finished houses. In a typical episode, they buy a neglected property for $35,000, spend $190,000 to renovate it, and then sell it for $239,000 for a $14,000 profit. A modest profit, to be sure, but even so, these costs place this house beyond the reach of a majority of the Indianapolis middle class.

By contrast, Tarek and Christina of *Flip or Flop* fame are explicitly bubble pushers, always looking to push comps in a neighborhood to their very top. They are indifferent to the social consequences of their actions. Similarly, in the real world of real estate these days, each new resale of rehabbed properties seeks to push up to, or past, the most recent top. And yet the greater this inflationary spiral, the more difficult it becomes to continue finding homes dirt cheap compared to the market The gap between potential and capitalized ground rent shrinks to the extent that too many investors compete to exploit that gap, pushing some investors further out, looking for the next area where discounted properties may again fit their strategy.[27]

In its early seasons, *Flip or Flop* chased foreclosures bought at bank auctions. But the doctored stories of chasing risk to make money diverted attention from the more significant story about bubbles and housing affordability in the wake of the financial meltdown. Lenders foreclosed on ten million home mortgages in the years following the housing crisis, vastly multiplying the inventory of devalued properties throughout inner- and middle-ring suburbs, as well as the exurbs. Foreclosures and evictions were not limited to the predatory subprime loans that targeted poor people, especially poor people of color, but also encompassed conventional prime mortgages that became vulnerable to the vortex of devaluation that swept housing markets. As the recession deepened, the burgeoning tally of vacant and blighted houses played havoc with plummeting market valuations of homes across urban and suburban geographies. Combined with rising rates of unemployment, many families found themselves under water on their loans. Thirty-five percent devaluations in housing markets paved the way to the next phase of accumulation via dispossession.

Foreclosures triggered by the crisis prompted significant demographic displacements that reshaped the geography of opportunity for flipping and gentrification. The abrupt housing market meltdown turned into a new phase of bank-imposed structural violence that created the possibilities for widely dispersed rent gaps. Structural violence and gentrification have gone hand in hand since the 1970s' displacement of the poor to enable gentrifying neighborhoods. The "shells" developers sought to renovate "do not simply appear as part of some naturally occurring neighborhood obsolescence and decay," they were "actively produced" via tactics that have historically included redlining, disinvestment, eminent domain, discriminatory policing, lack of property maintenance, obscene rent spikes, evictions, and predatory lending practices.[28] The 2007 mortgage market collapse was hardly a tactic, but the recession that ensued proved to be strategically opportune for speculators armed with cash. A few years later, a leading Arizona realtor confirmed that "institutional investors are siphoning the wealth and the ability for wealth accumulation out of underserved communities."[29]

Following the 2007 mortgage crisis, the groundswell of defaults, foreclosures, and evictions reshaped the spatial redistribution of opportunities for profitable rent streams, for large scale developments, flipping, and renovation. The sudden surplus of foreclosed properties contributed to new opportunities for flipping, but these opportunities were differentially scattered throughout the urban core and postwar inner-ring suburbs, and out into the exurbs. REO designates foreclosed properties that became bank or lender owned. In Los Angeles after the mortgage market collapse, "one-third of REOs purchased by investors were flipped.... Flipped properties were more common in poorer neighborhoods with relatively lower foreclosure rates, more renters, poorer schools, and, most strikingly, much larger non-white populations."[30]

Investors and investing strategies in the REO marketplace varied from buy-to-rent investors, including milkers, who purchased the poorest quality houses and rented them as is, to buy-to-sell investors, who ranged from rehabbers to flippers who purchased houses in reasonably good condition and turned them over quickly, to predatory flippers, who purchased houses in poor condition and turned them over without improvement within a year.[31] Emily Molina's study of foreclosure investments in the Los Angeles area found that investing strategies varied with the scale of capital. Individuals classified as owner-occupants were more likely to purchase REOs in the exurban fringe, while corporate capital that circulated at a national and global scale concentrated on urban and inner-ring suburbs characterized by less-concentrated foreclosure rates. Large investors were "significantly more likely to flip REOs in neighborhoods with relatively fewer white residents" and lower poverty rates, as they sought properties in suburban neighborhoods with a reputation for better elementary schools because such neighborhoods contributed to higher flipping profits.[32] Suburbs "that were once sources of mass wealth-building for homeowners of color shifted to places of mass wealth-building for financial institutions during the subprime boom and then for real estate investors via the purchases of REO properties during the Recession."[33]

The young and attractive Christina and Tarek portray themselves as mom-and-pop investors who have been savvy and successful in exploiting the REO market in the midst of the recession. The fact that they usually invested with cash to acquire REO properties suggests they had backing from deep-pocketed speculative investors. Such mom-and-pop investors were incentivized to perform as bubble pushers while playing a role in the transfer of wealth that began with the upsurge of subprime mortgages and intensified with the value-added flipping of REO properties.

The Return of the Repressed (the Class Character of Gentrification)

Shielding neighbors and neighborhoods from view is not only a matter for prospective homeowners who do not wish to see or be seen by their neighbors; on HGTV people who live and work nearby are given neither voice nor corporal form. However, a 2017 vehicular accident in Waco involving a

Fixer Upper home opened a window (so to speak) on the conflictual relationships that derive from gentrification but are repressed from the reality of the spectacle. A drunk driver crashed his car through the front wall of a house that Chip and Joanna Gaines had renovated during the show's third season. The homeowners (the Downs) then accused the city of Waco and the Gaineses of "deceiving" them about the social character of the neighborhood they bought into.[34] They complained that the neighborhood "is loud and filled with a seedy element due to nearby bars." They also criticized what they saw as inadequate police response to their noise complaints and concerns about "safety." Perhaps having watched too many HGTV shows, the homeowners apparently never imagined their fixer-upper cocoon might have to contend with urban space defined by regional cultural forms that cater to working-class whites, Hispanics, and blacks. The neighborhoods of North Waco where the home is located had a median income of $33,000, a relatively low education profile, and a predominantly white working-class population.

The couple bought the shabby, run-down remains of a 1905 Craftsman house well past its prime at a bargain-basement price of $35,000. It was sharply discounted because it needed a lot of work and was located in an area labeled as "unimproved." The couple did not deny their status as gentrifiers—perhaps they were just counting on gentrification taking a speedier course through their neighborhood. Were they led to believe there would be a quicker pace to the replacement of working-class cultural establishments with the infill of cafés, boutiques, restaurants, yoga salons, and a grocery rather than a convenience store? The Downses grabbed for the promise of a deep-discount upper-middle-class residence, but they evidenced little appetite for any of the social risks of gentrification: noise, safety concerns, resentment, and cultural discomforts in a possibly gentrifying neighborhood that still lies in the orbit of a poorer habitus. They appear to have been so eager to cash in on the rent gap between Dallas (where they moved from) and Waco real estate opportunities, especially with Joanna Gaines factored in as a value multiplier, that they looked past the nitty-gritty of living in a transitional neighborhood. Perhaps they overestimated their political clout as gentrifiers to quickly reshape the neighborhood infrastructure and culture—after all, they had just purchased one of the highest value homes in the neighborhood.

Suppose they had done their due diligence. They would have learned that this was an aging working-class neighborhood where more people than not live close to poverty. With median incomes 40 percent below the national median, 41 percent of residents in the neighborhood are renters. The neighborhood's Hispanic-Latino population is growing, while white and African American populations, especially the latter, have been shrinking

Figure 4.1 A "seedy" working-class convenience store that sits across the street from the Downs's house offended their vision of the proper environmental habitus for their gentrification experience. (Photo from Google Street View. © 2017 Google.)

slightly over the last fifteen years. Despite this neighborhood diversity, the closest elementary school is a model of segregated schooling with almost no white children enrolled.[35] Despite the usual biases against poor people, poverty does not necessarily translate into an unsafe neighborhood. The Downs's complaints about crime were not born out by the data. The crime rate—both violence on people and theft—is comparable with the rest of Waco. The couple's primary complaint seems to focus on the convenience store across the street, where young men play loud music and sometimes gun their engines.

The accident prompted the Downses to go public with their perspective of entitlement that we routinely see manifested on HGTV in the "I will not compromise" attitude that clients display regarding must-have interior amenities. Outside of HGTV, gentrifiers such as the Downses extend their attitude of entitlement to that which has otherwise been sliced away by HGTV, the neighborhood. The Downses expected that the city of Waco should, through public expenditure and regulatory activity, sweep out the culture of working-class poverty and facilitate transformation of the built environment to accommodate the sort of amenities that would draw more of their cultural kin to the neighborhood. This accident revealed that the jurisdiction of their entitlement extends to the outdoor spaces where they really don't want to spend time in the neighborhood among their neighbors. One of their unspoken must-haves seems to have been that the neighborhood should look more like them, and not like their poorer neighbors.

Writing about this story, Richard Lawson set the accident in a broader context that reveals a schism set in motion by the fixer-upper effect. Gentrification carries with it conflicts shaped by palpable class inequalities, but it can also set off tensions with surrounding middle-class businesses and homeowners who blame the gentrifiers for tax hikes that follow inflated property values. Lawson writes that *"Fixer Upper* has riven a town in two, ushering in a new flood of upstart home renovators looking to score dilapidated houses in dodgier parts of town so they can make them shiplapidated instead. There's always an assumption on these colonizers' part that they will be greeted warmly, because they're adding value to the neighborhood, beautifying it some."³⁶

Waco's recent economic prosperity received a boost from the *Fixer Upper* brand, and this has contributed (though it's certainly not the only factor) to a general upward pressure on property tax assessments. The TV show's popularity has translated into heavy media coverage that attracts investors from outside Waco "who are willing to put far more money into older homes than was once thought prudent" because the home prices seen on *Fixer Upper* are substantially more affordable than those in other refurbishing hot spots.³⁷ Indeed, the Downses moved to Waco from Dallas, motivated by a desire to cash in on the gentrification possibilities that came with a Joanna Gaines–designed house. Of course, locals are going to feel some antipathy toward outsiders, whom they blame for driving up the cost of housing in Waco. While some Waco locals have been encouraged by the tide of development that has visited Waco, others feel as if they are losing their place. It makes sense that the Downses might have heard harsh sentiments from longtime Waco residents who are unhappy about escalating property taxes: "People have complained about their taxes going up because we moved here. Store owners have complained about taxes."³⁸

Whether the homes renovated by the Gaineses are responsible for the spike in appraisals or not, the perception itself is a crucial piece of the valuation coin. A fixer-upper effect extends well beyond the specific properties they've worked on. The Gaines's influence, dubbed by many "the Magnolia effect," is also responsible for a dramatic influx of tourists—a threefold increase, from 789,000 in 2015 to 2.5 million in 2017—in a city whose economy now depends more on tourism than the agricultural commodities of lumber, cotton, and cottonseed oil that once anchored the Waco economy.³⁹ Already famous for their TV show, the Gaineses moved from home renovation to the renovation of Waco's abandoned cottonseed silos, making them the anchor for their expanding retail empire—the Magnolia Market at the

Silos is now the city's prime tourist destination, drawing three-fifths of total Waco tourists, or 30,000 per week.[40] In turn, the presence of the Magnolia Market has attracted enough capital investment to build out an additional one thousand hotel rooms, along with a cottage industry of amenities, ranging from food trucks and cafés to art and antique boutiques. The Gaineses are themselves a major contributor, along with Baylor University football mania, to Waco's story of postindustrial transformation, a motor driving something akin to a generalized process of gentrification. It seems fitting that the rusted iconic shells of Waco's industrial past have become the marker of Waco's revitalized brand identity—a built environment that shares a primary feature of Joanna Gaines's interior design look—an aesthetic of salvage modernism rooted in hybridizing rustic with industrial.

Like numerous other *Fixer Upper* alumni, the Downses also sought to capitalize on Waco's growing tourist trade, renting their home through the short-term home rental sites of Airbnb and Vrbo. The Gaineses themselves devoted an episode of their show to transforming an older home into a bed-and-breakfast vacation rental that they named the Magnolia House.[41] The Downs's listing on Vrbo eagerly identifies their "HGTV Fixer Upper house," while in a previous version acknowledging, with some cultural circumspection, that their fixer-upper is located in an area "undergo[ing] the growing pains of neighborhood revitalization. We are working with the City of Waco, council members and planners in hopes of adding improvements to this part of town."[42] This admission that they are without the cultural amenities that visitors may relish confirms their status as colonizers intent on "bring[ing] up the neighborhood" so that it conforms to their own cultural self-image while promising to command higher tourist rents in the future.[43]

Along with other owners of *Fixer Upper* pedigree homes, the Downses count on the show's fans being willing to pay a premium short-term rent to say that they stayed in an original Joanna Gaines design. That they do not yet reside in a gentrified neighborhood is not a barrier to the owners still seeking to realize the potential ground rent that comes with gentrification, since each Gaines-renovated home is perceived as the perfected incarnation of gentrification unto itself. In Waco as elsewhere, the owners of these renovations complete the gentrification loop by seeking to capture a piece of the lucrative Airbnb and Vrbo short-term rental cash streams. While the Downses bemoan noise and the lack of friendliness in their neighborhood, they are continuing to benefit from the Gaines effect that has transformed their TV home renovations into something akin to art pieces whose value shoots up commensurately with the celebrity of Joanna.

Efforts to reap the financial benefits of the value generated by the *Fixer Upper* franchise extend into the resale of houses at extravagant markups to the renovation prices paid. A tiny shotgun house salvaged from a teardown lot that represented a total investment of $130,000 is asking $950,000, while the owners of season three's "barndominium" (a barn makeover) want to flip it for $1.2 million. Another virtual teardown swathed in emotion and sentimentality was the Paw Paw's house episode in which a young woman committed $250,000 to transforming her grandfather's abandoned ranch house inhabited by squirrels. Her grandfather's memory notwithstanding, the house went on the market for a "whopping" $1.45 million, a 580 percent markup.[44]

The irony, of course, is that none of this really respects the Gaineses' spiel about renovating these houses for families to dwell forever in their dream home. Their ideological pitch about devotion to the sanctity of family and place, however reassuring it may be, has difficulty competing with the lure of "callous 'cash payment,'" which, gently tweaking Karl Marx and Frederick Engels, "has drowned" [familial] "ecstasies" of [middle-class] "sentimentalism in the icy water of egotistical calculation."[45] The deeper HGTV message is the one that is heard and acted on: commodification of lifestyle comes before family; these homes represent a new engine of valuation. Per HGTV, renovation and gentrification comprise a personal investment strategy.

5

Creative Erasure

All reification is forgetting.
—Max Horkheimer and Theodor Adorno, *Dialectic of Enlightenment*

Flipping a rent-gap discount isn't enough on HGTV, though it sometimes was in the frenzied markets leading up to the crash. On HGTV, the tainted and the obsolete must next be unequivocally torn down and all outward signs of devaluation negated. However, it is also not enough to merely demolish the outdated material features of the house. Reflecting gentrification's pattern of culturally displacing those whose race and class no longer fit with the neighborhood, HGTV erases all visible traces and signs of social and cultural histories of houses and neighborhood, along with the geography of space, financial institutions, and our imposition on nature and its coming revenge. But HGTV extends symbolic erasure still further. Reflecting the spirit of neoliberal urbanism, HGTV tries to imagine the landscape surrounding the renovation as an empty space devoid of as many limiting or regulatory forces as possible. This erasure renders the emptiness like a frontier to be colonized and tamed. But erasing the history of house, inhabitants, neighborhood, and city to get a fresh start also means the loss of those unique traits that are said to be valued in renovated homes—organic charm, character, and authenticity. Sometimes history, geography, or social reality do find their way into a story, and here they must be wrested into the victorious narrative, often hiding an uncomfortable paradox. Hence HGTV must not merely revalorize the home, it must also recast history as a set of curated commodity accents that are consumed under the rubric of charm and character.

Erasure, abstraction, and decontextualization converge to define HGTV's narratives every bit as much as what is foregrounded. The concept of creative erasure is meant to reference both the material and ideological forms of creative destruction that enable the TV renovation process. The ritual tearing down of walls is the most obvious method of opening spaces, along with the elimination—or erasure—of previous ways of living in the house. All vestiges of former cultural imprints and character are wiped away in this process—creating an open visual palette for the designers, a precondition for the blank canvas that will allow the expression of fresh aesthetic values. Open here equals empty, a reminder of the Lockean conceit that appropriating unsettled and empty lands is a necessary condition for individual freedom—in other words, primitive accumulation. As a moment of symbolic violence, the staging of demolition is a prerequisite to the reinvention of space—just as the appropriation of the American frontier required the symbolic erasure and material displacement of indigeneity, so too flipping as gentrification has been dependent on discourses of erasure.[1] "With gentrification, the central act of violence is one of erasure. Accordingly, when the discourse of gentrification isn't pathologizing communities of color, it's erasing them."[2] In the television version of home renovation, erasure moves from urban geography to the interior spaces of houses. A renovation host eager to expel the former life-spirit of the house confirms that "this place not only needs demo; it needs an exorcism."

Erasure doesn't stop there. The home is dislocated socially from surrounding neighbors and community. We've already noted the reluctance to visually or conceptually consider the immediate neighborhood as factors that might influence consumer value. The blank slate is necessary to the promise of unburdened future memories while lending itself toward the cultivation of social amnesia—a forgetting of social histories. The potential of the renovated home is conditional on disembedding the household from society—in fact, the separation and estrangement of the isolated house from social life is the prerequisite for the HGTV utopia of erasure.

Indeed, the list of what has been erased from the visual frame far exceeds the list of that which is present in HGTV's formula. Abstraction and decontextualization form the crucial determinants of home renovation storytelling. A blank slate is also a depoliticized slate, purged of considerations of debt, subprime loans, racial discrimination, banks, securities and derivatives, the defaults and foreclosures thus precipitated, a mortgage market collapse, and a bailout. Such blank slates are meant to be reassuring to consumers—an opportunity for a fresh start—even though we know the slate of personal credit histories is never wiped clean of notations about old debts or late payments.

By repressing the contextualizing histories of foreclosed houses—who lived in them and for how long, why they moved—HGTV also avoids the thorniest political issue that has surrounded gentrification since 2008. Especially in the aftershocks of 2008 and the ubiquity of subprime loan defaults, mentioning the history of houses and neighborhoods might open the narrative door to troubling geographies of redlining, disinvestment, reverse redlining, dispossession, and evictions. To put it bluntly, without all these erasures, clients who wish to become *petit* gentrifiers, and viewers who identify with the fantasy, might have to confront the webs of exploitation that stand between them and the realization of renovation value. The miracle of HGTV is that surplus value can be had without ever taking advantage of others. In this regard, the spectacle's erasures of power, privilege, and the spatial relations of inequality and domination might be thought of as special effects.

HGTV imagines the sphere of home renovation and flipping as a neoliberal marketplace largely free of government interventions, regulations, and barriers to value extraction. In fact, its version of a neoliberal housing market is devoid of politics altogether. References to local regulations, permits, and inspections to ensure compliance with building codes do occasionally arise in HGTV stories, but these rarely amount to anything other than a minor inconvenience. The reality, of course, is that landscapes of housing and gentrification have been shaped by histories of municipal, state, and federal involvements covering land-use rules, subsidies that have favored so-called redevelopment plans, loan availability (Freddie Mac and Fannie Mae), as well as the U.S. Department of Housing and Urban Development's (HUD) checkered history of supposedly fair housing enforcement and desegregation rules. Though redlining was outlawed by the Fair Housing Act of 1968, governmental agencies looked the other way to permit lenders to engage in reverse redlining and predatory lending. In fact, while HGTV's ideological misrepresentation of flipping, gentrification, and "neoliberalism aspires to create a utopia of free markets, liberated from all forms of state interference, it has in practice entailed a dramatic intensification of coercive, disciplinary forms of state intervention in order to impose versions of market rule and, subsequently, to manage the consequences and contradictions of such marketization initiatives."[3] Both before and after the 2008 crisis, the intensification of high-risk lending prompted political battles to regulate and limit predatory lending. The politics of financialization came into clearer public focus after the crash as regulators sought to address the crisis of leverage by tightening up banks' liquid capital requirements.[4] Erasure is the ideal representational form for neoliberal suburbanism, clearing the way to view the flipping of houses as apolitical, rather than as a function of a class struggle over the politics of financialization, gentrification, and the reallocation of housing resources to wealthier strata.

The erasure of power that is most historically pertinent to the HGTV narrative is also the most recent: the volatile contradictions of financialization, the housing bubble it supported, the consequent financial damage that inflicted housing precarity on families across a wide swath of working-class and middle-class populations when the bubble imploded, and the transfers of wealth made possible in the aftermath. How in the world did financing disappear from HGTV's neoliberal stories? Though questions about money always seem to nag at the story line, banks, loans, and market negotiations are curiously screened out. "We buy, renovate, and sell homes. We need loans in order to operate." That's how Chip Gaines opens a TV commercial for First National Bank McGregor. Of course. And yet this obvious subject of loans and operating capital is never mentioned in episodes of *Fixer Upper*. Where are the money lenders and banks in HGTV stories? Only *Flip or Flop* offers even superficial references to financing a house flip, though the source and the terms of the El Moussas' funding remain murky and undeveloped. The *Flip or Flop* philosophy is repeated show after show—find the most distressed and discounted houses and exploit the hell out of them. Tarek and Christina make cash-only offers ranging from $200,000 to $600,000 for properties they buy at auction, or via a broker, or in a short sale. Where's that cash coming from? A rare episode mentions a hard-money loan or partnering with another flipper. Such story lines are dramatized to call attention to partners squabbling over how much to spend on renovations, or to highlight emotional anxieties about delays eating into profits when interest payments must be paid to the nameless money lenders. Even when Tarek glibly refers to behind-the-scenes monied interests whose hirelings bid against him at auction for properties, he leaves unidentified whose interests those are. Banks manage to remain veiled and safely off-screen with regard to short sales—the subject of foreclosure is tacit but elided. Leaving banks outside the story frame ensures that they are invisible and hence that they cannot be held politically responsible.

No less telling in *Flip or Flop*'s narrative deceit is the erasure of the wider Los Angeles–area real estate market. Tarek's anxiety-fueled bravado about premium pricing, and his confidence that he can get away with it, has to do less with the quality of value they've added to the residence than with what a distorted market can bear. What Tarek knows but won't share with us is that by 2013 Los Angeles was the most rent-burdened city in the United States. He can show off as a price maker because Los Angeles–area housing prices appreciated by 15 to 18 percent year after year, driving up mortgage payments across Southern California by 16 percent in 2017–2018 and pricing neighborhood after neighborhood out of reach, with median home prices surging past $635,000 in 2019.[5] With even barely affordable Los Angeles housing in tight supply, families desperately searching for a way out of exorbitant rents find themselves shut out and vulnerable to the market. What Tarek knew was that generally there will be someone frantic enough to bite on an overpriced flip in a less attractive neighborhood.

Erasure and the Abstracted Curation of History

Set in Indianapolis, *Good Bones*' mother and daughter duo, Karen Laine and Mina Starsiak, run a home renovation company called Two Chicks and a Hammer. Their show is unique among home renovation and flipping shows in its almost-but-not-quite-open acknowledgment of participating in the central-city gentrification of Indianapolis, although without mentioning the word itself. Introducing their ninth episode, the women reflected on their acquisition of properties in the "East of State" neighborhood beyond the "frontier" of the Fountain Square neighborhood that has been in the process of gentrifying since the financial crisis. Artists had started the process by bringing cultural value back to Fountain Square. Indianapolis fits an almost classic textbook illustration of neighborhood gentrification. The ninth poorest big city in America, Indianapolis felt the crunch of the 2008 Great Recession acutely. Decades of disinvestment, deterioration, and devaluation in central-city neighborhoods attracted hipsters and artists, drawn by cheap rents for vacant spaces that became studios where they could afford to experiment and innovate without concern for the risks of failure. Fountain Square thus sprouted "scrappy" galleries and studios where hipsters pursued creative arts, from the visual to the culinary, from craft production to digital design. Out of the cultural vibe sprang an art museum, along with a cottage industry of curators and the usual hipster establishments of "craft breweries, achingly cool art galleries, bike shops and high-end local produce stores."[6] With popularity came public investment in streets, sidewalks, lighting, and transit systems that spurred commercial capital flows. Rents surged, and the pioneer artists became priced out, along with the poor. Two Chicks had been among the early rehabbers in the area, but they too found themselves priced out by their own successes in Fountain Square as the low-hanging opportunities disappeared and a swarm of other competitors crowded in to push purchase prices higher. So the women moved their focus to the "East of State" neighborhood and then to the Bates-Hendricks neighborhood to the south.[7]

MINA: We have a big project ahead of us. We're taking this duplex and turning it into a single-family home, and it's just east of State, which is an area that's a little . . . [*looks at Karen*].
KAREN: It's transitional still.
MINA: Yeah.
KAREN: It needs some love.
MINA: It's coming around, though. This house we're going to is one of two that we've bought on this block on Woodlawn.
KAREN: The challenge for these two properties is that they are east of State. I feel like if Fountain Square is the frontier, East of State is the territory beyond the frontier.[8]

This dialogue is sufficiently unusual on HGTV that it deserves reflection. Instead of erasure, let's call it semigloss, a hesitant effort to locate their project within an unfolding local geography of gentrification. It goes against the HGTV grain, departing from virtually every norm that governs the production of HGTV, briefly illuminating the network's usual way of not seeing disinvested urban spaces. Decades ago, Neil Smith wrote about a "gentrification frontier" that divides "areas of disinvestment from areas of reinvestment in the urban landscape."[9] The frontier metaphor suggests a risk boundary beyond whose territorial partition lurk financial risks imposed by an absence of middle-class settlement, where instead there are spaces defined by poverty, neglect, broken windows, crime statistics, and an absence of infrastructural amenities. The optimistic tone of Mina and Karen's comments about nurturing a rebirth of middle-class aesthetics is thus quickly followed by their realistic assessment that they may not turn a profit in this location.

Good Bones' stuttering acknowledgment of the hosts' participation in gentrification steers the conversation back toward beautification and restoration and away from displacement and dispossession. Why they dance around the "G" word is a matter of speculation: probably HGTV regards it as a Pandora's box. Karen and Mina present themselves not just as risk-oriented entrepreneurs but also as custodians of the civic good and evangelists of neighborhood reclamation motivated to renovate the entire neighborhood, not just the house they are working on. They are thus content to realize less ambitious profits on each home they flip. As they say, "We're making a difference in the neighborhood."

As they speak, a crude map appears on screen coupled with a photograph of unimproved row houses along State Street. This is another monumental inversion of the usual HGTV narrative practices. Geography is not entirely dead! For a split second, these images acknowledge the geography of a poor neighborhood. Yet notably absent in these pictures are any poor people. Though geography may not be completely effaced, society is. Lacking specificity, the map functions as a stripped-down indexical sign that points out a spatial divide between risk and profit but without explaining how these conditions came to be. If we were to freeze the map image for a moment, the unacknowledged line of an interstate highway that bisects the map actually provides an unspoken clue regarding the modern history of poverty and disinvestment that produced this Indianapolis frontier and initiated the processes of market devaluation that are a precondition for gentrification. "As were so many other neighborhoods in the US, [Fountain Square] was bisected by a badly-planned urban interstate highway (I-65) some 60 years ago" and then hammered by the "2008 housing crisis and national recession."[10] The interstate highway project aimed at revitalizing the downtown area by linking a downtown loop to the beltway. As suburbanization fueled white flight, this highway transit model invoked eminent domain to cut through older neighborhoods, severing Fountain Square from the downtown area. A once vibrant commercial district, Fountain Square quickly tanked, divided from the residential areas it served. Population declined, properties suffered from disinvestment, and poverty intensified in an area inhabited by poor artists and Southern whites. "The epicenter of Appalachian Indianapolis is Fountain Square."[11] When the mortgage crisis hit Indianapolis, over half of the houses sold in 2007 were listed as bank owned.

With the minimal information provided by the crude map, we can locate the census tract that corresponds to East of State. Census tract 3572 is classified as not yet gentrified. Population in the area declined from 4,341 in 2000 to 3,228 a decade later, along with a decline in median household income, an increase in the percentage of adults who have bachelor's degrees, and a slight increase in the median home value in the neighborhood.[12] The pace of gentrification in Indianapolis has accelerated, expanding from three census tracts during the 1990s to twelve census tracts a decade later. Census tract 3559, the Frontier Square area, shows median home values climbing to $76,500 and median income rising to $35,550 (compared to $48,700 and $22,000, respectively, in the East of State neighborhood) while the percentage of adults with bachelor's degrees increased nearly fivefold to 19.7 percent (compared to 4.7 percent in the East of State area) from 2000 to 2013. To keep these statistics in perspective, Karen and Mina purchased the duplex in episode 9 for $15,000 and invested another $130,000 in renovation costs before reselling the house for $175,000—extremely reasonable, but a sharp contrast to the median home value of roughly $48,700 in the surrounding area.

As the women tour the duplex they plan to renovate, a sequence of video edits shows them poking through the abandoned detritus scattered throughout rooms tilting toward disintegration. Karen and Mina comment in passing about their cursory and superficial archeology of these remains, the leavings of former occupants: "It's one of the weird things about what we do, is we get a little glimpse . . . into people's lives." The lifestyles of former inhabitants are not ordinarily (in fact, almost never) the subject of inquiry on HGTV flipping shows—who they were, how they lived, why they left, how long they lived there, none of this is permitted on-screen. This ten-second foray into an archeology of poor people's domesticity is another rare moment in the world of home renovation TV, even though it fails to tell us anything about who lived there before. To be sure, the duo barely skirt the question with their sound bite before the video editing relentlessly pushes our photographic attention along, and the subject disappears before we can even speculate about it. It's easier to ignore the personal histories of those who came before because the personal histories of impoverished strangers' bodies conflict with the illusion of building de novo dream spaces. Hence the need for demolition to wipe the canvas clean. It's another way that home renovation TV imagines itself constituting new frontiers. It's a narrative that comes straight out of the settler-colonial playbook featured in our mythology of pioneers who settled the American West. By ignoring the past, particularly the histories of displaced populations, poverty, aging, disease, familial dysfunction, racial inequalities, and primitive accumulation by dispossession, we are propelled into the imaginary of carving out an existence that bears only on our own wants and desires.

Decorating as the practice of dehistoricizing the past and present reiterates a parallel story of commodity fetishism. On HGTV, it is rare for books to appear on bookshelves as anything other than decorating props or, as Joanna Gaines likes to refer to them, "accent pieces." As such, books found in antique shops may take on the status of ornamental objects that lend charm and character. They are collected not for the purpose of reading, or even for their titles, but as display artifacts. "Charm" and "character" are code words for that which is not new—that is, that which has the appearance of a history of use. Books in this sense no longer represent knowledge but become referents for the patina of an earlier age. One decorates with them because they lend a feel to a space. In becoming a referent of charm and character, books become a referent of history as meaning not of the present; books have become what Roland Barthes would call a second-order signifier of past history visually divorced from the cultural practices of written literacy. On fashion TV, the book turns into a visual signifier, now considered within the framework of Gaines's home-decorating philosophy and deciphered within the home-fashion code. As readers of contemporary home-fashion codes, viewers are positioned to transfer the significance of the old book into a statement about decorating style (this is a second-order signifier that Barthes names Myth) that points to the status of the homeowner who takes pride in displaying a preference for character and charm.[13]

This pattern of selective dehistoricization is well suited to the televised spectacle of gentrification. In a manner similar to the erasure of urban spaces, charm and character are constructed via a two-step dance: first, sweep away (erase) markers of past inhabitants, and second, arrange and present a snapshot of a cultural life assembled out of curated memorabilia that have been fully separated and commodified from the social lives of now anonymous former owners and users. The designers' curated versions retain only an imaginary patina, wiping clean the once-lived meanings associated with objects in daily life but still semiotically capable of revealing their not-newness as a reminder of having been used in general. Plucked from the recycling bins of antique shops and flea markets, such found objects are repurposed as design pieces that signify vintage style within the refinished spaces that have been scrubbed of their history.

At its core, TV gentrification stories are about finding value in the recirculation of commodities. This process requires not simply the activity of historical forgetting (that is a by-product); it requires a cleansing of all the surfaces that are to be remade, so that the aesthetic imagination can run wild. The imprint of previous generations can cloud the necessary act of stripping away to create a fresh palette on which to craft fresh value. This may seem curious given the simultaneous demand for decorative charm and character. But the formula is clear: on the one hand, erase the marks of prior inhabitants, while on the other hand, honor the curated character of commodified patina, intentionally chosen and imported to fit an upscale semiotic palette. That which was organic needs to be erased to make room for the decoratively contrived appearance of ornamental value. As a marker of a previous era, the leather-bound book may become a quaint reminder of character, but it is a thin marker, a decorative façade that lacks the specificity to elicit any immediate or exact historical meaning. Whereas an heirloom builds value by virtue of the knowable genealogy that accompanies it, the decorative book has been fully abstracted from its cultural and social histories so that it may contribute to a staging of value.

In a similar fashion, tacitly invoking the settler-colonial framework positions viewers to think about places as lacking specifiable histories. The vacated houses shown to clients are already missing the biographies of former residents, but wherever semiotic traces of previous generations of dwellers remain inscribed on the walls, ceilings, or backsplashes, the invariable response is one of revulsion and a demand that such reminders of someone else's life choices be purged and covered over. "Beginning with *terra nullius*—the perception that lands in long-term use by indigenous peoples are empty or unused—settler colonisation proceeds to carve up indigenous-held lands into discrete packets of private property."[14] Though the TV version of the settler-colonial narrative is made to fit a dispersed and individuated model rather than a cultural model, purging the appearance of the past remains a necessary first condition of the narrative. HGTV shields viewers from the ouster or the erasure of those who came before as a necessary condition for recirculating the house as a commodity, a forgetting of what David Harvey calls "accumulation by dispossession."[15] When history remains absent, both in its general conceptual form and in its detailed specifics of houses and their former inhabitants, the processes of accumulation by dispossession quietly disappear from the equation and become a nonissue.

Barnwood Builders represents the most explicit ideological embrace of the settler-colonial narrative on the DIY and HGTV networks. The show focuses on the reclamation of a heritage building style using logs and barnwood as building materials: "We take old wood and make it new again." *Barnwood Builders* sees itself "sav[ing] history," rather than erasing it. Network promos for the show repeat these sound bites over and over. The show's host, Mark Bowe, explains that his business aims to "recover and restore antique log houses and old barns . . . with the craftsmanship, dedication and hard work that our forefathers put into their pioneer homesteads." While the show sells its admiration and preservation of history, its business model requires a focus on producing a forward-looking rustic commodity aesthetic. After deconstructing and salvaging a cabin, the work crew returns to their "boneyard" to give the cabin "a second life. . . . When we're in the field, we're thinking about history. We're thinking about the cabin and the pioneers that went before us. But when we bring the cabin back here, we're looking into the future on what this house is gonna become."[16] History must not just be preserved and sentimentalized; it must also be turned into a monetizable commodity—and here that commodity is an alternative design aesthetic. By necessity, *Barnwood Builders*' strategy must remove historic buildings from their rootedness in their places of origin to transport and rebuild these structures in geographies unconnected to those origins. Both as a building material and as an aura, history must be turned into a new form of capital at the boneyard. Despite its insistence on preserving history, *Barnwood Builders* must be willing to sever the relationship between time and space. In this regard, *Barnwood Builders* is of a piece with all the other sleight-of-hand gentrification programming, even if it also differs from the other programming on HGTV in salvaging and preserving building materials for reuse. It might be stretching the point to call this the rural analogue to gentrification, but it is contingent on a political economy of vacation homes and rural tourism.

Barnwood Builders searches for meaning and purpose by embracing nostalgia.[17] The salvaging of hillbilly culture that embodies character and integrity is tacitly set against another great unspoken of *Barnwood Builders*—the rape and pillage of Appalachia's geography and peoples by the coal mining industry's history of exploitative wealth extraction and a longstanding cultural stereotype of "hillbillies" as a "culture of poverty."[18] Appalachia bears the scars of this history, but the region as it appears in *Barnwood Builders* stories—as rural nature—bears no visual marks of that history. There is no mention of coal, no mention of unemployment, no mention of methamphetamine or opioid addiction crises, and no mention of grinding poverty. Once again, erasure is critical to the ironic product of the show—the fabrication and elevation of a novel commodity aesthetic joined out of the reclamation of wood and iron relics of the preindustrial and industrial eras. Contra Horkheimer and Adorno, our TV builder-philosophers can now declare that selective remembering is the precondition for a new (and apparently redemptive) commodity fetish.

Curiously, both the elision of history and its overmythification lead to similar stories of repurposing and renovating. *Barnwood Builders* celebrates the past masters of cabins and barns because they were able to construct durable structures from what they found on the land. Settler-colonial narratives justify erasing any consideration of those indigenous peoples who came before them because they did not have permanent architectural installations. The historyless stories of home renovation accomplish a similar figurative story—whoever was here before is gone, they were just passing through.

Thus on *Barnwood Builders* restoring history takes on a double meaning. The show's material focus is on salvaging and repurposing the logs as a commodity aesthetic, but the show symbolically dwells on an equation between the material artifacts and the remembering of a culture that otherwise must be archaeologically dredged up. The history invoked here is a reverence for a masculine work culture saturated in an ethic of self-sufficient hard work and craft. There is a self-contradictory knot in here that is difficult to untangle. Their deep respect for generations of producers who have preceded them celebrates a culture of building, allowing Bowe and his crew to conclude that by saving the logs put in place by their preindustrial forebears up to 175 years ago they are saving history. Salvaging history means saving material artifacts from a now largely disappeared culture. But *Barnwood Builders* knows that history won't tell itself, it has to be retold, and *Barnwood Builders* is more than ready to take on that task by reenacting the culture of production it most admires, but in reverse by deconstructing the decaying remains of the nineteenth and twentieth centuries. *Barnwood Builders*' exercise in salvaging history, however, reduces *history* to a one-dimensional mythology that averts its gaze from relationships of power, including domination, including the people those pioneers displaced, and for that matter, including any accounting for what forces eliminated those whom they celebrate. Renewed value, according to HGTV and DIY, is only possible if history is turned into an artifact as opposed to real relationships.

HGTV's Climate Change Denial

Erasure bleeds into other means of producing absence: HGTV represses, and effectively denies, even the faintest hint of climate change. In an era of heightened concern about climate change, HGTV renovations largely ignore energy resource options such as solar panels and tankless water heaters. Concern about energy efficiency is mostly a nonstarter (except for on *Holmes on Homes*, which stresses high-efficiency insulation). The dumpsters full of demolition-day materials destined for landfills are blatant reminders of a blind spot regarding questions of sustainability. Carbon footprints? Those are dirty words never uttered in the world of HGTV. Carbon footprints would actually seem a selling point, since renovated houses emit less carbon dioxide than new home constructions. Yet the 3D simulations of added value never visualize how the renovation will alter greenhouse-gas emissions. And there is nothing even among those who seek security for their families in their list of must-haves—such as, "I'd like to ensure clean air and water for my kids." The erasure here is that of our relation to nature.

Just as the screen severs the home from the surrounding geography of society, so too it limits the relationship between home and nature. Visually, we are always looking into the house, rather than out from it. Still, the erasure of nature is incomplete. Coming out of commercials, panoramic and calendar-like nature scenes function as transition shots back to the story inside the renovation. On *Fixer Upper*, it's a shot of the Waco River; in Southern California, it's an aerial view of a sunny coastline paradise. Picturesque and romanticized scenes of nature suggest a merger of the tourist gaze and the real estate gaze, each speaking to the consuming subject's desire for a sublime and uplifting reassurance by "natural scenery that never looked so alive."[19] If dislocated nature looks this inviting in the surrounding vicinity, why worry about the impact our investing and consumption choices will have on it?

Within the wider spectacle, there has been a knee-jerk corporate public relations support for green consumption. So-called greenwashing hails self-conscious consumers who might be sufficiently exorcized about the reckless overuse of fossil fuels throughout everyday life that they will choose environmentally conscious products that are symbolically more benign toward the environment. Inclinations toward green consumerism tend to overlap with populations that participate in green or eco-gentrification. Green consumerism seems to have its greatest appeal when it comes to relatively smaller price tags, but when it's a question of buying a Tesla or paying for a green-tinged solar-energy home renovation, consumers must be wealthy, true believers, or willing to accept the trade-off of immediate added value for deferred value accretion.

HGTV's narrative opts for the gratification of instant equity. Adopting green methods costs more than going the bargain-basement route of flipping shows that go cheap on material costs. The unwillingness to address questions about the sourcing and selection of building materials, the impact on landfills, or the misuse of energy resources thus misrepresents the calculation of renovated value. If we are simply making an older house look stylishly more modern and restoring it to its former suburban glory, we leave untouched the home's dependence on an economy of oil and gas. If we fail to calculate the environmental costs of burning fossil fuels to power our private paradises, we have not fully accounted for the true costs of adding value on the cheap. HGTV's refusal to consider how environmental costs are dispersed away from the flipper distorts the true value of a flip by failing to acknowledge how and where these costs and risks land on a wider community of inhabitants, on households and taxpayers, and of course, on nature.

Despite HGTV's insistence on upcycling the modern, there is no corresponding concern for moderating and managing risks associated with restoring the deadly era of modernity. The modern suburban paradise that HGTV is so keen to stylistically reimagine was—and still is—anchored in an infrastructure of oil privatism.[20] Sadly, in the HGTV universe, the fetish packages of lifestyle identities—midcentury modern and farmhouse modern styles—unreflexively recommit to a continuation of the fossil fuel infrastructures that underpinned an American way of life that depended on unquestioned domination over nature to satisfy unlimited consumer desires.

Of the hundreds of HGTV episodes that I've watched, only one addressed ecological considerations as part of the value-added calculus of home renovation. The annual *Property Brothers*' "Brother versus Brother" tournament of value took their 2018 competition to the suburban outskirts of the greater San Francisco area. Their contest has one goal and one goal only: each brother adds as much value (measured in before-and-after sales prices) as possible to his house via renovation. In this episode, Jonathan pitches the style of his competition entry as having an "eco-chic vibe." He reasons that this style should be a big selling point in Northern California, where ecological consciousness has demographic traction. His eco-chic housing package thus features a tankless water heater, foam insulation, and energy-efficient windows. Most importantly, for the camera, to make eco-chic feel visually and aesthetically cool, he proposes a feature wall that he calls a "sustainable living wall"—a vertical planter that resembles an ornamental hanging carpet. He purchases the house for $500,000 and sells it for a cool million to win the contest. The brothers do what they are best at—translating a lifestyle preference into a commodity style. The episode confirms that if ecological consciousness can be turned into an attractive commodity aesthetic (e.g., the sustainable living wall), it can add value to a renovation. It also reinforces the assumption that eco-consciousness is a luxury that few but the wealthy can afford: rendering eco-consciousness as a chic vibe turns it into a status commodity.

After erasure is accomplished, the creatives of home renovation TV seek to turn value into an aestheticized experience, subject to both expert and emotional validation. Chapter 6 peers into the cultural semiotics of commodity aesthetics that confirm the desirability of home renovation. The semiotic management of materials, colors, and styles yields a language of sign-value fetishism that HGTV identifies as the measure of value that may be realized both as financial instant equity and in emotional terms as personal security and freedom. The appearance, the class markers, and the broad appeal of a property are nimbly though opaquely valued by experts over their function or subjective meaning to the individual family inhabiting the home. Instant equity references HGTV's promise that if one follows all the steps outlined thus far, as well as the wise counsel of your renovator design guru, then a wealth effect is achieved as an immediate return on investment. Paradoxically, the forever-dream-home fantasy and the resale price of the house become enmeshed at once. But as the popularity of HGTV, and particularly its Waco-based show, *Fixer Upper*, has grown, the calculus of instant equity has moved beyond the premises of the show. In Waco, the celebrity of *Fixer Upper* with its particular rendition of the farmhouse aesthetic of modernism offers an empirical illustration of how the spectacle can become a force in influencing real-world real estate valuations, demonstrating in yet another way the close kinship between this kind of home renovation and the spate of effects that have come to be associated with gentrification, such as Airbnb tourism.

6

A Promised Land of Instant Equity

Speculation is no longer surplus value; it is the ecstasy of value, without reference to production or its real condition.
—Jean Baudrillard, *Paroxysm*

Every HGTV episode begins by noting where value is not and ends by offering a new value equation. Every fan of HGTV knows that the difference between before-and-after comparisons is the key to recognizing new value. Television's version of the renovated house gains value by becoming resplendent in a more prized set of sign values; it becomes as much an exercise in signification practices as it does an exercise in material construction practices. A deep dive into the semiotics of renovation signifiers and signifieds would reveal an HGTV renovation code analogous to Roland Barthes's revelation of the "vestimentary code" in *The Fashion System*.[1] Every selection—from color to texture to material choices to window placements—turns into a signifier organized by the classificatory system of the code. Oversized kitchens dominate, and the voice-over on *House Hunters Renovation* tells us that "whites, tans, and cool gray granites rule the day." Everything is oriented toward a visual aesthetic, toward the production of appearances. When budgets must be appeased, laminates can be substituted for hardwoods because, minus tight close-ups, on television laminates simulate the lifestyle status that is sought. As it has since the rise of the Renaissance, counterfeit surfaces threaten the signification of value when fashionability is democratized by opening it to the market.[2]

The more that fields of aesthetic value are crowded by counterfeits, facsimiles, and simulations laying claim to the status of the real deal, the greater the premium on expert eyes to discern the value of the true from the counterfeit. "Connoisseurship thrives where judgments are needed but measurement is hard."[3] Disconnected from the contradictions of inequality and kept at arm's length from market forces, politics, and power, how are we to answer questions about how much objective value has been added by renovation? HGTV turns to expert connoisseurs to appraise the nuances of true value.

Tournaments of value are familiar to viewers who watch cooking contests (e.g., *Iron Chef*) or baking competitions (e.g., *The Great British Baking Show*) in which expert judges rank performances.[4] HGTV has adapted the tournament of value to home renovations with shows like *Flipping the Block* and *Beach Flip*, judged by HGTV and DIY celebrity hosts who lecture contestants about what not to do value-wise, with Nicole Curtis exhorting contestants on *Beach Flip* to "think value, value, value!" Winners are determined when the judges draw on their experience to divine with precision the commodity basis of value added: "Congratulations to the season one winners . . . who increased their beach house value by a whopping 36 percent."[5] Or so they claim.

Series hosts periodically share with the audience the semiotic rules-of-thumb they rely on to maximize value equations in their flips. On *Flip or Flop*, Christina conjectures about what will yield the most value when deciding on her material and color choices for bathroom and kitchen designs. She understands that maximizing exchange value is the goal of making aesthetic choices and carries in her head a calculator of "what buyers in this area are looking for." She is apt to point out that going cheap on materials, the default strategy for her husband, does not always pay off, especially with buyers who have adopted discerning fetish tastes regarding interior design materials. When her combination of signifiers visually pop in a room, the *Flip or Flop* hosts express confidence about their articulation of value.

In the age of sign value, the home renovation spectacle consists of a circulation of signs to be converted into the measure of money. Circuits of value draw on glossy design magazines and websites like *Renovation Style*, *Better Homes and Gardens*, *Reveal*, *House Beautiful*, *HGTV Magazine*, *Houzz*, and *Dwell*. But HGTV also draws on itself—hence Joanna Gaines's style of home decoration lends a facsimile of her tastes to Miller Paint and Wayfair, reinforcing the revalorization process. Her packaged style is denominated by her own semiotic specialty, "rustic modern." The influence of the remodeling and furnishing industry on the desires of prospective buyers receives expression in the wish lists that define house searches. A prospective buyer on *House Hunters* insists on having "modern, open and white" spaces, beautiful windows, "large everything," white cabinets and high-end finishes. Above all she is adamant that she wants to live within an aesthetic that she references as "coastal," a color and design style defined by a white and aqua palette. She wants to express her identity through this coastal commodity aesthetic in a space that, she says, "I could accent with my coastalness."

The perfect dream home is a house commodified through and through, where questions about aesthetics, desire, style, subjective value, and market value intersect. Taken collectively, HGTV's programming validates a hierarchy of commodity value that confirms entry into a hyperreal world of status. Take the world of flooring choice, in which the current perceived value of hardwoods over carpet owes to a shift in sentiment among upper-middle-class taste makers. Laminate flooring is to the more privileged end of knowledgeable buyers a taboo, a synonym for fake or, worse yet, simulated status-seeking, which, paradoxically, in the hyperreal world of HGTV, is a sin. For the slightly less discerning, simulations are okay if they look good. "The aesthetics of it is what we want," explains a young woman when asked by her contractor to choose between a $6,000 fireplace rebuild or a $1,500 ventless fireplace. So saying, she chooses the ventless fireplace aesthetics over more expensive functionality. The fireplace façade is sufficient if it looks stylish.

The Arithmetic of Instant Equity

HGTV's renovation formula generally concludes with either the host or a voice-over tallying the purchase price and the sum of the renovation costs to exactly match up with the original budget. Renovation shows then offer a new appraisal value of the home that is higher than the sum of the purchase price and renovation costs. This value-added dimension is the payoff of the risk-reward narrative that has played out through the episode. Value has been added beyond the price of investment. Is the value of a renovated home automatically greater than the sum of its parts? On their respective shows, Chip Gaines and Scott McGillivray dwell on the financial implications of the big reveal, reminding the new homeowner of how much he spent to purchase the house and renovate it before sharing with him one more crucial piece of realtor information. Beyond the total costs of purchasing the house and the renovation, the newly veneered space has already generated equity for him in the house—that is, the house has already built a wealth effect for the owner before he has even lived in it. *Income Property* is emphatic about calculating new home equity as a result of the client's return on investment, coupled with the promise of regularized monthly income checks. *Fixer Upper* congratulates homeowners on their "wise investment" that has yielded a surplus of "new value" beyond the investment costs, what Chip calls "instant equity." Chip's on-air property valuation

Figure 6.1 During the big reveal, Chip Gaines's calculation of "instant equity" prompts a young couple to share a smug, knowing look that they made a smart decision. After all, their investment of $325,000 into a fixer-upper has yielded them an additional $95,000 in equity prior to their even taking occupancy. (*Fixer Upper*, season 2, episode 3, "Homebuilder's Dream Home" [High Noon Entertainment, HGTV, Discovery, 2015].)

adopts a standard real estate market multiplication of dollars per square foot to estimate the equity position of the new homeowners. Chip performs this role in a gendered division of labor. Joanna never handles this on-camera duty because public discourse about maximizing the return of money dirties the hands of a woman, especially one who has so carefully curated herself as a mother and a creative. Joanna is the perfectionist who imagines new value; Chip is charged with counting it.

As real as its portrayal might seem on camera, instant equity imagined this way is an abstraction achieved by isolating the renovation from a constellation of forces that bear on the social construction of real estate value. HGTV's vision of home renovation as a path to security and happiness takes place within a geography and a history narrowly framed by the tunnel vision of HGTV's video work. I want to interrogate the meaning of instant equity by jumping outside its television boundaries for a moment. Because Waco is a relatively small city and the Gaineses have become local celebrities, it is possible to reconstruct a bit of spatial and social context by searching the *Waco Tribune-Herald* for stories about several early renovations that they accomplished. During the first season of *Fixer Upper*, the Gaineses worked on houses in both the Brook-Oaks and Sanger Heights neighborhoods, just west of Waco's downtown district. Situate these episodes in Waco's real estate geography and an alternative narrative of instant equity emerges. By 2008, nearly 15 percent of Waco's total housing inventory consisted of vacant properties. The mortgage market debacle coupled with the ensuing recession threw many more Waco houses into foreclosure. There was, in short, a large inventory of foreclosed, red-tagged, green-tagged, and vacant houses in Waco by the time *Fixer Upper* debuted in 2014.[6] Early episodes of *Fixer Upper* faintly alluded to the gentrification possibilities that awaited in the material conditions of neighborhoods in the North Waco housing market while glossing over the economic climate that shaped Waco's then-wounded housing market. The state of Waco's housing market in 2014 made possible a rent-gap story, and Chip's calculations of instant equity confirm a rent-gap narrative of gentrification in Waco.

Waco had a substantially higher rate of poverty at 29 percent than the U.S. average of 14 percent. Median household incomes for Waco were approximately $33,000 in 2015 compared with $55,000 nationally, while the census tracts that cover Brook-Oaks and Sanger Heights indicate substantially lower median incomes than that. In 2015, Sanger Heights had median incomes of $27,300, while Brook Oaks median incomes hovered around $24,000. Low-income households in these neighborhoods ranged from 69 percent to 73 percent of the total population, and African Americans and Hispanics comprised the vast majority of the low-income households. In 2015, Waco's 46 percent rate of home ownership was substantially lower than the national average of 64 percent. Home ownership rates were even lower in Brook Oaks and Sanger Heights. Though the rate of home ownership for Waco's white households was 72.7 percent, by stark contrast, for African Americans it was 16.6 percent and for Hispanics it was 8.1 percent.[7]

The undervaluation of the Sanger Heights and Brook-Oaks neighborhoods also made them, at the time, among the "highest appreciating neighborhoods in Waco since 2000."[8] The site of century-old housing stock in central Waco, these neighborhoods include houses that once belonged to the Waco bourgeoisie. When those homes were originally built, housing in Waco was organized around a thoroughly racialized system of apartheid-like segregation. Like so many cities, as the more privileged residential areas close to the downtown business districts aged and fell into disrepair, succeeding generations moved out to the suburbs. Without investments to maintain these properties, deterioration set in, resale values continued to erode, and owners chose instead to charge rent from the poor until the buildings were condemned. Brook-Oaks and Sanger Heights languished for decades, defined by poverty. However, by 2000, these neighborhoods began falling under the spell of neoliberal revitalization strategies, even though the gentrification process proceeded slowly and without the cultural transformations to the built environment that we have come to expect with gentrification. Though vacant houses and lots still dot the map, the movement of population between 2000 and 2010 suggests the early stages of a process. In the Brook-Oaks census tract, the white population doubled from 12 percent to 25 percent, while the African American population declined from 64 percent to 51.5 percent.

But the recent history of revitalization attempts in Brook Oaks and Sanger Heights can hardly be classified as straightforward gentrification economics. Since the late 1990s, Brook Oaks and Sanger Heights have been resettled by numerous churches and followers of these churches. The *Waco Tribune-Herald* reported that a hundred families seeking to build an intentional faith-based Christian community had moved into these neighborhoods between the 1990s and 2010. "More than anywhere in Waco, the neighborhoods north of Waco Drive have been magnets for social justice-minded Christians who see neighborliness as part of their theology. They're building relationships, renovating homes and bucking conventional wisdom that says Waco's inner city is unattractive to middle-class families."[9] This movement parallels ministry-driven place-based strategies of "anti-poverty praxis" in other cities such as Atlanta. Advocates sometimes refer to this as "gentrification with justice," a slogan that recognizes both that urban poverty and racism go hand in hand and that the "value of neighbor" must be elevated over the "value of property."[10] An Atlanta-based leader in the Christian movement to build intentional faith-based communities in otherwise crumbling urban neighborhoods expands on his ministry's critique of gentrification's roots in racist housing practices.

> Racism is a system that removes people from land and land from people. The story of race is a story in which people who look like me—white people—control and profit from land, and remove the ability of people of color to be grounded in the earth. That's what colonialism is all about, who's in charge of the land. Gentrification is the new way of settler colonialism. It removes the people who have lived on that land, sometimes for generations, and it's the natural progression of late capitalism and the roots of it go way back. What does racism look like in this community? Right now, the instability of people's housing.[11]

Faith-motivated settlers accounted for a significant percentage of whites who returned to the Waco neighborhoods in the first decade of the twenty-first century. In Waco, faith-based or evangelical gentrification mobilized an early wave of gentrifiers motivated by their faith and a desire to realize some measure of local social justice alongside the intensity of shared community. Waco's new vibe of urban living was at least initially sparked by spiritually committed families more interested in social justice than accumulating wealth. While neither artists nor hipsters spearheaded the initial push to reenergize these neighborhoods, the dawning of the "Magnolia Effect" suggests that a new kind of settler may be drawn to the neighborhoods. Speaking about "Gentrification with justice," Jimmy Dorrell, executive director of Mission Waco and pastor of Church under the Bridge, observed in 2017 that

> about one-fourth, maybe one-third, of our neighborhood now are middle-class kind of hipsters. They're the one who want to live in multicultural neighborhoods. They don't want to live in a homogeneous group just like us [middle-class whites]. And so they're coming, they're involved, and they come to the grocery store. And there's excitement that's going on in Waco . . . [about] this new urbanism that's happening. And they're looking at things through different lens, and they want the kind of neighborhood that we've become. What we don't want to happen, especially with the Magnolia effect [referring to *Fixer Upper*], . . . is the possibility that outside people come in and buy houses in my neighborhood and make them into B&B's, and the houses become expensive, and the poor who live down the street now can't maintain their house.[12]

Faith-based responses to urban crises of poverty represent a dramatically different model of gentrification—indeed, the very opposite of the rent-gap model that is coupled on television with the seductive lure of living a comfortable simulation of petty bourgeois lifestyles. These models are so ideologically and practically divergent that it may explain why *Fixer Upper* has gone to such lengths to suppress any reference to the faith-based model. It is worth considering why *Fixer Upper*'s production team deliberately omitted this Christian narrative of neighborhood revival. The Gaineses are recognized for their committed Christian faith, and they belong to Antioch Community Church, which is located in the neighborhoods under discussion. Indeed, some fifty members of this church have joined in the return migration to homes in this same neighborhood. Perhaps HGTV was concerned that bringing Christianity (or any religion) into the narrative might compromise total viewership. Or perhaps it recognized that the faith-based intentional community model of gentrification unsettles the ideological coherence of the HGTV model of gentrified home transformations because the faith-based model emphasizes community, the sharing of resources, and neighborliness over property valuations and Airbnb opportunities.

The inaugural episode of *Fixer Upper* featured a once-grand historic home in Sanger Heights at 2001 Gorman Avenue. "We're in the Sanger Heights area. This is a really old historic neighborhood. We're really excited about this neighborhood because there's been a lot of revitalization that's happened in this neighborhood in the last couple of years."[13] While the clients, Charmaine Hooper and Chuck Codd, can be heard calling the house "scary" and a "catastrophe," Chip launches his gentrification pitch: "I get that it's a mess, but they're only asking $35,000 bucks for this place. This neighborhood is in desperate need of somebody taking a first chance on a house like this."[14] As they tour rooms strewn with garbage and dead rats, Chip reminds them that value lies behind the appearances of filth and grime: "But the point I need to keep reiterating is that they do not build houses like this anymore. The stairwell, the railing, the French doors."[15] The clients would purchase this house, green-tagged and owned by the city of Waco, for $24,000 and invest an additional $150,000 in renovation costs. From a crumbling garbage heap to the reincarnation of 1920s Texas bourgeois architecture, the renovation effect accomplished by the Gaineses was off the chart. It set them on the path to TV glory, especially insofar as they claimed to have accomplished this aesthetic leap from impoverished teardown to stylish bourgeoisie for what seemed a pittance anywhere else in urban America.

Fixer Upper next took on the Harp house, located on North Fifteenth Street, just blocks away from the Gorman Avenue house, in another inner-city tract defined by depreciated housing prices and lower incomes than the general Waco area. Clint and Kelly Harp are proprietors of a start-up custom furniture shop focused on rediscovering value by using salvaged, reclaimed woods. Clint is familiar to viewers because he plays the salvage-wood custom-carpenter artisan on *Fixer Upper* who crafts Joanna's made-to-order dining room table ideas for clients. With the camera on the couple while they drive, the Harps survey the residential neighborhood and point out houses undergoing renovation as "a good sign" that they are making the right investment decision. Kelly then identifies "the area we are looking at is Brook Oaks. That's where our shop is."[16] This reaction to other renovation projects suggest they are attuned to gentrification possibilities in Brook Oaks. For HGTV, this is a rare locational clue, more than most home renovation shows permit, but pictures of social geography still remain off limits. Clint offers a fuller accounting of his motivations in a *Waco Tribune-Herald* interview.

> Clint Harp, 36, said he's excited to be part of the revival of North 15th Street, a once-blighted area that now has dozens of new homes, a school and two restaurants. But he said moving to the area wasn't

part of any grand plan. He and his wife recently bought a former Habitat for Humanity workshop on North 15th Street for their new business, Harp Designs, which makes high-end furniture out of reclaimed wood. He said the house next door at 822 N. 15th St. was the "kingpin" of bad houses on the street. "I didn't come over here thinking I wanted to fix 15th Street," he said. "But I saw this house day after day. It was in horrible shape. I wanted it to be nice because of the shop. We're going to be opening up a showroom, and I didn't want to have what looked like a crack house next door."[17]

The shop was perfect for their start-up business because its location meant that overhead costs and rents were incredibly cheap, an opportunity created by disinvestment in the area. Its downside was the eyesore with broken windows sited directly opposite to it. The Harps accepted the risk of restoring this abandoned wreck of a 1913 home, which had lost almost all market value except for the land itself, to make their showroom more appealing to the upscale sensibilities of those who might afford their custom furniture but might also be deterred by the immediate surroundings. Clint saw the wisdom of investing in a storybook vintage home next door that would erase the visual of violence and poverty. When the couple initially approach the house for the *Fixer Upper* filming, it becomes obvious that their reaction to the exterior has been staged. Instead of calling it the "crack house next door," Clint jokes that "what really struck me at first were the bullet holes" in the side of the house.[18] His bullet hole reference might still signify a crack economy, but minus the interview, uncontextualized pictures of neglect, decay, and the inference of gun violence are simply folded into a series of second-order signifiers arranged to testify to a devalued pre-renovation improvements stage.

After the renovation, Chip launches into his fixer-upper summation as everyone relaxes in the comfort of the appealing post-renovation scenes. He asks us to consider the valuation metric that applies to Brook Oaks: it's just half of the average Waco real estate valuation metric of $100 per square foot. For the moment they've got more house than the neighborhood's worth, but still they have gained an upside equity position of $135,000. Chip wraps up this accounting:

> There was a $110,000 budget. You guys were able to secure this house for 10,000 bucks. That left us with about $100,000 to do these renovations . . . so you guys are all in this thing for $110,000. We're talking about a 2,700-square-foot house and this neighborhood at $50 a foot, which is, you know, $50 a foot sounds offensive to me—you know I wouldn't sell it for that—but given a $50 a square foot evalu-

ation, 2,700 square feet leaves you with a valuation of $135,000, I mean, all day long. So you guys could sell this thing and make you $25,000.[19]

Chip playfully winks as if to hint he'd be interested in buying it back at that price, but Kelly Harp shuts the door on that idea pretty quickly: "We're not gonna!" Beneath the banter, a bind surfaces between the forever dream home and instant equity. Instant equity embraces an ideal of wealth and its potential recirculation as capital. Capital always seeks to acquire more value than it has paid for. We call this surplus value. And, of course, capital generally seeks to maximize its rate of return on investment, a calculation that is considered over the elapse of time. What Chip describes here is a 22 percent return on investment that is realized instantly (via time compression). This journey toward instant equity began with acquiring this house at a massive discount to the market. Why were properties in this neighborhood so undervalued relative to the broader market? Its record of drugs, crime, neglect, and poverty are the long-term results of disinvestment in Waco's historically segregated housing market. But Chip's wink tells us that he recognizes (as do the Harps) that the Brook Oaks neighborhood is in the midst of turning, and this first bit of instant equity likely heralds the promise of more equity to come.

Fixer Upper enacts instant equity both visually and rhetorically, first in the ecstatic moment of the "Oh my gosh" reveal and then in Chip's discursive treatment of how new value translates into instant equity. Sitting voyeur-like with them in their picture-perfect living room, we are encouraged to try on the client's point of view. *Fixer Upper* addresses clients and spectators as both consumers who seek satisfaction of their desires and as smart investors who come out ahead financially. Consume and make money at the same time. This is some promise.

Seated in their remodeled front room, the Harps have not just realized their desires for a family dream home; they have beaten the market in their investment's rate of return. Perhaps recognizing the future value of their house, Kelly's emphatic refusal to think about selling immediately suggests that in her first exhilarating moments of occupying her family's aestheticized dream space, she holds more dearly to its use value as a home than its commodity equivalent. As for the latter, the abstraction of instant equity is itself a product and a measure of commodity fetishism. The "definite social relations" of race, class, disinvestment, and poverty are made to "assume . . . the fantastic form of a relation between things."[20] To create a real estate tool that can function as an objective valuation measuring stick, the neighborhood history of race and class relations has been translated into a thing-like abstraction. Though HGTV has done its best to erase both the presence and the memory of race and class conflicts from the visual representation of value produced by the big reveal, their history sneaks back in to haunt the valuation metric. With the Harp house, the valuation multiplier references the condition of the surrounding neighborhood that we have not been allowed to see. Thus, the abstracted measure of valuation per square foot does seem insultingly low when all we as viewers can see is the sculpted interior surfaces of desire. The narrative of instant equity surrounding the Harp house is caught in a contradiction between two competing measures of commodity fetishism that have been called forth by the show. From the production side, fetishized value is expressed in relations between quantitative things—a multiplier effect, square feet and money. From the consumption side, value receives qualitative expression in the commodity fetishes inscribed in the appearance of objects. By visually excluding everything that surrounds the house, the focus of our consumer desires stands primarily in relation to our own alreadyness of desire, thus confirming David Graeber's hunch that "in fetishizing an object, one is mistaking the power of a history internalized in one's own desires, for a power intrinsic to the object itself."[21] If HGTV is correct in pressing the view that true added value lies in the aesthetic transformation wrought by Joanna, the market value of the Harp house will likely go up when the neighborhood gentrification metric catches up to its comfortable and nurturing interior spaces.

This story has a postscript: a few years later the Harps were among a growing list of former *Fixer Upper* client-homeowners in Waco who have elevated economic self-interest over (or alongside) the love of their dream home. The Harps turned their home into an Airbnb rent-generating money machine (at $550 per night) and purchased another fixer-upper elsewhere in Waco, away from the tourist gaze that came with their celebrity renovation house. The tourist gaze may have compromised their family's privacy, but it permitted them to turn their dream home into a lucrative rent machine. This unanticipated but substantial source of additional revenue stems from *Fixer Upper*'s celebrity. In Waco, it is called the Magnolia Effect. The fame and celebrity that attaches to houses renovated by Joanna and Chip Gaines has generated an impressive tourism engine. A recurring pattern in many cities links Airbnb and short-term rentals with gentrification. From New York City to San Francisco and now to Waco, an Airbnb effect compounds the impacts of gentrification, reinforcing spikes in home prices and rents, exacerbating a crisis of affordable housing, and reinforcing the racialized effects of gentrification. With "Airbnb-fueled gentrification, desirable neighborhoods are turning into de facto tourist districts."[22] In part because of the Magnolia Effect, this new correlative between gentrified housing, Airbnb, and the tourist economy has taken hold in Waco.

Instant equity is a commodity abstraction. Like any commodity abstraction, it is premised on real relationships, but those relationships disappear in the telling of these stories. In the context of Waco, a history of poverty and racially segregated housing created an urban ghetto. The preconditions for the formation of new value began with decades of racially motivated disinvestment. As a result, the now devalued remains of 1920s middle-class homes can be turned into sources of value by salvaging them and making them look sumptuary again. Once again, we see the workings of a salvage-and-recycle economy that has grown up as a secondary circuit of capital.[23]

Capitalizing on the Magnolia Effect

On HGTV, the appearance of value is rooted in a set of photographic practices that obscure what sits to the left or right of a house. TV geography conceals the fact that renovations such as the Harp house or the shotgun house, discussed next, remain more than a bit stranded next to unimproved structures or vacant lots surrounding them. HGTV's camerawork limits the scope of viewing and skews and distorts the coordinates of value and gentrification. However, the backstory of the shotgun house reveals a constellation of value effects. A third-season episode of *Fixer Upper* featured a dilapidated shotgun-style house scheduled for teardown that was instead moved to another unspecified location nearer to Waco's downtown rebuilding project, where it underwent a complete makeover.[24] Juxtaposing the TV version with newspaper reports of this move and renovation reveals multiple strategies for extracting surplus value via the duality of salvage and gentrification capitalism. With this episode, Chip's tally of the costs and the new valuation is more circumspect than usual. The clients obtained the house for nothing but spent $31,000 to acquire another vacant lot where they could relocate the structure and spent an additional $108,000 on renovations. By adding a second-story loft to the original structure (turning it into a "camelback shotgun"), Gaines increased the square footage from 720 to 1,050. To make a new real estate value work, Chip conjures up a valuation of $126 per square foot, which is more than double any other comp in the immediate vicinity. Still, that would put the new valuation below the costs, so Chip deviates from his usual spiel about instant equity. Instead, he observes that "this is a new area and someday this neighborhood is going to take off... one of these days you may have $20,000 to 30,000 in this thing."[25] What explains his reluctance to talk new value here? No matter how stunning this renovation, the real estate professional in Chip knows that the comps do not yet justify a pronouncement of instant equity, even if he can imagine the conditions of value in Waco making this a decent investment down the road. Neither does he explain why this new location might take off, since for the purposes of the show the new street location is kept under wraps.

Their clients, Cameron and Jessica Bell, however, were working from an altogether different script as far as the pursuit of value goes. They never sought value in a happy-ever-after dream home but rather treated it purely as an investment vehicle. Once the house was renovated, they did not occupy it, instead making it available on the short-term rental market via Airbnb at $325 per night with (they claim) a 90 percent occupancy rate.[26] Young and hipsterish, the clients spoke of being enamored with shotgun houses in the Deep South. The shotgun house architectural style is associated with African Americans and urban poverty. Particularly identified with New Orleans, this vernacular architectural style has witnessed a revival in recent years, especially in post-Katrina New Orleans, where it became architecturally reappropriated to score style points in gentrifying districts. At the same time, decades of gentrification-like practices wiped out a majority of these structures, making them sufficiently scarce that their potential renovation value had risen. Indeed, this scarcity was on the minds of the clients who discovered that only two shotgun houses still stood in Waco, and this one would be razed to make way for a retail, hotel, and restaurant development. To the developer, the shotgun house had no remaining value—in fact, it had become an obstacle to the formation of new value where it stood, a casualty of an impoverished African American neighborhood soon to be leveled. The clients recognized an investment opportunity in the otherwise disposable shell of the old shotgun house and moved it to a location nearer to where they hoped to take advantage of the economic momentum driven by the agro-urban aesthetic of the Magnolia Silos and the new Baylor football stadium. A downtown riverfront development proposed to bring in capital investments to build loft apartments, along with a leisure and shopping infrastructure replete with restaurants, cafés, boutiques, and a fancy new rebuild of the downtown Farmers Market.[27]

Narratives of instant equity as well as narratives of the forever dream home presume a certain kind of imagined subject who brings a specific motivation to the home renovation process. HGTV production formulas smash time—fracture it—and then fuse it back together to simulate chronology. To fit the formula to the particulars of each client and their search for a house, the sequencing of lived experience is dissolved and reorganized to match the overarching narrative that gaining possession of a forever home space equals a wealth effect. Thus, while adding value hinges on taking advantage of homes priced at a discount to the market, in the *Fixer Upper* version of the narrative, gaining a financial advantage is pitched as a means to the forever family sanctuary rather than as an end in itself. Clients who have already purchased a house, or made a choice regarding the house they want renovated—as happened with the Gorman house, the Harp house, and the shotgun house—must pretend to pursue a good-faith search for a house that they have not yet seen. Charmaine Hooper, Clint Harp, and Cameron Bell each approached the risk-reward renovation scenario with different motivations and objectives, and a house in mind, when they contacted *Fixer Upper* about guiding them through the gentrification process. The show's strategy of omitting diverse motivations is, however, crucial to maintaining the ideological purity of the show's narrative about commitment and community.

That imagery took a hit when, in 2017, the Bells put the restyled shotgun house back on the market with an asking price of $950,000.[28] Such pricing seemed predicated on a wildly avaricious embellishment of assumed future valuations: (1) the celebrity value of Joanna Gaines's aesthetic wizardry and the tourism driven by the Magnolia Effect, (2) an urban revitalization scheme predicated on an influx of regional capital investments in a central-city gentrification model, (3) appropriating the hot sign value of African American vernacular architecture with a gentrified makeover, and (4) the erasure of a built environment of poverty and vacancy that premises appropriation via dispossession. The shotgun house turns into a self-aggrandizing story aimed at exploiting TV gentrification. The grossly inflated price tag put on the shotgun house shattered the fairy-tale account that *Fixer Upper* has so assiduously crafted. Locally, realtors scoffed at the price tag, while nationally the pop culture media noted with cynical glee the moral gap between the *Fixer Upper* depiction of family, home, and place and the callous efforts to exploit the *Fixer Upper* effect via Airbnb, Vrbo, and flipping to maximize exchange value.

The unforeseen twists of a capitalist marketplace in property values not only provoked moral shock; it also highlighted how much the renovation economics of building home equity on television remains a black box. Even though HGTV's modus operandi makes value subjectively dependent on framing the visual contrast between before-and-after images, the utter lack of accountability about real-world capitalist economics frequently unsettles the narrative. The arithmetic of new value presumes a calculation of costs, but on HGTV the costs of production are in no way made transparent to viewers. Despite the ritualized punctuation mark that concludes each episode with an objective declaration of the value gained via home renovation, the actual economics of televised renovations remain murky at best. While Chip at least offers an oversimplified methodology for arriving at the new valuation, on shows like *Love It or List It*, the post-renovation real estate value of the home seems conjured arbitrarily out of thin air, usually an automatic $20,000 over the total costs—take the initial estimate of market value, add in the costs of renovation, and a new value-added number materializes as an unsupported asseveration of fact. Shrouded in the supposed expertise of hosts, are these numbers guesses based on comparison home sales in the neighborhood, or are they simply one more closing sales pitch for home renovation? When hosts do allude to comps to justify a market price, the comps themselves remain largely an unverifiable abstraction. Viewers are never shown side-by-side images of what neighborhood comps look like, either at episode's beginning or end. Though the *Flip or Flop* formula depends on reading off two comparable listings in the area as a means of setting an asking price for the property, even here viewers are denied any tangible visual evidence of what defines the comparisons. The comps have no reference point other than a dollar figure.

If indeed this is reality TV's version of a neoliberal housing landscape, it's all the more curious that HGTV offers only the barest outlines of a capitalist accounting regimen, much less any accounting transparency. The costs of skilled and unskilled labor are unknowns. Costs of materials are sometimes a matter of concern and sometimes not. When costs are mentioned, as they sometimes are on *Flip or Flop*, they don't add up. How can one do a complete kitchen makeover with new cabinets, stainless-steel appliances, flooring, backsplashes, sinks, island, and granite countertops and claim to spend only $12,000 unless migrant labor is being ruthlessly exploited and inferior black-market materials are being used?

Because these estimates tend to be so flimsy, the moments of magically materialized exchange value at episode's end must, it seems, be the result of the imaginative reordering of aestheticized spaces. On *Property Brothers: Buying and Selling*, Jonathan and Drew Scott inform clients that their current house would currently fetch $395,000, but with a modest additional investment of $15,000 and the skills of the contractor/designer brothers, their house will be worth $440,000 when put on the market. What accounts for this multiplier effect that guarantees a 200 percent return on investment? The shows imply that the wow-factor image automatically doubles or triples the return on investment. We are back within the hyperreal model of HGTV in which an applied understanding of commodity aesthetics is key to instant equity. In the world of HGTV, the sign economy trumps other variables in the calculus of valuation.

Signs of Aesthetic Modernism

In the HGTV sign economy, modernism translates into a variety of flavors. Its aesthetic styles range from the fully commodified like-new knockoffs of midcentury modern furniture designs featured by the *Property Brothers* to

Fixer Upper's embrace of farmhouse modernism with its rearrangement and repurposing of materials salvaged from the early modern era (think shiplap). To an even greater extent, *Home Town* throws down salvage modernism, reworking discarded materials from the past via a variety of craft skills—carpentry, sewing, and art mediated by the practices of imaginative bricolage to produce a homey yet clean modern look. HGTV's other variants of aesthetic modernism include nods to imagined historical referents. The conversion of warehouse spaces into lofts introduced the industrial chic look of exposed brick, beams, and heavy metal valves, a look that aimed at signifying there's nothing hidden. It suggests a rejection of older codes of formality, pretense, and class privilege, especially important in an era when the lines of class privilege have grown more pronounced. Industrial chic celebrates the surfaces of relics from the era of heavy modernity, less as a celebration of industrial labor than an embrace of the exposed patina of rusted infrastructure. Worn and used materials take on greater importance as signifiers than as materials. Reclaimed wood equals rustic, and as an aesthetic myth, industrial rustic exalts the unadorned mix of wood, iron, and glass as textured surfaces to signify a rejection of plastic with its aura of inauthenticity. Especially when she decorates for a male client, Joanna likes to fit in a piece of metal salvaged from the rural industrial history of Texas— say, a weathered windmill blade turned into a burnished wall ornament. By contrast, her trademark farmhouse rustic chic look has a more feminine aesthetic appeal.

Aesthetic modernism reflects the general popularization of aesthetics as a category of daily life. Aesthetic capital ascends to the center of our cultural preoccupations because it focuses our experience of being consumers. For decades, the primary way to differentiate parity consumer goods (say, sneakers) has been to brand them to make them stand out in aesthetically appealing ways. As aesthetic judgments take on increased significance in shaping consumer perceptions of value, they chip away at the importance of old-school production-centric modes of valuation. It's all the more ironic then that HGTV promotes the rebirth of modern styles that grab hold of production-tinged signifiers from the eras of industrial and preindustrial capitalism. The farmhouse modern aesthetic popularized by *Fixer Upper* projects an earthiness and a realism that joins an appreciation for agrarian values with a respectful resurrection of craft skills that appreciate the work of the hands. Both figures of farmhouse modern and industrial chic speak to the spirit of remoralizing value by recuperating symbolically a "time when the future was more optimistic, and economic security seemed stronger. Both aesthetics involve the idea of labor as a means to living: one embraces the simplicity of rural life, and the other of machine-age optimism that life can be made more efficient in order to make people happy."[29]

Figure 6.2 The differences between the farmhouse modern aesthetic (*top*) and the industrial modern aesthetic (*bottom*) are primarily a matter of sourcing upcycled materials that have differing significations. Farmhouse modern generally has a more rustic feel, featuring reclaimed barnwood, architectural salvage details, antique-feel accents, and, of course, farmhouse sinks. The industrial modern aesthetic bends toward clean lines and the inclusion of retro-look metal surfaces that seem as if they had a previous life in factory settings. When these signifiers of no-nonsense durability are coupled with the textures of stucco-like walls and concrete countertops, the look signifies a discerning acceptance of the beauty of imperfection. (*Fixer Upper*, season 3, episode 4, "A Home Away from Home for the Holidays" [High Noon Entertainment, HGTV, Discovery, 2015]; HGTV, "Joanna's Take on Modern Design," *YouTube*, August 10, 2018, https://www.youtube.com/watch?app=desktop&v=LupnuDz2k0 M&list=PL3ciaInkqyXDbsiR3ehFDbHSRoKiM2Xtl.)

Wayfair is representative of consumer capital rooted in the commodification of aesthetics. Its on-screen doppelganger, *Property Brothers*, performs a preconstituted version of aesthetic labor—consult the furniture and interior design industry's catalog of choices, then put together combinations those options permit, and—voila!—you have an HGTV aesthetic of Wayfair modernism, which simply means that it looks newish. *Property Brothers* and *Flip or Flop* are the shows that are most fully tied into the e-commerce interior design and home goods definitions of aesthetic values. By contrast, the other renovation shows braid in at least some of their hosts' own handmade flair and creativity into the commodity mix in an effort to signify authenticity. In the end, the difference is mostly a wash because we can still pick out replicas of Joanna Gaines–inspired tables via her own Magnolia catalog or, once again, find it incorporated into Wayfair's business of aesthetic imperialism.

"Curation is a word long associated with the performance of traditionally feminized labor: A putting together, an assembling, a nurturing, a taking care of things and people."[30] The decorators who stand out are those who excel as curators of a look, a style, and an ensemble of objects that express and excite consumers' aesthetic sensibilities. If we construct a hierarchy of design and décor value within the world of HGTV, Joanna Gaines is the queen. In HGTV's galaxy of renovation stars, she stands for the neo-Americana home décor, with her farmstead modern aesthetic that is the sum of its key signifiers—farmhouse sinks, repurposed shiplap, industrial lighting fixtures, and lots of salvaged (i.e., reclaimed) wood. Through her, HGTV has managed to translate elements drawn from a regional style of vernacular architecture into a globally acclaimed interior design look defined by clean (but not streamlined) lines and simplified forms. The question, of course, is why has this particular curation style garnered so much cultural traction in the decade following the financial crisis? Certainly, its agrarian connotations hit the nostalgia mark, but there is more to it than that. Gaines's work captures a simple elegance that says, "I have arrived, but I do so without fussy pretense." In the wake of the financial crisis and during an era marked by a burgeoning wealth gap, we want the comfort but without marking ourselves as class outliers.

Joanna constructs rooms that feel sanctuary-like where one can find a Zen moment but with a down-home feel. Call it Zen domesticity, a Christian feng shui that counsels the appropriate aesthetic ensemble that fosters a space within which to find yourself. With her design and decoration choices, home can be where you find your truest self. This is confirmed at the Magnolia Market, where a consumer can choose her own ensemble, within the framework set by Magnolia's carefully curated collection of commodities accompanied by pithy philosophical aphorisms about self, faith, and home. Taken together, these aphorisms make up the "Magnolia manifesto." About the home, the manifesto declares, "We believe in home, that it should restore us from today and ready us for tomorrow."[31] Home is thus identified as the site where we may freely recuperate and prepare ourselves to meet the recurring stresses, strains, and alienations of everyday life quotidian in our capitalist society. *Fixer Upper* renovations strike a chord because, in addition to the constructed and designed renovation, they are, more significantly, selling a concept of home as the ownership of identity.

On the Magnolia website, "Signs" is a shopping category listed under "Wall Decor." There, an array of inspirational signs—homilies, epistles, testimonials, and other words to live by—are framed and printed on leather and metal. Each sign is available for purchase. I want the sign identified as the "Authenticity Leather Sign" because it speaks to the commodification of both signs and authenticity. It costs $68 and makes an attempt at philosophical reflection—loosely a pop-culture rendition of Ralph Waldo Emerson's "Self-Reliance." Designed by Joanna, the Authenticity Leather Sign is an encouragement to live fully as the person "you were meant to be."[32] Thus signified, authenticity rendered as a *commodity sign* reveals its self-contradictions. Does the *Fixer Upper* curated model of farmhouse modernity not also signify a similar aesthetic authenticity? The unity of house, décor, and self lies in the commandment that thou shalt seek to be one with oneself as an empowered self-directed person capable of caring for self and family in a space designed and curated to permit you to tell your story. The Leather Authenticity Sign urges the consumer to reach for the real in herself, eschewing the artificial and always distinguishing the real from the fake. The appeal of the Magnolia brand on both *Fixer Upper* and the website rests on the merger of philosophy (authenticity) and aesthetic style (rustic farmhouse look) as a set of mutually reinforcing signs. While the sign of authenticity can be mistaken for authenticity, and the signs of rustic modernism can be mistaken for identity, the question is no longer weather the faux and real can be kept apart; they can't in an economy of reproductions. As a signification project, the success of aesthetic modernism depends on how effectively sincerity and simulation can be made equivalent.

7

HGTV's Value Theories of Labor

Value resembles a dance, not a statue.
—**RAYMOND RUYER**, *La philosophie de la valeur*

Though HGTV doesn't explicitly talk much about labor, it routinely *pictures* labor in the reconstitution of value. This casual visualization of labor lends itself to a generalized gendering of the division of labor. Women's work focuses itself on reimagining the look of value. The fact that HGTV's audience is predominantly female may also lend itself to foregrounding the performance of affective and emotional labor since so much of HGTV's appeal rests on the emotional management of sign values. It is worth noting that if we think about the behind-the-scenes work that produces the HGTV shows themselves, most of that labor also seems aimed at performing aesthetic affect. HGTV's more male-oriented cousin, the DIY channel, visually emphasizes the intensity of demanding physical labor necessary to reclaim value. As a narrative, salvage capitalism is both backward and forward leaning in its preferred labor forms. It calls forth myths of muscular labor necessary to conquering a landscape of distressed housing while praising the triumphs of immaterial labor that reconceptualize spaces and the artisanship that produces distinction. Because HGTV tells its stories laterally, ricocheting across time, space, and task, labor on HGTV rarely appears unified in form, instead leaping back and forth between varied and fleeting expressions. HGTV makes a distinction between independent, self-employed, and artisan labors as a source of value and common wage labor, which may be necessary but does not, in and of itself, yield new value without an investor and an innovative design plan. Entrepreneurial labor is foregrounded, while generic labor is kept in the background via visual techniques of time compression that turn it into ghostly labor. As with everything else that touches on lending, mortgages, and finance, the transactional labors associated with these activities once again form a void, the significance of which renders invisible questions of exploitation surrounding the decisions that determine who does not get to play in the HGTV narrative.

The forms of labor that HGTV affirms most strongly are the labor of the heart, the labor of the hands, and the labor of the mind. The leading edge of capitalist industries depends on creative labor, immaterial labor, affective labor, linguistic labor, symbolic labor, informatics, and cognitive labor.[1] In HGTV's stories of neoliberal prosperity, such labors present themselves simultaneously as capital—after all, these forms of labor are all imagined as entrepreneurial. "These new forms of capital foist the responsibilities of entrepreneurship on their putative owners, reconfiguring the wage as a return on investment rather than the result of a struggle with management for a fairer share of the surplus. One way of understanding neoliberalism, then, is to see it as the passage to real subsumption."[2] The image of passionate labor for the few is requisite to HGTV's representation of itself as the unalienated spirit of entrepreneurial capital. To a person, every renovator on HGTV expresses a love of what he or she does. Each finds joy in creativity and professes to take gratification from giving pleasure to others.

Ghostly Labor and the (Spectacular) Materialization of Value

Thus far we have met the hosts of the shows, big personalities who design, renovate, buy, and sell. We are most aware of those effects performed by the designers and contractors who are introduced to us by name. They provide creative vision and purpose. By contrast, common laborers—hired hands—tend to be faceless and nameless. On some shows, generic workers wear T-shirt uniforms that label them as "CREW." Scurrying across the screen in sped-up flurries of activity, hired bodies appear as part of a laboring background—they are glancing images of arms, backs, and shoulders bent on tasks at hand. With rare exceptions, these are figures without personalities who lack any apparent subjectivity. We cannot substitute for Chip and Joanna Gaines—it wouldn't be the same without them. The crew members, however, are functionally interchangeable, cogs in the machine. This continues a long-standing division between conceptualization and execution in the capitalist division of labor. The ghostly labor of hired hands represents an unspoken cost of production; they are often imagined not as the source of value but rather as costs.

Figure 7.1 A freeze-frame captures an instant of phantom labor from a time-lapse sequence of time-compressed labors on *Flip or Flop*. These floor installers become labor abstractions in an effect rendered by speeded-up motion. In *Ghostly Matters* (Minneapolis: University of Minnesota Press, 1997), Avery Gordon treats ghostly apparitions as dialectical signifiers of what hegemonic discourse suppresses. These apparitions of labor simultaneously capture both labors' phantom presence and phantom invisibility as a labor source of value in the home renovation narratives. We recognize that labor was present only by the contrails left behind. (*Flip or Flop*, season 2, episode 1, "Foreclosure Shock" [Pie Town Productions, HGTV, Discovery, 2014].)

HGTV often visualizes the performance of labor as a series of blurs compressed into tightly edited time-lapse montage sequences. Time-compressed labor is an effect of accelerated motion; stringing together labor signifiers in rapid-fire chains creates the appearance of hyperactive labor. Photographically chopping up laboring activity and then recombining it into a mini montage turns labor into an abstraction—a molecule of Karl Marx's "labor in general." This imagery is perfect for articulating how "the secret of the expression of value" lies in treating "all kinds of labor" as "equal and equivalent" insofar "as they are human labor in general."[3] The video practice of ghostly labor captures the gist of Marx's argument about "the value of a commodity represent[ing] human labor in the abstract, the expenditure of human labor in general. . . . It is the expenditure of simple labor power, i.e., of the labor power which, on an average, apart from any special development, exists in the organism of every ordinary individual."[4]

Time-compression techniques are a staple of the home renovation genre, used to signify the passage of time, hours, days, and weeks—for example, the familiar time-lapse blur of highway traffic coursing from day to night and back again. These visual metaphors often segue into the similarly intensive intervals of labor time, visually rendered by the speedup of laborers in motion—thus abbreviating the necessity of construction labor into concentrated bursts of laboring activity. In this way, the many requisite laboring activities that go into a home renovation—including the work of carpenters, electricians, plumbers, framers, drywallers, tilers, painters, and roofers, as well as installers of subflooring, flooring, cabinets, and windows—all become mashed into what Marx calls "abstract general labor." Construction labor (both skilled and deskilled) is thus compressed as much as possible into a sequence of fleeting instants; it is not repressed so much as expressed as a visual sign of itself. While no single act of construction labor is followed to completion on the shows, the generalized work must be done to finish the project. Bursts of busyness thus signify progress toward the goal of transformation. Accelerated action stands not only for intensified labor but also for a speedier time to completion, drawing consumers and viewers ever closer to realizing their desires. Laborers carry no subjective weight—they are turned into an ethereal ghostly, albeit necessary, presence, never in the foreground of creating value. On HGTV, abstract labor and ghostly labor become one and the same, represented as executing tasks but without a mind of its own.

Like most celebrity HGTV hosts, Chip Gaines's on-screen performance of labor is mostly limited to the photo ops when he comes on site to film scenes,[5] even though Gaines is depicted as a jack-of-all-trades (and he might be), portrayed doing much of the work by himself—from demolition to installing barn doors to custom concrete countertops. The same general pattern applies to Jonathan Scott, who claims to be involved in a hands-on way with every phase of the renovation project, and who takes credit for getting all the work done. To be sure, each host has subcontractors and work crews performing the construction work while they are busy elsewhere with businesses that have grown by leaps and bounds. A hectic and crowded work schedule may explain why the hosts are not on site daily, but it does not explain why their shows fictionalize who performs the skilled and unskilled labor on the renovation and flipping programs. The answer has to do with the distinction between abstract and concrete labor. On HGTV, abstract labor—ghostly labor—does not appear to immediately make a pivotal contribution to producing added value. Instead, HGTV producers spotlight the words and actions of the celebrity host's labor. Television's incarnation of concrete labor takes the appearance of named, celebrity labor—this is who is responsible for producing new value.

When Chip works on-screen, the camera dwells on his actions, mainly because the camera dwells on his persona cheerfully and energetically performing both skilled and unskilled tasks. Even though his scenes seem staged, like punctuating the completion of a task with his nail gun, nevertheless it is his expenditure of labor power (accompanied by the visual of his sweat) that defines the transformation of the house before he ritually passes the baton to Joanna, telling her to work her decorating magic. Representing the host's labor inverts the representation of ghostly wage labor. With Gaines, the narrative emphasis is on his visible expenditure of labor power. By contrast, nameless abstract wage labor is represented by the staccato notes of labor time.

HGTV crafts signs of labor that point to a hierarchy of labor and a hierarchy of value. Scenes of labor at hyperspeed address the necessity of concentrated labor time to reassure that projects are on time and on budget, but it's the scenes of concrete, celebrity labor that deliver oomph to a project. The work of the many is relegated to abstracted time-lapse scenes, while the contributions of the few correspond to camera close-ups. While the labor of celebrity male contractors outstrips the value of faceless abstract labor, the most valued form of labor on the home renovation show is the imaginative labor of the designer. The creative power is knowing where to put that labor, to what task, not the labor itself: "the cameras give us quick glimpses of workmen who labor away under Chip's direction, all of these men—laborers, artisans, foreman, husband—making manifest a woman's exacting vision."[6]

Without at least tacitly invoking this distinction between creative labor power and the labor time of hired hands, HGTV narratives don't hold together. Marx distinguishes labor power as the source of value, while labor time pointed toward the "measure of its magnitude."[7] Labor power is the stuff that enables dreams to materialize, yet it is only visualized in slower moments of artisanal labor. Instead, what we see are the visual representations of labor time translated into pure speed. Because labor time translates the measure of time spent on a task into its monetary equivalent, its depiction as speed of movement captures the ideal of limiting construction costs. Yet, on HGTV stories, the labor power of the creative star eclipses muscular labor power in terms of the value (measured in money) generated. Thus, HGTV's visual formula governing the depiction of labor chooses to present subcontractors and their crews as shadow labor, focusing instead on their labor time.[8] Intensified and abbreviated, the speed of labor time determines whether deadlines (contractual agreements) are met. In this scenario, general labor may be necessary to realizing the finished product, but it is hardly the motive force—the primary source of value is disciplined knowledge of the market coupled with the ability to fashion stylish spatial illusions and transformations.

The role of ghostly labor is performed mostly by working-class men. Representing wage labor as ghostly labor is symptomatic of wage labor's place in the system of contemporary financial capital. Acceptable profit margins no longer flow from what corporate workforce consultants call "transformational activities" characteristic of earlier stages of industrialization. In today's "economics of labor, workers who undertake complex, interactive jobs typically command higher salaries, and their actions have a disproportionate impact on the ability of companies to woo customers, to compete, and to earn profits."[9] The mechanical execution of wage labor is no longer a sufficient means of multiplying value to power a capitalist economy. Financial capital no longer looks to the value generated by workers' labor, but to the value that can be generated by harnessing the cash streams that workers' wages feed. What matters to the derivatives markets is what workers' wages can consume and the interest streams that can be generated by loans, rents, and mortgages—by debt. Both the phantoms of labor and the repackaging of material symbols are more than significant tropes within the shows, they are also representative of late-stage capitalism and its financial tools (e.g., securities and derivatives). While HGTV heralds creative and immaterial labor in the pursuit of repackaged value, Wall Street banks rely on creative and immaterial labor to create the leveraged financial instruments that repackage debt.

Feminized Labor, an Economy of Creative Design Value

On HGTV home renovation shows, the term "value" takes on a tangle of simultaneous meanings. When a flipper opens up a space and declares that "we created so much value here," the term functions as a shorthand for the economic calculation of price as an expression of exchange value. Value refers in this sense to an end-game calculation, but it also assumes that perceptual value translates into exchange value. Both visually and emotionally, the televisual renovation seeks the highest form of value in the subjectivity of personal value.

Home renovation shows orchestrate a spectacle of value hunting. On one side, HGTV programming feeds a continuous stream of commodity-sign fetishism. With polished visions of kitchens leading the way, the home renovation spectacle reinforces the idea that house values increase when the house itself undergoes an aestheticized makeover. This logic is not dissimilar from the endless television programming that counsels how personal makeovers can improve one's personal value.[10] As opposed to the impersonality of ghostly labor, design labor relies on judgments that link knowledge of the marketplace to nuanced aesthetic sensibilities. As such, the value return on this form of labor is significantly higher than any other labor involved in the renovation and flipping process. The labor of design and semiosis on HGTV is made to appear as the most salient, visible, and accessible means of imparting and controlling new value. "The system runs less on the surplus-value of the commodity than on the aesthetic surplus-value of the sign."[11]

Because the lens of television bends the representation of value toward visual aesthetic styles, HGTV programming promotes a postmodern variant of a value theory of labor focused on the mirror of sign value. But whereas the classical value theory of labor addresses itself primarily to men's labor, HGTV's value theory of design addresses itself to a feminization of labor—and with it, a more feminized vision of the meaning of value. Masculine labor defines the sphere of construction, while feminine labor defines the sphere of aesthetic interior design and décor. Questions regarding choices of color, texture, style, interior material surfaces, or spatial room design all automatically default to the feminine side. Staging, as noted earlier, represents the consummation of sign value—an opportunity to present the house as a piece of art.

HGTV both does and does not dissolve the typically gendered boundaries called forth between productive and reproductive labor, between work and home. This dissolution prompts a transition to a "fourth shift" in which "the core of creating and accumulating wealth shifts from material goods to immaterial ones, in which knowledge, education, communication, caring and taking care of the chain of services—all kinds of domestic management—are central, and the paradigmatic form of new work is domestic work."[12] Traditional notions of women's work as housework—cooking, cleaning, monitoring the kids—have been supplemented in the HGTV universe by definitions of women's work as designing the function, look, and feel of domestic spaces. Traditional representations of women's work may have partially migrated away from clichés about housework, but that work remains in the shadows of HGTV's ideal layout. In the ideal/typical HGTV dream home, the space is conceptualized both by feminized labor and for feminized reproductive labor, where a second shift still prevails. The creativity of redefining spaces includes turning the open concept into a gilded cage designed for the second shift. Housework activities, of course, may remain off camera during the shows, but one suspects that women are still performing the disproportionate amount of such work once they move into those households.

And this is precisely where heroic women show up during the commercial breaks interspersed between segments of the shows. The success of HGTV home renovation programming has prompted partnerships such as Sherwin-Williams' HGTV Home Paint Collection. Sherwin-Williams television ads offer miniaturized DIY reenactments of the home renovation dream and the women who accomplish it. The company's 2015 ad "Heroes of the Household" pays tribute to the busy mom who is the hero of the title.

The subject here is a woman's labor and her production of the social space of family life. She possesses a strong work ethic and a deep sense of responsibility to others. She takes on too much but still manages to come through. On her way through a hectic day, she performs necessary but unpaid household labor—getting the kids off to school and preparing meals. She is a whirlwind of energy who manages to squeeze in a professional career, all the while managing a friendly, cheerful relationship with her coworkers. Her inspiration, however, comes from neither career nor housework; rather, it occurs during her commute, when she spots a blue metal chair at a yard sale and imagines how she can upcycle it as an accent piece into the color makeover she is performing on her home. Her opportunity for creative expression—her artistic inspiration—stems from her vision of how to craft the canvas of her house into a harmonious and comforting interior aesthetic. Both materially and culturally, the Sherwin-Williams "hero of the household" is identified as the author of her home, the space for her family: "You're not just painting walls here; you're making homes." Locating her domain of creativity in twin domestic labors of painting walls and cooking dinner for her family, a sequence of interwoven match cuts intersperse mixing paint and pasta sauce, concluding in a parallel visual arrangement of colorful paint buckets and an identical arrangement of dinner on the table, turning the paint and dinner table into equivalent metonyms for home and the creative expression of female labor.

The most common gendered division of labor on flipping and renovation shows assigns men the jobs of real estate agent and contractor, while women are acknowledged to be preeminent at interior design and décor. Men are generally users of power tools, and women make performances of disdaining yucky, dirty, or vermin-related tasks. Generally, the HGTV formula treats a woman handling a power tool as a cute, comic moment, with the exception of Nicole Curtis of *Rehab Addict* and the women of *Good Bones*, who do not shy away from dirty jobs. Almost all flipping series model the woman's role after Christina El Moussa's on *Flip or Flop*, depicting her as the authority when it comes to reconceptualizing interior living spaces and always giving her the final word when it comes to material and color choices for countertops, backsplashes, cabinets, and flooring. She justifies this by claiming to have her finger on the pulse of the buying demographic that the property takes aim at. On *Masters of Flip*, the interior designer-wife guards her self-proclaimed authority by dismissively mocking her husband's suggestions about color, style, and design. On *Fixer Upper*, Joanna makes a point of bringing her daughters with her to the antique mall, or occasionally includes them as her staging assistants as a means of socializing them into the feeling arts of decorating. The moment of decorating—curating and perfecting—the home's interior always corresponds to the formulaic arrival of the adorable Gaines kids to motivate their mother with cupcakes so that she will have the energy and good cheer to complete her decoration of the space. This confirms a deep association between maternal value and decorative value. On HGTV, feminized labor imparts the most visible contribution to the added value of home. Even shows that offer variations on this rule about who performs this form of value-producing labor on television—for example, the metrosexual Scott brothers—seem to confirm the general tendency.

HGTV extols middle-class ideals of feminine domesticity, but with an ironic twist that presents domesticity not as a marker of patriarchal confinement but as the source of skills that are leveraged into the value-producing expertise most likely to generate a return on investment. The long-term historical consequences of G.W.F. Hegel's master-slave dialectic lurk in the shadows as the history of women's domestic confinement turns into the advantage of feminized labor in a new era of capital.[13] The commodity fetishism of HGTV's aesthetic makeovers comes wrapped within a revamped faith in a romanticized value theory of aesthetic labor. Lifestyle channels now consider women, long consigned to the sphere of household aesthetics, to be the masters of aesthetic design and, hence, masters of producing value. In HGTV's reportage of what it takes to be successful in the salvage renovation market, the visual articulation of value is everything and the contributions of designers, decorators, and house aestheticians are privileged in this feminized value theory of sign labor.

At first glance, HGTV's varied representations of labor as sources of value appear to have vaulted women's work to the top of the value chain. Does this disrupt traditional patriarchal hierarchies of labor and value? The ideal that women are the most skilled at doing aesthetic and affective labor recenters the feminine contribution to value back in the domestic sphere, but with a twist—this time around, affectively mediated aesthetic labor is no longer considered patronizingly unproductive labor (like housework) but rather seen as a highly productive value source, especially when it is turned in virtuoso commodity performances.

Emotional Labor and Affective Labor

A broad turn toward the androgynization of affective and emotional labor marks fields of immaterial labor such as corporate sales, marketing, and advertising in the post-Fordist era.[14] Affective labor includes those occupations that deal in the management of feelings as a commodity and as a form of labor. In the *Managed Heart,* Arlie Hochschild observes the gendered performance of cheerleading as a fundamental form of emotional labor, aimed at steering and amplifying the depth of gratifying emotional sentiments.[15]

Consumer-goods advertising, particularly branded advertising like that subsumed by HGTV, attempts to connect the exaggeration of desires with objects, thus relying on an excess of cheerleading enthusiasm. Endowing commodities with an aura of enthusiasm is essential to boosting the perception of renovated value. In this way, HGTV mobilizes the performance of affective labor toward the social construction (manufacture) of enthusiasm as a commodity value that is "future-oriented."[16]

Multiple vectors of emotional labor are performed in HGTV's stories. And its agents work on different objects. Hosts work on managing the client, while clients pour their emotional labor into a dialectic of anxiety, desire, and fetish realization. Viewers supply (or decline) the emotional labor that valorizes the fixer-upper in its spectacular image form. HGTV's story formula all but guarantees that the requisite emotional valleys and peaks will end on peaks, although whether viewers will cooperate and valorize this or that vision of spectacular desire is always an open question. Hence, a surplus of affective labor must be performed in every episode. HGTV producers routinely rely on music editors to orchestrate the energy and feelings excited by the aesthetics of revelation. Musically framing slow-motion scenes of the big reveal is a tried-and-true method of stimulating the emotional intensity experienced by spectators. This performance of affective labor is not directly visible to consumers as a form of labor; its presence announces itself in the sound and video effects. Without identifiable agency, the exercise of affective labor is built into the scaffolding of the show itself.

Clients supply a critical dimension of emotional labor. While financial investments tend to be better controlled when subjects do not let themselves become too emotionally invested in properties, home buying almost always carries an emotional commitment. This is, of course, a major difference between flippers on their own shows and the clients on renovations shows. Flippers minimize and control their emotional investment, while renovation clients swim in their feelings. Prospective clients on *Property Brothers* and *Love It or List It* are asked on the casting-call questionnaire about their personality and relationship dynamics because HGTV producers are eager to exploit and dramatize emotional conflicts, which in turn demands that the Scott brothers step forward to soothe anxieties and resolve emotional misgivings. Emotional responses are elicited by the design of the formula. The apex of the emotional drama comes with the big reveal and the "Oh my gosh" moment—without the clients' exaggerated facial expressions and body language there is no subjective valorization of the renovation and no added value. On fixer-upper programming, the discovery of surplus value is contingent on emotional value induced by the performative ecstasy of revelation. In the triumphal scenes of the big reveal, it's hard to distinguish between the therapeutic moment and the gift of newfound emotional capital. Hosts such as Joanna Gaines or the Scotts perform therapeutically as if the concatenations of tone, texture, and style that they have assembled mirror the innermost emotional selves of their clients.

On programs that feature clients, the emotional arc of the story predominates. Renovation programs such as *Property Brothers*, *Love It or List It*, and *Property Virgins* assign the hosts responsibility for managing their clients' anxieties and ministering with intimate care and concern for their clients' affective states. Egypt Sherrod of *Property Virgins* is described on HGTV's website as "Part REALTOR®, part therapist, friend and financial advisor." The show's description on the website stresses navigating the emotional peaks and valleys: "The series focuses on the roller-coaster journey of property virgins' first foray into real estate, offering tell-it-like-it-is entertainment and practical take-home advice."[17] On *Property Brothers*, the real estate agent brother acknowledges his therapist role when he addresses a couple's bickering over choices of style and taste—"I am not a psychotherapist, but I am not getting good vibes off you guys"—or the other brother cools out a semihysterical client meltdown by taking an ice cream break together. Having talked their clients away from the turnkey market to a riskier renovation project, Jonathan and Drew put considerable effort into what Erving Goffman terms "cooling out the mark."[18] After the credit default crisis dragged down millions of homeowners, politicians failed miserably to "cool out" the unhappiness and discontent stemming from the bank bailouts and the general financial misery twisted by the Great Recession. That unhappiness fueled populist anger and contributed to the rise of Trumpism. In HGTV's retelling of the postcrash era, the rejuvenation of homes takes place not by politicizing the economy but by emotionalizing it. HGTV's narrative formula sparks, and steers, clients' personal emotional dramas before shifting gears to reassurance. In HGTV's restoration stories, the cooling-out narrative consists of "nostalgia for the 'golden age of good old-fashioned capitalism' and a return to the bubble!"[19] Those who felt the wrath of the mortgage market collapse suffered not just financial loss but also emotional traumas that devastated families and neighborhoods. HGTV puts to rest emotional traumas that have preceded the renovation, first by repressing and erasing, then by compensating with an excess of emotional packaging.

Men's Hard Work, Nostalgia, and a Labor Theory of Justice

While HGTV attracts more women and emphasizes the critical importance of design and décor labor in generating renovation value, Scripps Networks' other channel, DIY, brings men's labor back into the discussion for a more masculine audience profile. DIY programs focus less on renovation and flipping, but rather tend toward salvaging and building anew. *Barnwood Builders* conjures up a mythology of rugged, problem-solving settlers and pioneers who overcame their environs with hand tools and technologies of wood and stone. "The television show follows the adventures of a group of West Virginia master builders as they deconstruct centuries-old buildings and re-craft them into modern buildings."[20] Every *Barnwood Builders* episode offers up moralizing discourses that heroize the practices of pioneer forebears while lamenting contemporary laziness and wastefulness. During a season three episode, a team member recovers giant nails from a barn being taken apart. In a moment of forensic speculation, he reflects on the builders of the cabin they are deconstructing. "It's amazing that they had to make everything. The logs, they had to carve the rocks off of the cliff over there, and they had to make these nails out of an old piece of scrap horseshoe or something they had laying around. They didn't let anything go to waste. Nowadays people throw so much away; it's a shame."[21] He joins an admiration of self-sufficiency to an ethic of stewardship of natural resources bolstered by a dual ethic of conservation and conservatism.

Unlike the HGTV shows that imagine a geography of nowhere, *Barnwood Builders* embraces the specificity of its locality and announces its West Virginia chauvinism with a proud self-embrace as hillbillies. As defined on the show, being a hillbilly signifies a man of moral character who gives 100 percent to his work and to his mates, a man who gets the job done no matter what the obstacle, a man who knows how to solve problems. Mark Bowe, the proprietor of Barnyard Living and host of *Barnwood Builders*, offers homespun aphorisms and philosophical observations about the quality of work, comradeship, and respect for old-fashioned values. The firmness of a handshake and the directness of eye contact when meeting are significant practices in this moral code. In a 2015 episode, after shaking hands with a stranger he greets near a barn site, Bowe exclaims, "I can tell by your hands that you've done hard work." In a moment of mutual recognition, they nod in agreement that their hands don't feel like "banker's hands." In their ensuing conversation, they banter about measures of wealth, with Bowe opining that "a lot of people don't get the meaning of 'rich.'" His fellow West Virginian responds that there are lots of ways to measure wealth, but "peace and happiness" are atop his list. The men reject the bankers' definitions of value as restricted to the money economy.

When Bowe greets other heavy-equipment operators doing difficult jobs in the rural mud that constitutes the usual work environment on each episode, he is apt to invoke his vision of an imagined community of hillbillies. His highest form of recognition about their shared identity occurs when he welcomes such strangers with "you're a hillbilly too!" These men are champions of a heritage ethic of white, Protestant, working-class West Virginians. The value system these Appalachian men embrace preaches solidarity with their fellow workers, stressing the camaraderie and caring that these men share: as one says, "I love doing it together with these guys." In other words, they refuse to reduce value solely to profits that accrue from salvaging barnwood and logs and transforming them into rustic-chic building materials. The barnwood builders find the highest value in their work and their lifestyle, which are to them synonymous. They locate value in the skilled and unalienated physical labor they exercise. Bowe can frequently be overheard bantering with other working men about the freedom and joy of choosing to work outdoors in the midst of nature, as opposed to the alienation of being "imprisoned in an office" or "toiling away at a desk in a cubicle." Their shared commitment to an ethic of hard work and working with their hands fits well with their desire for unalienated work. The show unifies their experience of unalienated labor with the egalitarian ethos that emerges from their fraternal order.[22]

The exchange about how to read a man's hands situates hillbilly labor as more honest than that of the privileged classes. Hard work is honest work, respectable work. The soft hands of bankers are evidence that bankers have not used their hands to create value. This moral distinction between material labor (hard, calloused hands) and unproductive labor (soft, smooth hands) stands in sharp contrast to most of what appears on home renovation TV. Especially when set against the backdrop of the 2008 recession, this can be read as a revalidation of old-school labor and the rebuilding of an honest salvage economy—or what these men might see as a moral economy. In an off-camera interview, Bowe speaks to his company's ethical policy about who they hire, work with, and work for: "We try to hire people who are kind and hardworking. That's about it—you've got to have a good work ethic and be a kind human being. Everything else is learnable. We have a 'no assholes' policy. We don't hire people who aren't nice. We won't do jobs for people who aren't nice. We won't buy from them, and we won't sell to them."[23]

Part of Bowe's running commentary each week has to do with his ability to size up a barn and evaluate whether taking it apart will cost more than the parts can fetch in the marketplace. He does not eschew the measured realities of markets at all, yet the show does not dwell on, or even mention, the monetary valuations realized from the product of the team's labor. One senses that his company's margins are tight, but money is not their only measure of value, so they abstain from the alienated language of money that measures real estate value in dollar amounts. Bowe acknowledges that the TV show gives their margins a bit of a buffer: "When it's over we'll just have to reach a little deeper and figure out how we're going to keep making a living doing what we like. We're always thinking about it, and we've got some ideas. We've got a furniture line coming out. We've got a line of tiny houses."[24]

The code words that recur throughout *Barnwood Builders* episodes construct a deep narrative that needs to be situated vis-à-vis the 2008 financial crisis. Their sincere admiration of the heritage construction practices of their Appalachian forebears impels Mark and his team to model their business after their idea of what that ethos looked like. Hence, they have fashioned for themselves a business founded on being independent producers committed to a moral code that embraces authenticity, hard work, honesty, perseverance, physicality, reliability, kindness, and being there for one's brothers. This ethos hearkens back to nineteenth-century ideologies of craft producers and mechanics who confronted the deskilling of their labor that accompanied the growing power of industrial capitalists and their control of workplaces. In the nineteenth century, workers sought to defend their status as craft producers against the control of industrial bosses. Instead of bowing down to bosses, they chose to safeguard their dignity by adopting a code of manliness ("a 'manly posture' toward the boss") rooted in "a mutualistic ethic of 'unselfish brotherhood'" and a "defiant egalitarianism which put the producer-craftsmen on the same plane as the capitalist-manufacturer."[25]

The barnwood builders are not just fans of their nineteenth-century laboring ancestors; they also endeavor to take a page from that history. Following the 2008 banking crisis that imperiled the well-being of hardworking women and men and their families, these men made a choice that privileges independent, hard work over the exploitation and vulnerability of industrial wage labor. Consider again the conversation about the respect these men have for the calloused hands that go along with honest work as opposed to the hands of bankers who cannot be trusted. It is almost as if this is the underlying message of *Barnwood Builders*—you cannot trust the money exchangers, those who seek only to extract value from the circulation and capture of money as opposed to those who produce material value with their hands and their backs. Honest labor produces honest value rooted in a moral code, while the effort to sidestep labor yields only the mirage of distorted values.

There is a moment of contestation in *Barnwood Builders* episodes about what constitutes value and how it might be measured. Yet by the end of each episode this critique has been folded back within the framework of commodity fetishism that is the raison d'être of HGTV and DIY channels. Their pride of work and their pride of product is sold in turn around the newly minted fetish for barnwood chic that the show seeks to burnish. In each episode, a formulaic detour takes Bowe away from his crew to visit artisans and entrepreneurial craftsmen dedicated to turning reclaimed wood into fine furniture and woodwork. These visits allow Bowe to promote a wider barnwood industry and a consumer market for barnwood by selling us on an aesthetic that joins the rustic textures of recovered wood with relics of industrial metal. Other weeks, he visits cabins that have been newly framed by barn logs that his crew salvaged. These rebuilds reflect extraordinary craftsmanship, along with modernist sensibilities about mixing materials. Stunning, rurally sited modernist architecture mixes barnwood with salvaged metal and stone that pays homage to the materials from the past while promoting the artisanship of contemporary craftsmen and artists. There represents a curious merger of praise for working-class values with finished products that reflect the development of contemporary bourgeois aesthetics and rural gentrification. No less than his HGTV counterparts, Bowe ends up selling a commodity aesthetic premised on the recycling and upcycling of nostalgic signifiers.

Artisan Labor—Simulating History

Barnwood Builders' work crew is made up of skilled woodworkers who perform exacting salvages and rebuilds. Johnny Jett, a grizzled, devoutly Christian member of the crew is weekly lauded for his virtuoso skills as a heavy-machine operator, especially cranes and forklifts. Jett is defined as a man who possesses artistic and artisan skills, it's just that one of his tools of choice is one of industrial capitalism's mechanized behemoths—a machine associated with multiplying human efficiency and productivity, but without soul. Sherman Thompson, another member of the work team, also demonstrates expert skill making precision notch cuts with a chainsaw, an outdoorsman's tool, another automated tool that we rarely associate with artisanship or virtuosity. Artisanship here represents a dedication to the quality of work, along with pride of ownership. As virtuosos, each man performs his labor solo—it doesn't hurt that television cameras are there to bear witness to the performance. Each man confronts a challenging material task. Thus motivated, his adept performance tames the task at hand, and he gains the admiration of his fellows.[26]

Clint Harp performs as the resident persona of artisan labor on *Fixer Upper*—whenever Joanna wants a custom table made, she turns to Harp to craft a weighty showpiece made of reclaimed wood for the home she is designing. *Fixer Upper* (and all its imitators) maintains a small cadre of local artisans who are introduced to execute a Joanna Gaines custom design concept. The genealogy of artisan labor on television goes back to the now venerable *This Old House* franchise (a didactic show that followed the tools and skills necessary to remodel high-end homes without ever talking about how much value was added). Consistent with the ethos of *This Old House*, Harp never speaks about his furniture as commodities, and Joanna gifts these pieces to the client families, whereas all the other commodified furniture pieces used to stage the big reveal goes back to the company after the cameras leave. This connection between artisan labor and a gift economy is no accident.

On *Fixer Upper*, the customized, one-of-a-kind dining room table is treated as a material signifier of the sanctity and centrality of family life. In Joanna's vision of the forever dream home, the imposing presence of a rustic-mediated dining room table establishes a shrine to the unification of heritage, family, and home. Her particular stylistic treatment of how to marry the character of antique styles to modern aesthetics is a testament to the feminine power that imagines it, designs it, and sets it. After scrubbing the house of its past, a legacy of inheritance must be invented. A home that is now without a history must be given one. Recognizing the home as a site for making new memories, Joanna lets her imagination of an older way of life, rooted in place and family, redefine the modern home as a site for the constitution of familial bonds and memories. While the imagination and care that empower such heritage artifacts are feminine, the finished product appears excessively masculine. The solidity and weight of these tables adds substance to equations of place making, signaling the achievement of petit-bourgeois affluence and status while also introducing a symbolic restoration of a renewed social order focused around the dining table. The handmade heft of these tables suggests the opposite of globalization with its production of disposable furniture. Symbolically, this gift that she bequeaths to each homeowner represents a recentering of family life, a hopeful reassertion of family and faith as durable and lasting relationships that must transcend the fungibility of the commodity.

On the DIY channel, artisan restoration expert Jeff Devlin hosts *Stone House Revival*, a show about venerating and restoring historical homes in Pennsylvania. Devlin introduces himself by declaring that his "job is to save history." When a homeowner asks him to "bring the history back to this place," the artisan strategy for saving history relies on semiosis and simulation. Devlin explains that installing "Shaker-style cabinets will give it a historical feel," so he adds pegs "to make it feel rustic." A few simple carpenter tricks are added for appearance, enabling the craftsman to dissimulate the feel of history as a means of preserving it. As always with questions of representation, there is a difference between the sign and the thing it represents. The TV craftsman reproduces a fine simulation of the look of history, further confusing the category of history with its mode of signification. He reproduces history by knowing the coding rules: want to feel rustic, use pegs.

TV artisanship pitches itself as purposive labor, the aim of which is to combine function with feeling. Artisanship and craftsmanship as they are represented on television signify a desire for authenticity along with a sincerity of purpose unsullied by the motivations of commercial standardization. Shows like *Good Bones, Fixer Upper, Nashville Flipped, Barnwood Builders, Rehab Addict,* and *Stone House Revival* are imagined antidotes to the celebration of surfaces over depth even though they perpetuate a fixation on surfaces that offer the illusion of depth. Ideologically, artisan labor and craft labor suggest a moral attitude of dedication, skill, and commitment to artifice—the authentic recreation of enduring value. The performance of artisan labor on HGTV and DIY lends itself to the impression that an alternative commodity aesthetics represents a higher, truer form of value than is available in the morass of commodification itself because it is capable of customized effects.

Another quasi-artisanal labor form has to do with salvage and the mainstreaming of bricolage. Dick Hebdige adapts Claude Lévi-Strauss's concept of bricolage to show how punk culture rearranged conventional signifiers and signifieds to contest the hegemony of commodity culture. Celeste Olalquiaga hails the vitality of postmodern culture that built on a cultural economy of kitsch, a reordering of signification that played on the afterlife of commodities.[27] HGTV abandons the era of postmodern kitsch for the midcentury-modern aesthetics of shabby chic, farmhouse modernism, and rustic industrial, but it has not abandoned the principles of recombinant aesthetics—expressed here as apolitical bricolage. It surrenders the political contestation of commodity culture, seeking instead to appropriate the imagination of the bricoleur to discover new veins of novel commodity values. Drawing from the well of salvage economies—antique malls, flea markets, and architectural salvage bars—the theme of salvaging and repurposing objects into creatively unpredictable mash-ups runs through a range of salvage and renovation programming from *Salvage Dawgs, Home Town, Fixer Upper, Good Bones,* and *Rehab Addict*. The language here is about creativity, upcycling, and repurposing. On shows like *Good Bones* and *Home Town*, unlocking value from scraps whose value has been spent and even abandoned offers a testimonial on how new value can be made affordable, and it can be found everywhere. *Flea Market Flip*'s value creation contest premised on repurposing scraps from the commodity afterlife is, however, a feeder back into alienated commodity culture: when that rusted trough gets upcycled into a shiny coffee table and sells for a profit, we can be assured that mass-produced knockoffs of steampunk coffee tables will soon be available at Wayfair.com.

The Invisible Labor of Agents, Brokers, and Financiers

On HGTV, real estate agents maintain a relatively unobtrusive profile. This may seem odd given that the real estate industry revolves around buying and selling properties. Though television flippers hurriedly allude to the vagaries of closing costs, the work of buying and selling real estate takes place in an off-screen universe. Market transactions and conflictual price negotiations tend to be invisible. Real estate agents on HGTV renovation shows generally seek to soften market forces by assuming the role of Realtor-as-friend who tours houses with clients and gently manages the emotional balance between desire and possibility. A running joke on promos for *Property Brothers* revolves around the brothers' sibling rivalry, with Jonathan poking fun at Drew the real estate agent: "What do you do?" Apparently, his work is so immaterial and abstract that it is unseen. Indeed, this is how HGTV wishes it to be. Similarly, on *Fixer Upper* the decision to select a home is functionally equivalent to buying it: wish for it and it is yours. It's not magic; the absence of negotiations is because clients have generally secured the house before they ever come on the show. But that merely begs the issue. On *Flip or Flop*, the formula abbreviates an initial price offer into a phone call to the disembodied voice of an intermediary agent who relays the offer to a seller. It might as well be an ATM, it's that automated and routine. Still, at the very least, *Flip or Flop* shares with viewers an oversimplified set of calculations used by its host to divine an appropriate offering price for a property if he is to garner a profit after renovation. Because these deals too have already been secured in advance, El Moussa never fails to make a winning offer. Almost the only time viewers see the active performance of transactional labor on HGTV is on *Texas Flip N Move* when an auctioneer solicits bids for properties at public auction, but even this is staged.

Why does HGTV obscure the labor of financial transactions? Supposedly, the art of the deal lies at the heart of success in financial markets these days. The highest compensations and bonuses in the neoliberal system are often associated with bankers, financiers, investors, and arbitrageurs. Yet bankers, loan officers, and mortgage brokers are banished from the shows. On the feel-good side of HGTV's renovation shows, the exposure of the more crassly alienated elements of buying and selling might tarnish the emotional investments that make the remoralization of value in gentrifying real estate projects so appealing. Expose the inner machinations of these market transactions and we are left with a callous cash nexus. While value may be everything in the HGTV universe, haggling over money carries dirty connotations.

Cloaking the financial side of the mortgage economy is a choice that HGTV continued to make following the collapse of mortgage markets in 2008. HGTV could have chosen a very different route to reality TV—make transparent the role of financial decision makers and their institutions in residential real estate markets. While television ads for Rocket Mortgage, Lending Tree, and Quicken Loans claim to empower consumers shopping for loans via the transparency of their online platforms, a truer transparency might compromise the power of banks to pick and choose who gets loans and who gets which interest rates. Simulated transparency facilitates the HGTV narrative of remoralized markets, while opening up the accountability of banks and lenders might compromise the story—reminding viewers that all loan applicants are not created equal and that, indeed, opportunities to participate in the processes of wealth production hinge on far more than desire.

Not only is financing a key precondition for buying a home; its absence is also the most important structural limit on building value through home ownership. HGTV narratives suppress the real-world interactions between banks, discriminatory lending practices, and gentrification. When African American households were systematically denied access to capital to repair, renovate, or purchase homes in urban neighborhoods that are under pressure from developers and gentrifiers, their properties became increasingly subject to dispossession. Reporters at the *Wall Street Journal* examined 38 million loan applications dating from 2007 to 2014 and found that "the percentage of overall mortgages issued to African Americans fell to 5% from 8%, while the overall percentage of mortgages issued to Hispanics fell to 9% from 11%. During the same period, the share of loans going to whites increased by 5 percentage points, while Asians also saw their share of mortgages increase."[28] The article, "Banks' Embrace of Jumbo Mortgages Means Fewer Loans for Blacks, Hispanics," reported that big banks met government mandates to lower their risk profiles by tightening up loan requirements and relying more on jumbo mortgages, "or loans that are too expensive to be bought by Fannie Mae and Freddie Mac. These loans have been popular with lenders since the financial crisis because the wealthy borrowers who use these products have seen their incomes rise of late, while the vast majority of American workers have been struggling to improve their financial situations."[29]

Such lending practices compound swelling wealth and income disparities. In the context of urban neighborhoods undergoing revitalization, withholding loans from small borrowers while putting jumbo loans into developers' pockets boosts the likelihood that the latter can buy up discounted properties in bulk. Over the years, the material effects of disinvestment accumulate in devalued properties until they become perceived as discounted. But unlike the stories told by HGTV, these discounts are not equally available to all who wish to join this property marketplace. In fact, the banks and their sister financial institutions function as the gatekeepers of these marketplaces. Discriminatory lending blocks many working households from investing in their own neighborhoods, sometimes in the very homes in which they live. Discriminatory lending thus does not just do damage to the life chances of less privileged borrowers; it is invariably a prelude to accumulation by dispossession by those who already have access to capital.

What difference does it make that HGTV representations divert attention from a banking system that stacks the deck against middle-class and working African Americans and Hispanics (in particular) in gaining access to home loans? By quarantining questions about lending patterns, HGTV stories profoundly mystify how value, gentrification, and wealth building fit together. HGTV maintains an intentional posture of visually highlighting multiculturalism. Superficially, if we are to believe its video testimonials, HGTV embraces racial, sexual, and ethnic diversity. So too, advertisements for mortgage lenders and real estate agents don't just feature African Americans, Hispanics, Asians, single women, and interracial couples, they have recently overrepresented these demographics. But the façade of commercial multicultural imagery has been exposed by investigative reports that document continuing patterns of discrimination against African Americans and Hispanics when it comes to home loans.[30] What are we to make of the whopping gap between media representations and marketplace realities? Are these TV shows and the ads in between anything more than ideological masks? Since these stories are made to entertain, it's easy to imagine the standard response to the kind of ideology critique I suggest: "HGTV is *just* entertainment. Everybody knows that." But this is precisely Slavoj Žižek's point when he observes that "cynical reason, with all its ironic detachment, leaves untouched the fundamental level of ideological fantasy, the level on which ideology structures the social reality itself."[31]

HGTV's practiced misrecognition of a real estate market saturated in inequitable racist practices is explained by the fact that HGTV's business and media strategies aim at expanding consumer markets for the goods and services associated with home renovation. HGTV's leading advertising sponsors include retailers like Home Depot and Lowe's who have an obvious corporate self-interest in encouraging consumers to consider taking on debt to consume products for home improvements. To encourage both the consumption and the debt, firms like these offer branded credit cards. Corporate marketing today requires crafting an inviting inclusionary posture that opens up the marketplace to previously untapped demographic constituencies. In short, HGTV and its advertisers must attract an omnicultural Other if a globalizing home improvement market is to keep growing. Of course, HGTV has crafted a strategy for reconciling the difference. No one ever needs to get a loan on HGTV. No one. This is because anyone who is selected to appear has already been preapproved for a loan. Obviously, no client of color who appears on HGTV is among those who are denied financing based on race, ethnicity, or sexuality, but only 5 percent or less of the total population of African American loan applicants were approved for loans in 2016, even after controlling for income. Needless to say, those who are denied loans will never be seen on HGTV.

Debt, bankers, and loan officers may be obscured on HGTV but are given an optimistic twist in the ads. Consumer ads generally compose a site of commodity fantasies, yet in 2017 real estate and lending ads specially crafted for HGTV remind consumers to consider a wider view of "realty reality." Commercial campaigns from Chase Bank, Zillow, and Trulia Real Estate counsel consumers to keep in mind the realities of getting a loan. Trulia's campaign even includes a not-so-subtle swipe at HGTV's tunnel vision approach to video editing that cuts out surrounding social risks that might compromise the value of a house. Ads for Chase Bank gently pose the question of loans, suggesting a meeting with a banker to discuss credit and debt profiles. The mere acknowledgment that a home renovation will necessitate a bank loan stands in striking contrast to HGTV's cone of silence about banks, loans, and financing. While the subject of budgets on HGTV might prompt viewers to consider matters of affordability, without any references to interest rates, mortgage payments, and debt, the politics of bank lending remains invisible. Amid the growing popularity of *Property Brothers*, the duo entered into a 2017 advertising partnership with Chase Bank to talk about loans, still keeping the politics of debt and lending safely tucked away behind their affable TV personas to introduce viewers to a friendly female Chase home loan "expert." It is no accident that the couple seeking a loan are thirtysomething African Americans and the lending expert is an approachable young woman. In this world of soft home finance, caring and interested Chase representatives will "personalize" home finance packages to fit the needs of everyone regardless of race or sexual orientation. There are no hints here of an unforgiving lending system that relies on supposedly objective but already racially tinged credit histories to discredit African American loan applicants. The universe of HGTV and corporate ads in the wake of the 2008 mortgage market collapse appear to herald progressive reforms that claim to have freed the marketplace from its historic biases. Chase ads like this put an inclusive spin on contemporary bank practices, emphasizing the exception to the rule rather than the pattern itself. Consider that the climate for African American loan applicants darkened considerably between 2005 and 2015, dropping from 1.1 million in 2005 to 132,000 in 2015. If statistical patterns are any indicator, then the personalization of loans is more likely to refer to the fact that blacks are far less likely to be considered for conventional loans and far more likely to pay higher interest rates on the loans they do obtain.[32] The wealth gap between white and nonwhite households has expanded since the crisis and subsequent recession of 2008, and the chief factor responsible has to do with discriminatory lending practices that build off the history of segregationist and redlining practices that put nonwhite populations at a significant disadvantage.

> The disproportionate denials and limited anti-discrimination enforcement help explain why the homeownership gap between whites and African Americans, which had been shrinking since the 1970s, has exploded since the housing bust. It is now wider than it was during the Jim Crow era. This gap has far-reaching consequences. In the United States, "wealth and financial stability are inextricably linked to housing opportunity and homeownership," said Lisa Rice, executive vice president of the National Fair Housing Alliance, an advocacy group. "For a typical family, the largest share of their wealth emanates from homeownership and home equity." The latest figures from the U.S. Census Bureau show the median net worth for an African American family is $9,000, compared with $132,000 for a white family. Latino families did not fare much better at $12,000.[33]

For their part, bankers have moved the fulcrum of discrimination from subjective prejudices into a black box of proprietary credit scores, such that the accumulation of disadvantage can be justified as a result of objective economic facts. Thus, recent Rocket Mortgage ad campaigns actually overrepresent nonwhites in depicting a fully automated loan application process that visually eliminates white bankers and their surrogates from appearing to decide who gets what.

> Lenders and their trade organizations do not dispute the fact that they turn away people of color at rates far greater than whites. But they maintain that the disparity can be explained by factors the industry has fought to keep hidden, including the prospective borrowers' credit history and overall debt-to-income ratio. They singled out the three-digit credit score—which banks use to determine whether a borrower is likely to repay a loan—as especially important in lending decisions.[34]

The secret sauce of credit scores thus functions as a classification, or sorting, mechanism that reproduces the effects of discrimination on the homeowning chances of the working poor, particularly people of color. Access to credit is today dependent on "an increasingly mechanized reporting system" that supposedly works on the basis of impersonal and nonsubjective criteria. Though this yields the appearance of a "colorblind" system of determining creditworthiness, it draws on the historical record of past inequalities of race and class to "objectively" renew those inequalities of access.[35]

Histories of mortgage discrimination are thus simultaneously masked and reproduced. In particular, where class and race converge, those who are disadvantaged in the marketplace will never be seen participating in HGTV's recession-recovery narrative of securing value (wealth, equity) via home renovation and gentrification. This has not, however, deterred HGTV from featuring African American couples as the hosts of flipping shows. Nor does it block nonwhite couples—though they remain minorities—from being clients on the renovation shows—they just have to able to clear the credit score hurdles before they can appear. What HGTV and its advertisers purport to show is that we live in an era of postracial discrimination, when historical forms of discrimination seemingly dissolve away for anyone who comes on the show. There is just one obvious but unstated catch, prequalify for a home loan and one might be chosen to appear on *Property Brothers* or *Fixer Upper*, where no matter one's ethnicity or skin color, one can join the ranks of the *petit* bourgeoisie who participate in the benefits of owning property. By keeping those who cannot qualify for a loan out of sight, the crisis of home affordability is also concealed. By keeping the work of loan origination out of sight, the generation of debt that has become a linchpin of how finance capital makes its money also remains outside the conversation.

Restoring a Myth of Labor and Value

In HGTV's hierarchy of labor, the greatest contributions to the value-added equation appear to be creative labor—aesthetic and design—and entrepreneurial self-motivated labor. It should come as no surprise, however, that just as deep discounts in the purchase price of properties are key to profitable flipping, profits also depend on the wage exploitation of general construction labor. What I term ghostly labor is, in fact, the spectacle's way of simultaneously representing and not representing poorly compensated labor. Ghostly labor is the television equivalent of abstract labor.

Who are those ghostly figures kept in the shadows? Research on renovation labor pools both before and after 2008 indicates that poor and noncitizen workers, often undocumented immigrants, are overrepresented among the day laborers who perform the strenuous deskilled physical labors such as demolition, drywalling, and painting—and because of their vulnerable status, they work for wages well below what union and competitive non-union workers can command.[36] HGTV's stories permit neither the conditions of employment nor the matter of wages to rise to the surface. Television's representation of renovation labor as a shadow labor force inadvertently mirrors how "the workplace for residential renovations labor—the home—is often rendered informal and invisible."[37]

Many of the earlier TV renovation shows were Canadian—in particular, *Property Brothers* filmed a lot of its early episodes in Toronto. Thinking about *Property Brothers* in light of Michelle Buckley's Toronto studies of renovation labor suggests another possible explanation of how the hosts were always able to bring their upscale-looking renovations in on budget: the availability of low-wage laborers drawn from a pool of workers whose lives are marked by conditions of precarity. Buckley finds that Toronto renovators have been able to realize very substantial wage subsidies as a result of a differential in wage rates between the formal and informal labor markets for construction workers: a discount of between 42 percent and 57 percent. Let's suppose a $200,000 renovation budget includes a 35 percent allocation for labor costs. A 50 percent discount on labor would reduce labor costs from $70,000 to $35,000. In Toronto, "de-skilled and informalized noncitizen renovations labor" made the turn toward home renovation a viable strategy to "asset wealth-building and house buying."[38] This story is no less relevant in Waco and Los Angeles, where informal labor markets are weighted heavily toward migrant labor from Central America.

The profits secured via flipping houses become less magical when we factor in the exploitation of vulnerable pools of migrant workers in conjunction with the discounts secured on foreclosed and/or aging, deteriorating houses (especially in neighborhoods that have the potential for *petit* gentrification). Toss in smart spatial redesigns and aesthetic flair, and we can account for most of the new value to be found in renovations. But there is one more piece to accounting for stories of wealth building, and once again it is missing in HGTV's storytelling. As invisible as HGTV keeps low-wage racialized labor, it is no less vigilant at repressing the world of loans, debt, and mortgage discrimination, not to mention the structural violence imposed by the millions of foreclosures. Stories of dispossession and wealth transfer haunt the HGTV version of the American dream reborn. The same workers whose wages are suppressed in informal labor markets cannot qualify for home loans (even for homes heavily devalued by the recession) and are thus forced into rentership. Indeed, after the mortgage crisis, impoverished working-class residents condemned to renting substandard and deteriorating housing have found themselves further dispossessed by the very forces that make their neighborhoods ideal for reappropriation by rentiers and flippers who fix to rent for a bigger slice of pie. Exploited by their vulnerability in informal labor markets, dispossessed by virtue of mortgage market collapse, and structurally excluded by their credit histories from seeking their own piece of asset wealth building after 2008, the precariat seeking shelter would make for sobering reality television.

HGTV aims at the heart of individualism. Its stories often feel like a latter-day retelling of the myth of the yeoman farmer, with salvage-savvy flippers and gentrifiers cast in the starring role. It's an imperfect fit, given HGTV's reliance on the immaterial and performative labor that appears essential to the production of added value. But HGTV never allows the sturdy muscle and inventiveness of material labor forms to drift far from the scene. In fact, by casting husband-wife teams as the preferred labor unit for flipping value, a division of labor between material and immaterial labor can be preserved, and with it the myth of heroic labor that produces value without exploiting anyone else is also salvaged. Revisioning the myth of the yeoman farmer, like the myth of neoliberal individualism, relies on refusing to recognize those whose lives have been made insecure by the precarity of their labor and the uncertainty of their living situations.

Throughout this book I have chosen to stress a value theory of labor rather than the more familiar labor theory of value. Marx's study of capital emphasizes the commodity form as the organizing logic of capital and value as capital's unceasing pursuit. Writing during the nineteenth century, Marx asked why the constitution of value depended so heavily on the organization of labor. Today, we ought to ask why the constitution of value leans so deliberately on the organization of technology and finance. Four decades ago, Diane Elson persuasively critiqued the notion that Marx championed a labor theory of value, theorizing instead that Marx's study of capital's *value form* centered on a value theory of labor.[39] Elson's recovery of a value theory of labor draws out the distinction that capitalism's *value form* is not an unbending statue but rather takes shape historically within each era, subject to its own internal contradictions. Today's capitalism continues to require a value theory of labor, but one that is set in relation to value theories of technological innovation, of debt, and of signs. "As capitalism changes, so too will the way in which value operates."[40] Chapter 8 contrasts HGTV's mythology of a value form associated with our past with the new rules of a value form that now encircles the financialization of housing.

8

Masking the New Rules of Value

Man is no longer man enclosed, but man in debt.
—Gilles Deleuze, "Postscript on the Societies of Control"

Operating as a camera obscura, HGTV tweaks, bends, and warps narratives of value that circulate throughout our culture. Nonetheless, home renovation TV expresses important cultural themes and anxieties for the era surrounding the housing mortgage crisis, even if it does so, as the spectacle often tends to do, in ways that emotionally reroute our cultural anxieties and desires into commodity form, redirecting them back into commodity consumption. HGTV's format hails viewers with an appealing narrative that reinforces what Lauren Berlant has dubbed "cruel optimism," which she describes as an attachment to desires that may actually be counterproductive to the realization of those very desires and turn instead into "an obstacle to your flourishing."[1] Despite all the signals that neoliberal market societies have become less conducive to supporting the dream of the happily-ever-after home built on a foundation of emotional economic stability, HGTV tells and retells a fairy tale of capturing an eternally appreciating asset and thus realizing true social security.

A central HGTV narrative is one of nostalgia for an American residential paradise made more modern—for a past made present achieved through updating fetish pieces from modernity's ideological and material catalog. The story it tells is one of navigating the flipping marketplace without ever encountering those who have been displaced and turned into renters, or worse, the houseless. It weaves together a story of gentrification as a personal investment strategy, not as urban policy. The tales HGTV spins are not just about homes but about unlocking the conditions of speculative value that lie in those housing stocks, and crucially, its shows are about remoralizing (think Émile Durkheim) a shifting landscape of access to single-family residences. Indeed, these are stories about salvaging homes in disrepair while also salvaging the morality of a badly tarnished market that has become challenging to decipher. As allegories about value, HGTV's narratives come together in the braid of the big reveal at every episode's finale: value lies in the realization of spectacular instant equity; value lies in the personal freedom that comes with unfettered open space designed with you in mind; value lies in a familial ethics that equates home and love (a condition that ought universally to be the case, if only housing became a human right, as opposed to being treated exclusively as a commodity).

No less telling are the narratives left out. In the years leading up to the financial crisis, home ownership was a key piece of the much-touted George W. Bush ownership society, presented as a bulwark against an increasingly precarious landscape of everyday life in globalized capitalist societies—a landscape characterized by uncertain and casualized labor, accompanied by a rising tide of debt amid the burdens of privatizing social reproduction costs. Because all of HGTV's stories are dictated by predetermined narrative formulas, the bias of one show is the bias of every show in that series, such that the ideological and affective weight accumulates with viewings. HGTV's frames are not unmotivated, the network has a commercial interest in selling more products for house and home, and its interests are aligned with those of the real estate industry, so it's unsurprising that HGTV chooses to exclude household tragedies of subprime loans and the foreclosures that trailed behind. Themes of precarity and affordable housing do not mix well, so HGTV removes without a trace the culpability of those who pillage speculative housing markets. The strategy of this book is to make such sociological and financial absences weigh heavy on HGTV's story, rather than allowing their erasure to go unnoticed.

It's no accident that HGTV turns a blind eye to the discrepancy between the woes of debt borne by the household and the financial benefits of debt when it falls into the hands of financial speculators. Because personal debt connotes disorder and moral defect, its utterance is forbidden on HGTV, its place taken by the more disciplined and reasoned calculation of the budget.[2] By 2008, measures of total household debt, which had been climbing for years, peaked at 98 percent of U.S. gross domestic product (GDP).[3] That's not a misprint. While economists recognized this as unsustainable for the long haul, finance capital saw in this condition of household indebtedness an opportunity for generating more enticing rates of profit by packaging the debt, slicing and reassembling it into bonds priced by their degree of default risk. The greater the risk, the greater the yield. How much of this total was mortgage indebtedness? In the fourth quarter of 2008, the ratio of mortgage debt to total household indebtedness (which includes student loans, credit card debt, medical debt, and auto loans) stood at 79.4 percent. At that time, mortgage debt was the prime candidate for repackaging into the securities known as CDOs.

While the financial industry's strategy aimed to leverage the accumulation of households' debt into high-yield investments, homeowners as consumers bought into their own role in spiraling pursuits of stunted value. Buoyed by the perception that housing prices just seemed to go up and up, homeowners who had seen wages and salaries stagnate for years sought their piece of the wealth pie by jumping into the remortgage market. There are surely many reasons for taking out second mortgages, but the two most popular motives from 2001 to 2006 were (1) to convert existing home equity into a line of credit that could reopen channels for general consumption, thus supplementing wages; and (2) as a means of financing home renovations that might yield higher returns in the booming housing markets—flipping. The rules governing the refinance market were fast and loose during this time—home appraisers working with the loan industry would miraculously appraise house after house at just the right valuation necessary for the home loan to come in on target. The narrative of value was that it could be what you wanted it to be. Anything was possible. "American mortgage indebtedness" drove economic growth and the real estate bubble, and converting equity into debt bolstered the market for durable-goods consumption. This stimulus to the economy was the product of an intensified "acceleration in household indebtedness and a sharp decline in savings."[4]

Every binge has a downside though—homeowners gave up equity in their houses to inflate their personal consumer credit balloons and thus became more vulnerable to the debt monster. By 2007, appraised values had lost all measure of relationship to the risks of default. If homeowners were using the equity of their homes as a replacement for wages and salaries, how were they going to pay off the loans? At best, they were pulled into the vortex of perpetual debt while the risks of default escalated. As the rate of home mortgage defaults inched past 8 percent in the autumn of 2007, the riskier tranches of mortgage-backed bonds began to collapse.

Governing Credit, Trading Debt: Who Gets to Play?

In addition to lots of low-wage jobs, the accumulation of debt has been a pivotal force fueling the wealth gap. For the individual household, debt has become a necessary burden, especially in the wake of government deregulation of markets and the privatization of benefits. The latter in particular, coming during an era when economic prospects were dimming, leaves individual households holding the bag when it comes to absorbing social reproduction costs—education, health, transportation, and so on. To investment bankers, household debt beckons as a risk asset that once securitized can pay handsome dividends, while for most workers debt means the constant anxiety of chasing the interest payment cycle. The havoc that followed the 2008 tsunami of mortgage defaults further contributed to a transfer of wealth from the working class to those who had cash to accumulate portfolios of distressed homes. Enabled by debt, this transfer of home ownership has changed the landscape of power over the housing economy. The securitization machine, which went so terribly awry, was not simply a momentary excursion into greed; it has rather become a deeply rooted feature of the neoliberal investment system.

Decades of job insecurity, burgeoning inequality, and a disappearing safety net have magnified doubts about the fairness of capitalist markets and made households more vulnerable to debt. A crisis of faith about how to share in the opportunities for value acquisition that have fueled economic inequality and the wealth gap has been amplified by the fact that finance capital's newfound methods of extracting value remain mysterious to the vast majority of the working population. By contrast, HGTV recommends a new coat of paint to restore the luster of value and nostalgia for a restored past as the path to finding a place among the value privileged. While HGTV's programming suppresses discussion of debt, its advertising interest lies with promoting big-ticket items to its audience via retailers such as Home Depot, Lowe's, and Wayfair, whose business models depend on consumers who buy on credit. HGTV shares their commitment to encouraging a structural tendency toward overconsumption—not only consumption that tends to exceed savings rates but aggregate consumption that must expand each year if economic growth rates are to be sustained.

While debt doesn't exist on HGTV, credit score ads do. They run frequently, a reminder of the true business at hand. Credit score ads aim to dispel mistrust of the unseen machinations that govern consumer credit score calculations that may have injurious consequences for borrowers. Individuals' credit and debt histories have emerged as crucial variables influencing how well households do in the broad consumer economy. The history of capitalism can be viewed as a train of increasingly dense institutional practices that channel and integrate the laboring classes into commodity dependency for addressing their reproductive needs. In the nineteenth century, wage labor enforced the hegemony of universal currency, rerouting the fulfillment of household needs through the social practices of the commodity form, structurally enforcing individualism.[5] As the weight of consumerism began to dominate everyday life in the twentieth century, consumer credit (as opposed to capital credit) took shape, expanding the range of commodification. Credit eventually took on an institutional presence that has turned it into a powerful mode of subsumption, every bit as structurally imposing as wage labor has been over social life. No one questions any longer the centrality of credit in our lives, it's a given. Whereas once we worked to live (old-fashioned, uncomplicated alienated labor), now we work to pay off the creditors on whom we depend to live (an elastic, more sublimated alienated labor).

By masking the allocation of life chances, HGTV can portray an emotionally charged narrative of how well-being can come to fruition in the renovation of spaces marked as safe and secure and dedicated to the pursuit of self-fulfillment. HGTV elects to gloss over the rules of bureaucratized discrimination that determine who has been selected to the everlasting life of a repurposed space, as opposed to who has been condemned to the everlasting hell of cost-burdened rentership. Those rules are governed by how one's credit scores have been assembled, marked, and used.[6] An individual's profile is gathered without the voluntary consent of the individual, and yet such data have become central to the governance of the consumer credit system and the management of debt relationships. "For households, this absorption of financial system risk is increasingly just part of daily life—incidental to consuming and paying bills—in the way that producing surplus value is thought incidental to wage labor."[7] Information gathered about the individual is translated into a mathematical quotient, a metric of a person's history of taking on and repaying debts. Credit reports thus signal a gatekeeper function of making loans available, or not, on the basis of a surveilled credit history record. The FICO credit score became the linchpin that binds the assessment of personal risk of credit default to the system of securitization in both mortgage-backed and rent-backed forms.[8]

Whereas HGTV's stories are sincere in tone, credit report ads adopt amusing tones aimed at lowering anxiety thresholds about credit scores. As the Great Recession settled in, a 2009 television ad campaign for Free CreditReport.com chose dark humor to narrate the housing consequences of a mismanaged credit score. The message takes the form of a song by a young passive-aggressive troubadour who fronts a jingle-pop band, practicing in his in-law's cramped basement while his wife tries to maneuver around him to do the laundry. She's not a happy camper. The ad presents a story never told on HGTV: a young man bemoans his fate of not being able to live in a "respectable home" (dream house) in a "pleasant suburb" because he married his "dream girl" without doing due diligence about her credit history. If he had properly paid attention to her credit history, encapsulated in that report, he might have heeded the power of commodified personal financial data and made a different mating choice—"I'd be a happy bachelor with a dog and a yard." That considerations of credit scores should intrude into our decision making about who to include in our family life is insidious but sung with a rhyme. Sociologically, there's a lot going on in this claustrophobic scene space: he symbolizes the casual subject of the gig economy, contributing little but a ditty of complaint while she performs unpaid, and (to her) unwanted, domestic labor. Perhaps the ad imagines this as her penance for failing her debt obligations. Discursively, the ad reaffirms that "debt produces a specific morality" that has consequences. "The creditor's power over the debtor very much resembles Foucault's last definition of power: an action carried out on another action, an action that keeps the person over which power is exercised 'free.'"[9]

FICO credit scores represent a calculation that summarizes the quality of an individual's credit profile history. They are a means of surveilling consumers, monitoring their creditworthiness, and determining who gets what in terms of loans. The ads aim at reassuring consumers that they can view their own surveillance files without fear and suggest that knowing one's credit scores can enable individuals to empower themselves in the credit marketplace by learning how to manage their scores more effectively. In this way, FICO scores are turned from surveillance into a means of self-discipline, and a nontransparent form of governing stratification hierarchies gets normalized. Just as in the ad, "the credit score's algorithmic gaze incriminates the subject, while absolving the framing device, the credit score."[10] Normalizing the credit score as a just means of governing life chances throws responsibility for unhappy outcomes back on the negligent consuming subject, while the categorization of consumers through classificatory instruments such as FICO credit scores offers a self-policing tool for self-responsibility. In our neoliberal society, these so-called unbiased instruments sort consumers into the equivalent of self-reinforcing class rankings that become restrictive of individuals' life chances by marking them with their histories of debt and repayment. "By enabling and facilitating the differential pricing of people, scoring has expanded the reach of the market while opening the door to new forms of classification with powerful stratifying effects."[11]

HGTV surely recognizes that drawing attention to consumer debt does not serve its immediate market interests. Still, the manner in which it veils the commodity chain of credit-debt-securitization effects a significant allegorical accomplishment, the substitution of a romantic fairy tale about finding a way to live outside the relations of commodity dependency and vulnerability that daunt the greater number of us. What it offers instead is a picture of how to be a moral entrepreneur in an era of neoliberalism when most people are forced to take on more and more risks in the marketplace that finance capital can then harness to its new instruments of value extraction. HGTV's argument for an ethics of self-governance presents moral entrepreneurship as a route to salvation in the housing market.[12]

HGTV's efforts to remoralize the neoliberal real estate market resolutely avoids mentioning the amorality of a financial system that routinely values abstractions of abstractions (derivatives) over the human subjects who are squeezed out of the market. To be sure, when HGTV pictures consumers in poses that accord them agency and control—opting for the imagery of moral entrepreneurs and investors—there is some truth to this as a statement of class privilege, yet it ignores home buyers toward the lower, and the racialized, end of the income and credit spectrum who are actively denied the resources that might make them candidates for moral entrepreneurship. Obnoxious as it may be, the entitlement displayed by clients on *Property Brothers* corresponds to something real—those who make it past the credit bureau gatekeepers and the HGTV selection process are at least permitted the appearance of greater agency. In a rapidly changing economy in which following the old rules of production and value doesn't necessarily seem to hold anymore, the entrepreneurial rules of renovated value are couched in the depoliticized language of lifestyle. One must, in this narrative, take reassurance from the aura of affect because if there are any economic rules to be gleaned from HGTV concerning the rational calculation of wealth building, they reside in a mysterious black box shrouded by visual effects.

Rejiggering the Conditions of Value

It's time to step back and reflect on some of the theoretical questions that have animated my study. In the midst of the financialization revolution, and particularly the securitization of debt, Maurizio Lazzarato has urged that we rethink "the principles of valuation, the ways in which we understand the value of value."[13] I elected to study HGTV's discourses of renovation and flipping because it opened a window for me to situate questions about value in the wake of the 2008 mortgage crisis from the vantage points of both commodity semiotics and finance capital. How value has been ideologically recast in the realm of home ownership after the crisis requires a deeper understanding of changes in the political economy of value. Using HGTV as a lens for joining the study of a discursive economy of value with a political economy of value also opens up considerations of how the spectacle of HGTV as discourse and semiotic framework has itself become folded into a wider political economy of value.

A prominent question circulating within political economy both before and after the crisis concerns whether, and if so how, the structural mechanics of capitalism's value-extracting engines have changed with the rapid ascendance of finance capital in the global capitalist system. David Harvey reminds us that capital's value form "is not a still and stable fulcrum ... but a constantly changing and unstable metric being pushed hither and thither" by a multitude of historical forces, including the sweeping transformations wrought by digital technologies in the spheres of finance, production, and circulation, along with the full integration of sign economies into the core systems of capital accumulation (including capital markets themselves).[14]

Moments of crisis illuminate the moving contradictions of the "category of value itself" and focus attention on the fact that value is not simply "a 'good' that labor produces ... but rather, is the organizing principle of capital, and the essence of the commodity-form that wealth takes in capitalism."[15] Its reorganization has been in play over the past several decades. While the exploitation of low-wage labor remains essential to the profitability of capitalist agriculture, outsourced manufacturing, a plethora of service sector businesses, and even the home renovation industry, labor power does not offer the only route to the acquisition of surplus value. In fact, though necessary, it no longer seems to be the most lucrative route. How are we to make sense of the relationships between neoliberal globalism, salvage accumulation, high-tech knowledge economies, and the runaway train of securitization atop the finance system? The world of HGTV is sublimely insulated from the forces of contemporary capitalism; it's like a Disney World pavilion dedicated to journeying through the historical mythos of capitalism as if it were an eternal present extending backward and forward in time. Such a pavilion would, of course, avoid as much as possible the financial mining operations of its corporate sponsorship, say a Goldman Sachs. Four integrated relationships define the loop of value extraction when finance capital seeks to migrate its focus from the sphere of production to the sphere of circulation: (1) Risk has become a prime asset (2) that is rooted in methods of organizing credit/debt relationships (3) so that value may be pursued in speculative bets on future prices (4) that are dependent on the ability to transform risk into a liquid asset that yields surplus value by circulating and recirculating its permutations through the churning motors of electronic exchange.[16]

Risk has vaulted to the top of the most potentially profitable assets when converted into financial derivatives that give it liquidity and make it tradable. Ivan Ascher succinctly observes that for those who buy and sell securities, "risk, rather than labor, is now considered the fount of Value."[17] In the same vein, the writings of Dick Bryan and Michael Rafferty focus on risk shifting as one of the broad consequences of neoliberal marketization policies that push risks onto the backs of individuals and their households. To mine and convert this risk into value requires the financial vision to imagine the multiple dimensions of household wealth and expenditure that could be made profitable: to create a spectrum of liquid financial market assets built on the performance of (illiquid) household assets. Central to this process has been the securitization of household payments: a process of bundling up payments on loans . . . on insurance . . . on rent, and on utilities . . . and selling the income streams (the monthly payments) into global markets, but without selling the underlying asset. These are called asset-backed securities (ABS); those related specifically to mortgages are called mortgage-backed securities (MBSs). They involve selling the liquid dimension of households' exposures: not the fixity (the house) but the mortgage payment.[18]

MBSs constitute our era's most leveraged expression to date of what Karl Marx calls the "real subsumption" of the labor process[19]—in its most recent iteration, this is a technology of finance that structurally integrates the daily lives of the laboring classes into the machinery of capital. Wage labor may actually contribute less value for the goods it produces than for the generalized debt it incurs and the monthly bills that it must pay. In the financialized system, labor's role in the immediate production of goods and services ceases to be the most lucrative source of value, but labor's wages become a coveted asset when channeled through a system that converts debt payments into revenue streams that feed returns on investments in securities markets. To make this work requires the collection and storage of data about credit and debt risk, which are then put through the wringer of mathematical models to predict the probabilities of how to shape portfolios (assemblages) of debt that are worth leveraging and at what odds—the greater the risk, the higher the odds, and the greater the payoff.[20] Within this system, credit scores have evolved as the critical mechanism that integrates wage labor into these calculations of finance.[21] Under financialization, investors can thus harness the carrying capacity of household debt to open up new veins of "financial expropriation."

> Financialisation of advanced capitalist economies during the last three decades represents expansion of the sphere of circulation, while the sphere of production has continued to face difficulties of profitability and productivity growth. . . . The financial sector has become capable of extracting profit directly out of wages and salaries, a process called financial expropriation.[22]

In this regard, "the reproduction of labor power is itself a source of surplus value, in the form of interest payments."[23] Just as one's personal financial history is appropriated, compiled, and sold to construct and enforce FICO credit scores, so too one's personal debt stream is appropriated without permission and without compensation. Financialization does not eliminate capitalism's reliance on wage labor's capacity to produce value; it augments it by turning labor-at-rest into an additional lever for extracting surplus value. This is where the intersection with neoliberal policy has been so critical—clearing away state supports for the reproduction of labor mandates that a household's reproduction be turned into commodities. Labor's reproduction thus becomes ever more susceptible to, and further integrated into, the debt streams that are convertible into capital assets.

Bryan summarizes in theoretical language the pitch that HGTV has been presenting about the fixer-upper: "for workers, stagnant and falling living standards (an increase in the cost of reproducing labor power) created a clear message: the way to increase living standards is not via wage labor, but by claiming part of the surplus—that is, borrowing to purchase assets, and waiting for the asset values to appreciate."[24] Thus encouraged to join in the rush to cash in on the appreciation of real estate assets, workers were incentivized to diminish their vulnerability as wage labor by taking on the risks of capital in the reproductive sphere of the household. This is precisely what HGTV has been urging people to try. Instant equity is code for that ecstatic moment when the individual qua household joins in what it feels like to be an appropriator of value. With this payoff in mind, what HGTV lets slide is the double appropriation of labor's capacity for contributing to surplus value—both as wage labor to further the production of value and as bill payer to augment the return on value (to others) via circulation. Instead, HGTV presents labor qua capital as the triumph of the entrepreneurial spirit.

Liquidity is not a naturally occurring phenomenon, it must be discursively produced. The early history of capitalism required the abstraction of money to function as a universal equivalent that permitted otherwise incommensurable utilities to enter into an equivalence exchange. Trading in financial risk requires the creation of another type of a mutually acceptable fiction among traders—namely, a fiction of liquidity constructed via abstractions of risk that allow otherwise incommensurable risks to be treated as comparable. By definition, derivatives do not reference any actually existing commodity; rather, they are "socially imaginary objects" that signify abstracted predictions of risk and reward fabricated according to the specifications of mathematicised models and formulas.[25] Indeed, derivatives and securities become so abstracted from their underlying sources of valuation that they are no longer valued per se, but priced. Thus, unchained from their referents, prices of value circulate with wild abandon, tethered now only to interest rates and the models from whence they derive: in this whirl, as Jean Baudrillard once predicted, there seems to be no law of value whatsoever, only the fetish of price speculation. A student of financial markets, André Orléan arrives at a similar conclusion: "financial speculation" becomes organized around a logic that "is essentially self-referential (autoréférentiel) in nature. . . . Investors make their decisions not on the ground of what they think intrinsic value is—but on the ground of what [they wager] the price will be."[26] Once there is a shared agreement among traders regarding liquidity, wagers about price appreciation accentuate the contemporary importance of the sphere of circulation because signs of price must be able to fluidly exchange against themselves without friction or limit.

HGTV's stories prefer to locate the source of surplus value in both the savvy recognition of inefficiencies in salvage markets and in a repurposed value theory of labor that pictures nonexploitative labor. The fetishism of value that HGTV visually crafts rests on pretending that there is no political economy of securitized risk at work in our lives. HGTV's optimistic stories about neoliberal subjects who are in control of their own lives would be severely compromised if figures of investment bankers appeared deconstructing home loans as "tradeable risks."[27] Such derivatives were designed to be liquid—to trade easily and quickly between investors who seek the rewards of risk as well as those who short the risk by betting on higher than expected default rates. That's why there are no real estate investment trusts (REITs) on HGTV, because the forever dream home is a spatially fixed real estate property, not an interchangeable liquid asset. HGTV inverts the secret of finance capital—that it's the mortgage debt itself that has value among the investors who trade and circulate it through electronic networks. HGTV's story thus withholds the broad features of a capital investment system of organizing and exploiting value through the practices of securitization.

A Crisis of Hyperreal Capital versus a Paradise of Hyperreal Value

Value is ambivalent in its meaning—it points both toward the universal currency of exchange value and toward that which we hold priceless or immeasurable. Add to this our conceptions of value, which anchor our sensibilities of morality in everyday life. Implicit understandings of value as morality underlie economic exchanges, offering reassurance that exchanges are fair, just, and legible, rather than a rigged game. In the midst of a crisis that was financial as well as moral, HGTV undertook the project of restoring the mystique of the home as a viable economic asset, in part by recentering the home as the moral center for all that we deem personally priceless. The moral crisis of value brings to mind what Durkheim identifies as anomie, a condition he defines as occurring during periods of transition from one stage of societal development to another. At such historical junctures, Durkheim perceived that inherited moral codes no longer quite provide an adequate guide to action, while new rules are not yet clearly stated or understood.[28] The post-2008 crisis of value resembled an anomic crisis of value that expressed itself as a crisis of legitimacy because norms of fairness and justice regarding the allocation of value in a globalized-qua-neoliberal-qua-financialized market economy felt more convoluted than usual. The received nostrums about how to get on the plus side of capitalist value equations—work hard, save, invest for the long haul, buy a house—had long since eroded over decades of structural transformation driven by automation, outsourcing, global commodity chains, and speculative finance markets.

The instability of value has been as disorienting as not knowing the new rules, and the instability of value feeds a mounting sense of insecurity: "When security is missing, free agents are stripped of the confidence without which freedom can hardly be exercised."[29] While the new rules of value might remain a mystery to the multitudes, and the shifting relationship between labor and value a puzzle, finance capital had been busy crafting a new paradigm of value. Ascher summarizes this paradigm shift from a mode of production rooted in the expropriation of labor to a "mode of prediction" rooted in leveraging risk and placing bets on what might happen to prices in a speculative future.[30] Would the new rules of value seem so perplexing "if ours were not simply to be thought of as a 'civil society' mediated by monetized exchange, but as a historically unique portfolio society in which capital's relation to its own future (and hence everyone's relation to the future) is itself mediated by financial markets?"[31]

Bundling home mortgages and then treating those bundles as CDOs opened the door to a new era of value extraction premised on the circulation of risk as a tradable commodity. As this innovation gained momentum, investment banks carved reference portfolios of mortgage assets into segmented hierarchies of default risks before creating offsetting markets to hedge their bets against the risks of default. These insurance hedges were called CDSs, and like the sorcerer's apprentice, they triggered the appearance of monstrous duplications and replications of value. The adoption of computational modeling to represent and shape value at risk churned out a spiraling array of mortgage-backed bonds, synthetic CDOs, and CDSs. As these overleveraged financial instruments grew more elaborate, opaque, and abstract, it became increasingly difficult to identify a correspondence between these concoctions and whatever underlying material property values premised them. In this swirling mix of bundled debt assets, value became disconnected from the reference portfolios. "Each CDO contained pieces of a hundred different mortgage bonds—which in turn held thousands of different loans. It was impossible, or nearly so, to find out which pieces, or which loans."[32] We may never see a more robust illustration of the hyperreal than the securities that were fabricated from mortgage risks. Cooked up via computer modeling, CDOs ate the reference portfolios that ate the household mortgages, so that "referential value was annihilated, giving the structural play of value the upper hand."[33] In the high-velocity system of global circulation, these financial derivatives were exchanged over and over against themselves, feeding an "uninterrupted circuit without reference."[34] As competition accelerated among the banks vying for this lucrative investment practice, it became dizzying: "Trading derivatives could often seem like standing between two mirrors and seeing the reflection of your reflection of your reflection, ad infinitum."[35] Combine this with seriously flawed lending practices and a price bubble in the housing market, and the makings of a perfect storm were in place: a global crisis of hyperreal capital.

Wall Street banks sliced mortgage portfolios into tranches of risk to form mortgage bond-backed CDOs, and they sold like hotcakes. To meet the market demand for even juicier returns, the next move was to slice up the CDOs and repackage them as a CDO of CDOs—the CDO-squared—and next the CDO^2 got cut up and recombined in a CDO-cubed.[36] Even the marketing "names [attached to these products] were disingenuous, and told you nothing about their contents, their creators, or their managers: Carina, Gemstone, Octans II, Glacier Funding. They all had these random names."[37] These signifiers' primary purpose was to veil the underlying referents of family homes and mortgages that had been rendered dangerously immaterial, or beside the point, to those who invested them. "The original home loans on whose fate both sides [the CDOs and CDSs] were betting played no other role. In a funny way, they existed only so that their fate might be gambled upon."[38]

Though we have become inclined to think of the structural law of value primarily in terms of commodity culture and its aleatory remixing of images to form commodity signs (brand values), the contemporary political economy of finance capital is just as prone to the hyperreal as has been the cultural economy of value. In the world of finance, a comparable breakdown of referentiality has been a long time in the making. After all, "the 'scandal' of imaginary money in the nineteenth century was that it could be increased by fiat without backing by inconvertible specie such as gold or silver."[39] Eventually, this dissociation between the signified of value and its referent became normalized in everyday life. In bits and drabs, capitalist society has acclimated to the growing abstraction of value as it has been liberated from the fixity of being pegged to the intrinsic character of commodities.

However, there remains a distinction to be made between the hyperreal in the world of finance capital and in the spectacle. In Baudrillard's account, the hyperreal imposes a model of the real over the real, giving those models the power to redefine the real. We are particularly attuned to this in the realm of consumption in which HGTV's imagery of the big reveal confirms for viewers how people like us ought to live. On television, the hyperreal is seduction, an invitation to gloss over domination on the way to realizing our desires, whereas in the realm of financialization the hyperreal becomes another quiet tool for domination, a means of wresting surplus value from the circumstances of those who cannot defend themselves in a debt economy. If in consumption, hyperreal incarnations appear more vivid and lifelike than the real, in its financial derivatives, the hyperreal becomes maddeningly impenetrable to those who stand outside the model.[40]

Today, "the world of finance is inherently symbolic, like a language."[41] In combination with digital technologies, the structural law of value encourages the wild replication of value by an order of magnitude. Viral reproduction of value, the endless recursive looping through formulas, yielded a combinatorial explosion of fractal value—an "epidemic of value."[42] "The entire strategy of the system lies in this hyperreality of floating values. . . . Value rules according to an ungraspable order: the generation of models, the indefinite chaining of simulation."[43] Within this framework, a transition occurs from a value form "chained up to the real" to one shaped by "by reference to a set of models."[44] The difficulty begins when the sign is no longer chained to the real. The monstrous excesses of CDOs that became squared and then cubed to juice up rates of potential profit retrace the same tendencies that Baudrillard identified—financial instruments became abstractions layered on abstractions until investors could no longer identify which underlying assets were being referenced by the financial instruments.[45]

Since the 1970s capital has faced a persistent problem—how to absorb surplus capital in manufacturing. Of course, there were so many areas that could have benefited from capital investments—affordable housing being but one—that would improve the quality of life for many people, but those promised lesser rates of profit. Some investors moved their capital into unproductive large-scale real estate development projects that promised higher returns—hence the first round of big investments in central-city gentrification.[46] With the advent of the current iteration of hyperglobalization, rates of profit continued to be bogged down by intense price competitions and equally intense competitions to revolutionize technologies of production, communication, and logistics that yielded short-term competitive advantages but in the long run contributed to a higher organic composition of capital and once again sluggish rates of profit coupled with tepid wage growth, continued downsizing, and outsourcing of manufacturing jobs. Financialization beckoned as an alternative path to absorbing surplus capital while letting others foot the costs of production—the financialized pursuit of higher rates of return channeled a growing proportion of surplus capital through the now unregulated circuits of placing bets on securitized debt. This represents capital's dream fantasy of frictionless value extraction—"self-valorizing speculative capital"—derivatives exchanging against each other rather than the real in a self-referential loop.[47] This effort at resolving prior limits on capital has provoked an intensified tangle of social contradictions, not the least of which from the perspective of wage earners seeking a house they can afford is a downward pressure on wages while intensifying the demand for labor's wages.

For capital lenders and investors, straightforward credit no longer has enough oomph, but in its derivative form it becomes hyperreal debt—an investment in speculative value that becomes almost immeasurably abstract as a method of betting on the relationship between current risks and future uncertainty. As an attempt to short-circuit the dialectic of time value, the transition from credit to "derivatives as technique, and technique as a closed black box" requires (as does any black box) a certain amount of faith.[48] The point is not that derivatives are untrue because of the dissociation they accomplish from the referents of physical assets and people, or because they are rooted in complex differential equations—rather, their performativity makes them real in their consequences. With the backing of surplus capital, their discursive power turns into what seems like an autonomous market force.[49] We can hardly expect HGTV to explore the black box of the Black-Scholes model of pricing options and hedging risk (differential equations make for bad television), but the network's repression of it altogether veils its enormous transformative impact over the power relations of mortgages, credit, debt—and empires of rent.

Just because the capitalist system has mutated at its center, pushing to move beyond the primacy of production does not means that capital as a "mode of domination" is a thing of the past. It may only appear this way "because the structural law of value is the purest, most illegible form of social domination, like surplus-value. It no longer has any references within a dominant class or a relation of forces, it works without [apparent] violence."[50] And yet the 2008 crisis of referentiality eventually provoked a crisis of confidence and wrecked countless households. Capital had become illegible even to capitalist investors. The effects of the crisis registered in everyday life as panic, confusion, and uncertainty about the apparent excesses of a financialized economy—not just about its apparent lack of justice but about how exactly it worked. From above, the loss of market legibility triggered a crisis of confidence, and from below it registered as a crisis of faith in how to regain footing in a value system that did not support predictability in the workplace or the home. The financial crisis may have begun as a crisis of referentiality, but it manifested itself as a crisis of legibility.

HGTV's narratives aim to restore a sense of morality and agency to housing markets. HGTV does so, in part, by fabricating and situating "the illusion of production" closer to the private sphere of the home. Decades ago (before there was an HGTV), Baudrillard theorized about why an HGTV might someday become popular: "As long as we can still discover a 'production' corresponding (even if this is only in the imagination) to individual or social needs . . . the worst individual or historical situations are bearable because the illusion of production is always the illusory coincidence of production and use-value."[51] As the loss of reference becomes systemic, the collateral drift toward anomie is reinforced by the apparent abandonment of production as the central condition of new value. It's not accidental that HGTV pushes the DIY angle at the same time that fulfilling productive labor has disappeared for the greater number of us.

The mortgage meltdown and the recession that ensued are sharp reminders that the system of financialization not only has made home ownership more precarious; it also treats people as disposable.[52] HGTV tells stories about a spatial fix aimed at smoothing out the anomic perturbations prompted by an era of investment-driven housing. HGTV's stories embellish a myth of the forever dream home whose time is coming to an end, but how does restoring the myth of the single-family residence restore the legibility of value? HGTV has crafted a hyperreal residential paradise insulated from the taint of a value system now governed by the amoral iterations of algorithm-generated mathematical models. It does so by resolutely hiding the new realities of capitalist subsumption and the shifting character of accumulation by dispossession. It can only remoralize the home as the ur-site of value by abstracting it from the real relations of reproduction and a crumbling wage system. Epoch-driven upheavals in the constitution of value "index themselves on the immediately prior phase of the system. They arm themselves with a nostalgic resurrection of the real in all its forms . . . as ideal content, the phantoms which the system has devoured in successive revolutions and which it subtly resuscitates as revolutionary fantasies."[53] HGTV envisions a clean-slate landscape of modernity as the space for a do-over, a bubble inside which value does not float and is free of vicissitudes; a bubble inside which we can be free of the domination of both the state and finance capital in our pursuit of forever value. It is cruel optimism upcycled.

Epilogue

Must-Haves—Four Walls and a Roof

While HGTV models for viewers how a consumer-oriented speculative economy oriented around renovating and flipping houses can be manipulated for personal benefit, the hyperreal of finance capital has proven to be a powerful force shaping housing in contemporary society. Step outside the alternative hyperreal of HGTV, and real lives encounter the consequences of hyperreal finance in the oh-so-real relations of poverty, debt, rent, and homelessness.

Reverberations of the 2008 credit default and mortgage crises continue to play out across the housing landscape—resulting in transfers of wealth from the working classes to investors, swelling the ranks of renters, and intensifying the pressures of flipping and gentrification on the availability of affordable housing. In 2017, more than 18 million households of renters and mortgage holders were severely cost burdened, meaning that they spent 50 percent or more of their incomes on housing.[1] With employment uncertain in its duration and wages not tracking with rents and prices, those millions of households live in constant anxiety of meeting their bills, aware that an unexpected health care expense or rent hike or auto-repair bill can push them into the perils of homelessness.

Oakland, California, has been a petri dish for these processes, driven by the Bay Area's astronomical escalation of rents and home prices over recent decades. The creative tech economy has spawned a well-compensated stratum of techies who bid up already unaffordable housing, leaving the less affluent out of luck, forced to look farther and farther from the Bay Area to find housing. Long the poor stepsister of San Francisco, Oakland cannot escape entanglement in these market forces. After the foreclosure crisis, Oakland became an appealing site for those armed with cash—another place where houses of the working poor can be acquired at a discount to the market, flipped, and resold to the relatively well-off who cannot afford houses in San Francisco. Seeing this market opportunity, deep-pocketed companies have been scooping up nonperforming loans in neighborhoods hit hard by foreclosures, leaving the working poor scrambling to find housing.

In January 2020, the Oakland minimum wage of $14.14 per hour trailed the "housing wage—defined as the hourly wage that a full-time worker would need to earn to pay rent"—by a factor of three to one, or $40.33, on a median rent.[2] So it's safe to say poverty drives homelessness, but the dual forces of flipping and gentrification cannot be discounted where affordable housing stocks are scarce. California's deepening crisis of homelessness has turned the intersection between economies of flipping and homelessness into an urgent site of class conflict. In December 2019, a dispute between a group of women calling themselves Moms 4 Housing and a company named Wedgewood Property Management centered on a vacant house in West Oakland that the women illegally occupied. Wedgewood describes itself as a company that "acquires and manages bulk quantities of non-performing and re-performing residential whole loans purchased from banks, financial institutions, and US governmental agencies including the FHA and HUD. . . . The flip business is the backbone of Wedgewood."[3] Wedgewood and other similar companies' practice of "buying up properties in areas on the cusp of gentrification and sitting on them until their values surge" has effectively turned the flipping business into a "displacement machine."[4] Moms 4 Housing charged that because of such investor strategies nearly four thousand properties stood unoccupied in Oakland at the same time that houseless working families could find no shelter. In the idiom of our times, Wedgewood and the LLCs that trail behind them trade in precarity and then double-down on it.

With the state doing little more than neoliberal hand-wringing, Moms 4 Housing organized to contest the California homelessness crunch engulfing an ever-widening swath of vulnerable families. The particular house that Moms 4 Housing occupied had been acquired "at a foreclosure auction by a subsidiary of Wedgewood Properties."[5] The women and their children occupied the house because they needed shelter from the winter cold, and they chose to politicize its occupation to mount a public campaign focused on housing for profit versus housing as a human right.

Moms 4 Housing refused the only open-concept plan available to them, to live outdoors. As a human right, their housing must-haves begin with four walls and a roof. Wedgewood defended its property rights in court and prevailed. In short order, the county sheriff sent a heavily armed squad to evict two black single mothers. But Moms 4 Housing prevailed in the court of public opinion. Within days, the city of Oakland brokered a deal between Wedgewood and the Oakland Community Land Trust for the sale of the West Oakland home and others like it at "fair market value."[6] What this translates into going forward is unclear. What is clear is that the flipping economy has been pulled into a class struggle over the conditions of housing.

Notes

PREFACE

1. Julia Falcon, "Foreclosure Filings Fell to a Record Low in 2019," *HousingWire*, January 16, 2020, https://www.housingwire.com/articles/foreclosure-filings-fell-to-a-record-low-in-2019/.

INTRODUCTION

1. In fact, it's not just HGTV but a spectrum of television cultural forms (and now social media) that devote themselves in daily and weekly cycles to questions about value. Notable among these are makeover television about upgrading the value of the individual subject. Media coverage of the NFL Draft and fantasy football rival HGTV in the intensity of their discourse about chasing the conditions of value and are the most committed to developing a replicable methodology of valuation—witness the rise of analytics throughout the sports media.

2. My study is based on watching the following HGTV and DIY shows between 2014 and 2018: *Income Property, Rehab Addict, Property Brothers, Love It or List It, House Hunters Renovation, Flip or Flop, Fixer Upper, American Rehab, Flipping the Heartland, Good Bones, Texas Flip N Move, Barnwood Builders, Salvage Dawgs, Kitchen Cousins, America's Most Desperate Kitchens, Flipping Virgins, Sweet House Alabama, Sarah Sees Potential, Elbow Room, Rescue My Renovation, Building Hawaii, My Flipping Family, House Crashers, Kitchen Crashers, Bath Crashers, Sledgehammer, My Big Family Renovation, Renovate to Rent, Old Home Love, Miami Flip, Nashville Flipped, Masters of Flip, Desert Flippers, Stone House Revival, Listed Sisters, Home Town*, and *First Time Flippers*.

3. The relaxation of credit rules is often attributed to the 1999 repeal of the Glass-Steagall Act, which previously split commercial from investment banking, but the old "regulatory firmament" had already dissolved by then. Bethany McLean and Joe Nocera,

All the Devils Are Here: The Hidden History of the Financial Crisis (New York: Penguin, 2011), 109.

4. Lawrence Mishel, "The Wedges between Productivity and Median Compensation Growth," Economic Policy Institute, April 26, 2012, https://www.epi.org/publication/ib330-productivity-vs-compensation/.

5. Federal Reserve Bank of New York, "Total Household Debt Climbs for 20th Straight Quarter as Mortgage Debt and Originations Rise," August 13, 2019, https://www.newyorkfed.org/newsevents/news/research/2019/20190813.

6. Edward Wolfe, Lindsey A. Owens, and Esra Burak, "How Much Wealth Was Destroyed?" in *The Great Recession*, edited by David B.Grusky, Bruce Western, and Christopher Wimer (New York: Russell Sage Foundation, 2011), 155.

7. Fiona Allon and Guy Redden, "The Global Financial Crisis and the Culture of Continual Growth," *Journal of Cultural Economy* 5, no. 4 (2012): 375–390; James Hay, "Too Good to Fail: Managing Financial Crisis through the Moral Economy of Realty TV," *Journal of Communication Inquiry* 34, no. 4 (2010): 382–402.

8. Anna Lowenhaupt Tsing, *The Mushroom at the End of the World: On the Possibility of Life in Capitalist Ruins* (Princeton, NJ: Princeton University Press, 2017), 2.

9. Ben Bernanke, quoted in Edmund Andrews, "Treasury Chief Aims to Steady Credit Markets," *New York Times*, October 16, 2007, https://www.nytimes.com/2007/10/16/business/16rescue.html.

10. Julia Ott and Louis Hyman, "The Politics of Debt: How Labor Should Think about the Debt Question," *New Labor Forum* 22, no. 2 (2013): 28.

11. Eric Foner, *Free Soil, Free Labor, Free Men: The Ideology of the Republican Party before the Civil War* (Oxford: Oxford University Press, 1995).

12. Kate Wagner, "Behind-the-Scenes of Rustic Modernism: Your Complete Guide to Farmhouse and Industrial Chic," *Curbly*, June 22, 2017, https://www.curbly.com/rustic-modernism-guide.

13. Julie Guthman, *Weighing In: Obesity, Food Justice, and the Limits of Capitalism* (Berkeley: University of California Press, 2011), 18.

14. Hay, "Too Good to Fail," 392; Shawn Shimpach, "Realty Reality: HGTV and the Subprime Crisis," *American Quarterly* 64, no. 3 (2012): 515–542; Fiona Allon, "Speculating on Everyday Life: The Cultural Economy of the Quotidian," *Journal of Communication Inquiry* 34, no. 4 (2010): 366–381.

15. David Harvey, "From Managerialism to Entrepreneurialism: The Transformation in Urban Governance in Late Capitalism," *Geografiska Annaler: Series B, Human Geography* 71, no. 1 (1989): 3–17.

16. Neil Smith, "New Globalism, New Urbanism: Gentrification as Global Urban Strategy," *Antipode* 34, no. 3 (2002): 427–450.

17. "Today crisis has become an instrument of rule. It serves to legitimize political and economic decisions that in fact dispossess citizens and deprive them of any possibility of decision." Giorgio Agamben, "The Endless Crisis as an Instrument of Power: In Conversation with Giorgio Agamben," *Verso* (blog), June 2013, https://www.versobooks.com/blogs/1318-the-endless-crisis-as-an-instrument-of-power-in-conversation-with-giorgio-agamben.

18. See Neil Smith, *The New Urban Frontier: Gentrification and the Revanchist City* (London: Routledge, 1996).

19. See Neil Smith, "Toward a Theory of Gentrification: A Back to the City Movement by Capital, not People," *Journal of the American Planning Association* 45, no. 4

(1979): 538–548. See also Peter Moskowitz, *How to Kill a City: Gentrification, Inequality, and the Fight for the Neighborhood* (New York: Bold Type Books, 2017), 38.

20. See Diane Elson, "The Value Theory of Labour," in *Value: The Representation of Labour in Capitalism* (Atlantic Highlands, NJ: Humanities Press, 1979), 115–180.

21. Robert E. Scott, "We Can Reshore Manufacturing Jobs, but Trump Hasn't Done It," Economic Policy Institute, August 10, 2020, https://www.epi.org/publication/reshoring-manufacturing-jobs/; Fred Magdoff, "The Jobs Disaster in the United States," *Monthly Review*, June 1, 2011, https://monthlyreview.org/2011/06/01/the-jobs-disaster-in-the-united-states/.

22. Keeanga-Yamahtta Taylor, *Race for Profit: How Banks and the Real Estate Industry Undermined Black Homeownership* (Chapel Hill: University of North Carolina Press, 2019), 254.

23. Laura Gottesdiener, *A Dream Foreclosed: Black America and the Fight for a Place to Call Home* (Westfield, NJ: Zuccotti Park Press, 2013), 63.

24. See Dick Bryan and Mike Rafferty, *Risking Together* (Sydney: Sydney University Press, 2018); and Costas Lapavitsas, "Theorizing Financialization," *Work, Employment and Society* 25, no. 4 (2011): 611–626.

25. Dick Bryan, Michael Rafferty, and Chris Jefferis, "Risk and Value: Finance, Labor, and Production," *South Atlantic Quarterly* 114, no. 2 (2015): 307.

26. Allon, "Speculating on Everyday Life," 369. See also Annette Baldauf, "Betting the House," *Rethinking Marxism* 22, no. 2 (2010): 219–230.

27. Shimpach, "Realty Reality," 517.

28. Wenli Li, "Smart Money or Dumb Money: Investors' Role in the Housing Bubble," *Federal Reserve Bank of Philadelphia Business Review* Q1 (2015): 23, https://citeseerx.ist.psu.edu/viewdoc/download?doi=10.1.1.679.9560&rep=rep1&type=pdf.

29. Stefania Albanesi, Giacomo DiForgio, and Jaromir Nosal, "Credit Growth and the Financial Crisis: A New Narrative," NBER Working Paper No. 23740, August 2017, p. 1, https://www.nber.org/papers/w23740.

30. Gwynn Guilford, "House Flippers Triggered the US Housing Market Crash, not Poor Subprime Borrowers," *Quartz*, August 29, 2017, https://qz.com/1064061/house-flippers-triggered-the-us-housing-market-crash-not-poor-subprime-borrowers-a-new-study-shows.

31. To put the numbers into chronological context, the foreclosure rates for subprime loans also rose dramatically in 2007. See Dan Immergluck, *Foreclosed: High-Risk Lending, Deregulation, and the Undermining of America's Mortgage Market* (Ithaca, NY: Cornell University Press, 2009), 137.

32. Albanesi, DiForgio, and Nosal, "Credit Growth and the Financial Crisis," 50.

33. Li, "Smart Money or Dumb Money," 23.

34. Immergluck, *Foreclosed*, 133.

35. Allon, "Speculating on Everyday Life," 367.

36. David Harvey, *Marx, Capital and the Madness of Economic Reason* (Oxford: Oxford University Press, 2018).

37. Lauren Berlant, *Cruel Optimism* (Durham, NC: Duke University Press, 2001), 19.

38. Annie McClanahan, *Dead Pledges: Debt, Crisis, and Twenty-First-Century Culture* (Stanford: Stanford University Press, 2017), 54.

39. Allon, "Speculating on Everyday Life," 368.

CHAPTER 1

1. David Auerbach, "Georg Simmel's Philosophy of Money, Part 1: Value and Money," *Waggish* (blog), August 16, 2014, https://www.waggish.org/2014/georg-simmels-philosophy-of-money-1-value-and-money.
2. Ibid.
3. *Merriam-Webster Dictionary*, s.v. "value," https://www.merriam-webster.com/dictionary/value (accessed February 25, 2021).
4. David Harvey, *Marx, Capital and the Madness of Economic Reason* (Oxford: Oxford University Press, 2018), 51.
5. Daniel Miller, "The Uses of Value," *Geoforum* 39 (2008): 1122.
6. C. B. Macpherson, *The Political Theory of Possessive Individualism* (Oxford: Oxford University Press, 1962).
7. Michael Roberts and David Harvey, "Marx's Law of Value: A Debate between David Harvey and Michael Roberts," *Michael Roberts Blog*, April 2, 2018, https://thenextrecession.wordpress.com/2018/04/02/marxs-law-of-value-a-debate-between-david-harvey-and-michael-roberts/.
8. Dick Bryan, Michael Rafferty, and Chris Jefferis, "Risk and Value: Finance, Labor, and Production," *South Atlantic Quarterly* 114, no. 2 (2015): 313.
9. This phrase was coined by Diane Rubenstein in "The Mirror of Reproduction: Baudrillard and Reagan's America," *Political Theory* 17, no. 4 (1989): 582–606.
10. "In societies where modern conditions of production prevail, all of life presents itself as an immense accumulation of spectacles. Everything that was directly lived has moved away into a representation." Guy Debord, *Society of the Spectacle* (Detroit: Red and Black, 1971), 1. Debord is obviously referencing Karl Marx's opening lines about commodities in *Capital*: "The wealth of those societies in which the capitalist mode of production prevails, presents itself as 'an immense accumulation of commodities.'" Karl Marx, *Capital: A Critique of Political Economy*, trans. Ben Fowkes (New York: Vintage Books, 1977), 1:125.
11. Albert Camus, *The Myth of Sisyphus and Other Essays*, trans. Justin O'Brien (New York: Vintage Books, 1991), 119.
12. Ibid.
13. Jean Baudrillard, "The Destiny of Value," in *Paroxysm: Interviews with Philippe Petit*, trans. Chris Turner (New York: Verso, 1998), 4.
14. Jean Baudrillard, "After the Orgy," in *The Transparency of Evil: Essays on Extreme Phenomena*, trans. James Benedict (New York: Verso, 1993), 5.
15. Baudrillard, "Destiny of Value," 4.
16. Jean Baudrillard, "The End of Production," in *Symbolic Exchange and Death*, trans. Iain Hamilton Grant (London: Sage, 1993), 7.
17. Lawrence Grossberg, Carolyn Hardin, and Michael Palm, "Contributions to a Conjunctural Theory of Valuation," *Rethinking Marxism* 26, no. 3 (2014): 307.
18. Georg Simmel, *The Philosophy of Money* (London: Routledge, 2004), 98.
19. Ibid., 67.
20. Baudrillard, "The End of Production," 6.
21. Gilles Deleuze and Felix Guattari, *A Thousand Plateaus: Capitalism and Schizophrenia* (Minneapolis: University of Minnesota Press, 2007); Robert Goldman and Stephen Papson, *Landscapes of Capital* (Cambridge, UK: Polity, 2011), 121.
22. Karl Marx, *Grundrisse* (Harmondsworth, UK: Penguin, 1973), 690–712; Jeremy Rifkin, *The Zero Marginal-Cost Society* (New York: St. Martin's, 2014).

23. Kate Allison Granju, "Quartz: The New Countertop Contender," HGTV, https://www.hgtv.com/design/rooms/kitchens/quartz-the-new-countertop-contender (accessed December 28, 2020). HGTV considers the value of quartz from a consumer viewpoint, but from labor's vantage point, cutting this engineered stone has deadly consequences from breathing silica dust. See Nell Greenfieldboyce, "Workers Are Falling Ill, Even Dying, after Making Kitchen Countertops," *NPR*, October 2, 2019, https://www.npr.org/sections/health-shots/2019/10/02/766028237/workers-are-falling-ill-even-dying-after-making-kitchen-countertops.

24. Baudrillard, "End of Production," 2.

25. Ferdinand de Saussure, *Course in General Linguistics*, trans. Wade Baskin, ed. Perry Meisel and Haun Saussy (New York: Columbia University Press, 2011).

26. Baudrillard, "After the Orgy," 5.

27. Robert Goldman and Stephen Papson, *Sign Wars* (New York: Guilford, 1996).

28. Louis Althusser, "Ideology and Ideological State Apparatuses," in *Lenin and Philosophy, and Other Essays* (London: New Left Books, 1971); Judith Williamson, *Decoding Advertisements: Ideology and Meaning in Advertising* (London: Marion Boyars, 1978), 50, 51.

29. See Jean Baudrillard, *The System of Objects* (London: Verso, 1996).

30. Arjun Appadurai, "Commodities and the Politics of Value," in *Interpreting Objects and Collections*, ed. Susan Pearce (London: Routledge, 1994), 76–91.

31. Magnolia, "Premium Interior Paint," https://shop.magnolia.com/collections/premium-colors/color-beige (accessed February 25, 2021).

32. Caitlin Zaloom, "How to Read the Future: The Yield Curve, Affect, and Financial Prediction," *Public Culture* 21, no. 2 (2009): 264.

33. Karl Marx and Frederick Engels, *Manifesto of the Communist Party* (Peking: Foreign Language Press, 1970), 34–35.

34. Ibid, 35.

35. David Harvey, *The Condition of Postmodernity* (Cambridge, MA: Basil Blackwell, 1989), 105–108.

36. Joseph Schumpeter, *Capitalism, Socialism, and Democracy* (London: Routledge, 1994).

37. Jeff Andrews, "10 Years after the Financial Crisis, Is the Housing Market Still at Risk?" *Curbed*, August 29, 2018, https://www.curbed.com/2018/8/29/17788844/financial-crisis-2008-cause-housing-mortgage-lending.

38. Fiona Allon, "Money, Debt, and the Business of 'Free Stuff,'" *South Atlantic Quarterly* 114, no. 2 (April 2015): 291.

39. See Bruce Carruthers and Arthur Stinchcombe, "The Social Structure of Liquidity: Flexibility, Markets, and States," *Theory and Society* 28, no. 3 (1999): 353–382.

40. Kevin Fox Gotham, "Creating Liquidity out of Spatial Fixity: The Secondary Circuit of Capital and the Subprime Mortgage Crisis," *International Journal of Urban and Regional Research* 33, no. 2 (2009): 357, 359, 367.

41. Dick Bryan and Michael Rafferty, "Political Economy and Housing in the Twenty-First Century—from Mobile Homes to Liquid Housing?" *Housing, Theory and Society* 31, no. 4 (2014): 404.

42. Justin Steil, Len Albright, Jacob Rugh, and Douglas Massey, "The Social Structure of Mortgage Discrimination," *Housing Studies* 33, no. 5 (2018): 762.

43. Ivan Ascher, *Portfolio Society: On the Capitalist Mode of Prediction* (New York: Zone Books, 2016); Bryan, Rafferty, and Jefferis, "Risk and Value."

44. Dick Bryan, Michael Rafferty, and Bruno Tinel, "Households at the Frontiers of Monetary Development," *Behemoth—a Journal on Civilisation* 9, no. 2 (2016): 46–58.

45. Matthew Desmond, *Evicted: Poverty and Profit in the American City* (New York: Broadway Books, 2017).

46. Paul Sullivan, "Investors Push into a Resurging Market: House Flipping," *New York Times*, October 20, 2017, https://www.nytimes.com/2017/10/20/your-money/house-flipping-loans.html; Jeff Andrews, "How Wall Street, Silicon Valley Institutionalized Home Flipping," *Curbed*, May 9, 2018, https://www.curbed.com/2018/5/9/17319958/house-flipping-lenders-roc-capital-lendinghome.

CHAPTER 2

1. Daniel Mrozowski, "From Hoarders to Pickers: Salvage Aesthetics and Reality Television in the Great Recession," in *The Great Recession in Fiction, Film, and Television: Twenty-First-Century Bust Culture*, ed. Kirk Boyle and Daniel Mrozowski (Lanham, MD: Lexington Books, 2013).

2. Mary Douglas, *Purity and Danger* (London: Routledge, 1966), 48.

3. Zygmunt Bauman, *Liquid Modernity* (Cambridge, UK: Polity, 2000), 121.

4. Carrie Madormo, "The Untold Truth of Rehab Addict," *The List*, December 17, 2016, http://www.thelist.com/32115/untold-truth-rehab-addict/?utm_campaign=clip; Stephen Kurutz, "The Housing Bubble Burst All Over HGTV," *New York Times*, September 12, 2018, https://www.nytimes.com/interactive/2018/09/12/business/media/hgtv-housing-mortgage-crisis.html.

5. Daren Blomquist, quoted in Thomas C. Frohlich and Michael B. Sauter, "6 Best States to Flip a House," *USA Today*, February 2, 2014, http://www.usatoday.com/story/money/business/2014/02/02/6-best-states-to-flip-a-house/5115321/.

6. Richard Lawson, "Did a Car Accident Reveal a Darker Side of HGTV's Biggest Hit?" *Vanity Fair*, July 10, 2017, https://www.vanityfair.com/style/2017/07/fixer-upper-hgtv-car-drives-through-house.

7. Vic Ryckaert, "Two Chicks and a Hammer Nail HGTV Deal," *USA Today*, May 26, 2015, http://www.usatoday.com/story/life/tv/2015/05/26/two-chicks-and-a-hammer-nail-hgtv-deal/27988425/.

8. HGTV's embrace of whiteness as cultural capital is sufficiently obvious that *South Park* quickly parodied it in an episode titled "White People Renovating Houses," which merged renovation mania with a satire of white nationalism.

9. Georg Simmel, *The Philosophy of Money* (London: Routledge, 2004), 64.

10. Jean Baudrillard, *Simulacra and Simulation*, trans. Sheila Glaser (Ann Arbor: University of Michigan Press, 1994), 1.

11. After the on-screen reveal, the staging furniture goes back to the stores on *Fixer Upper*, while *Property Brothers* leaves the subsidized furnishings behind.

12. John, "Do the People on Property Brothers Get to Keep the Furnishings?" *Starcasm*, April 11, 2016, http://starcasm.net/archives/346920.

13. See Kate Wagner's analysis of "beige" and the political economy of flipping in "How Beige Took Over American Homes," *Atlas Obscura*, September 26, 2016, http://www.atlasobscura.com/articles/how-beige-took-over-american-homes.

14. Kerry Gold, "The Property Brothers Are Back Home—and on the Hunt for Bargains," *Globe and Mail*, March 18, 2013, http://www.theglobeandmail.com/life/home-and-garden/real-estate/the-property-brothers-are-back-home-and-on-the-hunt-for-bargains/article9870798/.

15. However, the HGTV formula also repeats the same dialogue and shots both before and after a block of commercials to resuture the viewers' place in the story.

16. Douglas, *Purity and Danger*, 12.

17. Marshall Berman, *All That Is Solid Melts into Air* (New York: Simon and Schuster, 1982).

18. Kat Rosenfield and Todd Jacobs, "Why Property Brothers Is Totally Fake," *Nicki Swift*, November 3, 2016, https://www.nickiswift.com/27699/property-brothers-totally-fake/.

19. Shawn Shimpach, "Realty Reality: HGTV and the Subprime Crisis," *American Quarterly* 64, no. 3 (2012): 37.

20. The commercial is available at https://www.ispot.tv/ad/ABwM/hgtv-home-by-sherwin-williams-color-collection-easy-decisions.

21. Schuyler Velasco, "'House Hunters' TV Show Is Fake: Does It Matter?" *Christian Science Monitor*, June 15, 2012, http://www.csmonitor.com/Business/2012/0615/House-Hunters-TV-show-is-fake.-Does-it-matter.

22. Aaron Glantz and Emmanuel Martinez, "For People of Color, Banks Are Shutting the Door to Homeownership," *Reveal*, February 15, 2018, https://www.revealnews.org/article/for-people-of-color-banks-are-shutting-the-door-to-homeownership/.

23. Daniel Langhorne, "Local Couple Star in HGTV Reality Show on Flipping Houses," *Orange County Register*, April 4, 2013, http://www.ocregister.com/articles/moussa-502466-tarek-houses.html.

24. Harry Bradford, "Foreclosure Vandals Threaten Prospective Homeowners: 'Only Going to Get Worse,'" *Huffington Post*, May 2, 2012, http://www.huffingtonpost.com/2012/05/02/foreclosure-vandals-threaten-homeowners-take-my-house_n_1471472.html; Susanna Kim, "Here's the Keys, and Some Cement Down the Drains," *ABC News*, January 18, 2011, http://abcnews.go.com/Business/million-dollar-foreclosed-home-vandalized/story?id=12638936.

CHAPTER 3

1. Stuart Hall and Doreen Massey, "Interpreting the Crisis," *Soundings: A Journal of Politics and Culture* 44 (Spring 2010): 57–71.

2. In their quarterly and annual reports, CoreLogic and ATTOM Data Solutions routinely address variations in regional and metropolitan flipping rates and profitability. See, for example, Ralph McLaughlin, "Special Report: House Flipping and Profits," *CoreLogic Insights Blog*, April 9, 2019, https://www.corelogic.com/blog/2019/04/special-report-house-flipping-and-profits.aspx; and ATTOM Data Solutions, "U.S. Home Flipping Returns Drop to Seven-Year Low in 2018," February 26, 2019, https://www.attomdata.com/news/most-recent/2018-year-end-u-s-home-flipping-report/.

3. Patrick Sisson, "Millennials, Priced out of Homes Locally, Shop for Investment Properties Online," *Curbed*, September 10, 2019, https://www.curbed.com/2019/9/10/20852849/millennial-buy-a-home-homeownership-remote.

4. Ivan Ascher, *Portfolio Society: On the Capitalist Mode of Prediction* (New York: Zone Books, 2016).

5. Manuel B. Aalbers, "Introduction to the Forum: From Third to Fifth-Wave Gentrification," *Tijdschrift voor economische en sociale geografie* 110, no. 1 (2019): 6.

6. Robert Brenner, *The Economics of Global Turbulence* (New York: Verso, 2006), 136; Paolo Gelain, Kevin J. Lansing, and Gisle J. Natvik, "Explaining the Boom-Bust Cycle in the U.S. Housing Market: A Reverse-Engineering Approach," Federal Reserve Bank of San Francisco Working Paper 2015-02, February 2018, http://www.frbsf.org/economic-research/publications/working-papers/2015/02/.

7. Benjamin Landy, "A Tale of Two Recoveries: Wealth Inequality after the Great Recession," Century Foundation, August 28, 2013, http://www.tcf.org/blog/detail/a-tale-of-two-recoveries.

8. Ari Shapiro, "A Decade after the Bubble Burst, House Flipping Is on the Rise," *NPR*, April 17, 2018, https://www.npr.org/2018/04/17/601925433/a-decade-after-the-bubble-burst-house-flipping-is-on-the-rise.

9. McLaughlin, "Special Report: House Flipping and Profits."

10. Patrick Bayer et al., "Speculators and Middlemen: The Strategy and Performance of Investors in the Housing Market," NBER Working Paper 16784, February 2011, https://doi.org/10.3386/w16784. This study documented a fourfold increase of inexperienced flippers in the superheated Los Angeles market between the late 1990s and 2006.

11. Andrew Haughwout et al., "Real Estate Investors, the Leverage Cycle, and the Housing Market Crisis," Federal Reserve Bank of New York Staff Report 514, September 2011, https://www.newyorkfed.org/medialibrary/media/research/staff_reports/sr514.pdf; Wenli Li, "Smart Money or Dumb Money: Investors' Role in the Housing Bubble," *Federal Reserve Bank of Philadelphia Business Review* Q1 (2015), https://citeseerx.ist.psu.edu/viewdoc/download?doi=10.1.1.679.9560&rep=rep1&type=pdf; Stefania Albanesi, Giacomo DiForgio, and Jaromir Nosal, "Credit Growth and the Financial Crisis: A New Narrative," NBER Working Paper No. 23740, August 2017, https://www.nber.org/papers/w23740.

12. Ralph McLaughlin and Arthur Jobe, "A Wild Flipping Ride: Economic Returns to U.S. House Flipping, 2002–2018," paper presented at 47th American Real Estate and Urban Economics Association National Conference, Washington, DC, May 31, 2019.

13. "In Montbello, Denver's most flipped neighborhood, 73.6 percent of all house flips involved a property that had been foreclosed on. In the second-most flipped neighborhood, Gateway–Green Valley Ranch, 74 percent of all flips can be traced to a foreclosure. But most of the flipping happens before 2011 in both neighborhoods." Megan Arellano, "In Booming Denver, the Role of Flipped Houses Is Changing," *Denverite*, June 9, 2016, https://denverite.com/2016/06/09/booming-denver-role-flipped-houses-changing/.

14. Teke Wiggin, "Fix-and-Flip Mortgage Bonds: Wall Street's New Housing Bet to Boost Home Flippers," *Inman*, February 15, 2017, https://www.inman.com/2017/02/15/fix-flip-mortgage-bonds-wall-streets-new-housing-bet-boost-home-flippers/. Traditionally, "hard money" was a euphemism for lending to poor people at higher interest rates with shorter time frames for repayment. A season two episode of HGTV's *Flip or Flop,* titled "Hard Money Blues," actually mentioned the constraints imposed by borrowing on hard-money terms. The flipper expressed anxiety about schedule delays because his "costly hard-money loan" was "a ticking time bomb," with interest calculated by days and weeks.

15. Rebecca Burns, "You Think Your Landlord Is Bad? Try Renting from Wall Street," *The Intercept*, January 20, 2018, https://theintercept.com/2018/01/20/you-think-your-landlord-is-bad-try-renting-from-wall-street/.

16. Felipe Ossa, "Why 'Build to Rent' Is Having Its Moment," *Asset Securitization Report*, February 14, 2018, https://asreport.americanbanker.com/news/why-build-to-rent-is-having-its-moment.

17. Dustin Dwyer and Kaye LaFond, "Pushed Out: A Documentary on Housing in Grand Rapids," *All Things Considered*, April 26, 2017, https://stateofopportunity.michiganradio.org/post/pushed-out-documentary-housing-grand-rapids.

18. Rachel Dwyer and Lois Lassus, "The Great Risk Shift and Precarity in the U.S. Housing Market," *Annals AAPSS* 660 (July 2015): 199–216; Maya Abood, "AFR Report: Wall Street and Single-Family Rentals," *Americans for Financial Reform*, January 17, 2018, http://ourfinancialsecurity.org/2018/01/afr-report-wall-street-and-single-family-rentals/; Dwyer and LaFond, "Pushed Out"; Steve Lopez, "As Renters Struggle to Pay the Bills, Landlords and Speculators Cash In," *Los Angeles Times*, November 4, 2017, https://www.latimes.com/local/california/la-me-lopez-housing-profiteers-20171104-story.html; Shapiro, "A Decade after the Bubble Burst"; Michelle Conlin, "Spiders, Sewage and a Flurry of Fees—the Other Side of Renting a House from Wall Street," *Reuters*, July 27, 2018, https://www.reuters.com/investigates/special-report/usa-housing-invitation/.

19. Abood, "AFR Report"; Elora Lee Raymond et al., "From Foreclosure to Eviction: Housing Insecurity in Corporate-Owned Single-Family Rentals," *Cityscape* 20, no. 3 (2018): 159–188.

20. For more on how racially discriminatory lending practices have widened the racial wealth gap, see Jacob Rugh, Len Albright, and Douglas Massey, "Race, Space, and Cumulative Disadvantage: A Case Study of the Subprime Lending Collapse," *Social Problems* 62, no. 2 (2015): 186–218; and Sarah Burd-Sharps and Rebecca Rasch, "Impact of the US Housing Crisis on the Racial Wealth Gap across Generations," Social Science Research Council, June 2015, https://www.ssrc.org/publications/view/impact-of-the-us-housing-crisis-on-the-racial-wealth-gap-across-generations/.

21. Laura Gottesdiener, "How Wall Street Has Turned Housing into a Dangerous Get-Rich-Quick Scheme—Again," *Mother Jones*, November 29, 2013, https://www.motherjones.com/politics/2013/11/wall-street-buying-foreclosed-homes/.

22. ATTOM Data Solutions, "U.S. Foreclosure Activity Drops to 12-Year Low in 2017," January 16, 2018, https://www.attomdata.com/news/foreclosure-trends/2017-year-end-u-s-foreclosure-market-report.

23. Les Christie, "Foreclosures up a Record 81% in 2008," *CNN*, January 15, 2019, https://money.cnn.com/2009/01/15/real_estate/millions_in_foreclosure/.

24. Aaron Glantz, *Homewreckers: How a Gang of Wall Street Kingpins, Hedge Fund Magnates, Crooked Banks, and Vulture Capitalists Suckered Millions out of Their Homes and Demolished the American Dream* (New York: HarperCollins, 2019). Aaron Glantz focuses on specific capitalists in the Trump orbit who preyed on the wreckage of the mortgage crisis to enrich themselves, including Jared Kushner, Steven Mnuchin, Wilbur Ross, Thomas Barrack, and Stephen Schwartzman.

25. "Blackstone manages more than $210 billion in assets, according to its 2012 Securities and Exchange Commission annual filing. It's also a public company with a list of institutional owners that reads like a who's who of companies recently implicated in lawsuits over the mortgage crisis, including Morgan Stanley, Citigroup, Deutsche Bank, UBS, Bank of America, Goldman Sachs, and JP Morgan Chase.... In other words, if Blackstone makes money by capitalizing on the housing crisis, all these other Wall Street banks—generally regarded as the main culprits in creating the conditions that led to the foreclosure crisis in the first place—make money too." Gottesdiener, "How Wall Street."

26. Ibid. With each successive SFR bond offering, Blackstone grew more aggressive, reverting to problematic securitization practices. Blackstone valued its fourth and largest offering in 2014 at $1 billion, but over 5 percent of the collateral pool consisted of vacant homes that carried no rental income. Blackstone further scrapped tenant affordability tests that "that capped annual rent at 40% of a tenant's income." Blackstone's prior SFR bond offerings realized returns between 19 and 24 percent. Despite its obvious

limitations, this fourth offering excited sufficient investor demand that it returned 17 percent to Blackstone. Joy Wiltermuth, "Blackstone Pays Up but Wins Big on New SFR Bond," *Yahoo! Life*, May 23, 2014, https://www.yahoo.com/lifestyle/tagged/health/blackstone-pays-wins-big-sfr-151926023.html.

27. Ryan Dezember and Peter Rudegeair, "The Future of Housing Rises in Phoenix: High-Tech Flippers Such as Zillow Are Using Algorithms to Reshape the Housing Market," *Wall Street Journal*, June 19, 2019, https://www.wsj.com/articles/the-future-of-housing-rises-in-phoenix-11560957036.

28. McLaughlin, "Special Report: House Flipping and Profits."

29. RealtyTrac, "A Flip of the Numbers," *Think Realty*, April 21, 2016, https://thinkrealty.com/a-flip-of-the-numbers/.

30. Fintech encompasses proptech (property technology) and CRE-tech (commercial real estate technology). "Since the housing bust 10 years ago, firms from Silicon Valley and Wall Street have nationalized and institutionalized the 'fix-and-flip' loan market by leveraging big data and technology. The transformation has attracted the type of big banks, Wall Street players, and venture capitalists that had traditionally shied away from making investments in home flipping, turning the once hyper-local business into a global FinTech industry." Jeff Andrews, "How Wall Street, Silicon Valley Institutionalized Home Flipping," *Curbed*, May 9, 2018, https://www.curbed.com/2018/5/9/17319958/house-flipping-lenders-roc-capital-lendinghome.

31. ATTOM Data Solutions, "U.S. Home Flipping Increases to 11-Year High in 2017 with More Than 200,000 Homes Flipped for Second Straight Year," March 7, 2018, https://www.attomdata.com/news/home-flipping/2017-u-s-home-flipping-report/.

32. McLaughlin, "Special Report: House Flipping and Profits."

33. Laura Gottesdiener, "Wall Street's Hot New Financial Product: Your Rent Check," *Mother Jones*, March–April 2014, https://www.motherjones.com/politics/2014/02/blackstone-rental-homes-bundled-derivatives/.

34. Enterprise value is calculated as the sum of the market value of equity plus long- and short-term debt.

35. Samantha Sharf, "Wall Street Firms Build a Single-Family Rental Giant, but It's Still a Minnow in Housing Market," *Forbes*, August 10, 2017, https://www.forbes.com/sites/samanthasharf/2017/08/10/single-family-rental-leaders-invitation-homes-starwood-waypoint-homes-to-combine/.

36. Philip Garboden and Eva Rosen, "Serial Filing: How Landlords Use the Threat of Eviction," *City and Community* 18, no. 2 (2019): 638–661; Dan Immergluck et al., "Evictions, Large Owners, and Serial Filings: Findings from Atlanta," *Housing Studies* 35, no. 5 (2019): 903–924. Serial eviction filings are also used to limit the power of renters to exercise their rights to code enforcement.

37. Dezember and Rudegeair, "The Future of Housing Rises in Phoenix."

38. Burns, "You Think Your Landlord Is Bad?"; Paul Sullivan, "Investors Push into a Resurging Market: House Flipping," *New York Times*, October 20, 2017, https://www.nytimes.com/2017/10/20/your-money/house-flipping-loans.html; Wiggin, "Fix-and-Flip Mortgage Bonds"; Amherst Capital Management, "U.S. Single-Family Rental—an Emerging Institutional Asset Class," November 2016, https://www.amherstcapital.com/documents/20649/22737/US+SFR+Emerging+Asset+Class/9d84e0da-4a9f-4665-9880-88a4515d9d2b.

39. Marcus Allen et al., "Impact of Investors in Distressed Housing Markets," *Journal of Real Estate Finance and Economics* 56, no. 4 (2018): 622–652.

Notes to Chapter 3 / 191

40. ATTOM Data Solutions, "U.S. Home Flipping Increases to 11-Year High in 2017."

41. Diana Olick, "Home Flippers Are Fleeing the Market as Their Profits Shrink," *CNBC*, November 1, 2018, https://www.cnbc.com/2018/11/01/home-flippers-are-fleeing-the-market-as-their-profits-shrink.html.

42. Deep-pocketed fintech ventures such as Opendoor and Aperture hope their technological sophistication will outmaneuver competition in the flipping market. Using computerized models and algorithms to assess probabilities of profit, slick personalized mailers from Opendoor have supplanted the scribbled mailers from local investors looking to take advantage of vulnerable homeowners. Fintech companies buy SFR properties to renovate and resell as well as provide short-term bridge loans to mom-and-pop investors. See Samantha Sharf, "Forbes Fintech 50 2018: The Future of Lending," *Forbes*, February 13, 2018, https://www.forbes.com/sites/samanthasharf/2018/02/13/forbes-fintech-50-2018-the-future-of-lending/#37a037051329.

43. Sisson, "Millennials, Priced out of Homes."

44. Hyojung Lee, "Who Owns Rental Properties, and Is It Changing?" *Housing Perspectives*, August 18, 2017, https://www.jchs.harvard.edu/blog/who-owns-rental-properties-and-is-it-changing/.

45. McLaughlin, "Special Report: House Flipping and Profits."

46. Daren Blomquist, "The Home Flipping Pyramid," RealtyTrac, June 9, 2017, https://www.realtytrac.com/news/the-home-flipping-pyramid/. This is consistent with studies of distressed housing markets between 2009 and 2013. A study of Miami-Dade County (covering 72,000 houses and purchases of $20 billion) found single-purchase buyers accounted for 66 percent of the purchases of single-family dwellings and 71 percent of the total value. Allen et al., "Impact of Investors," 624.

47. Adam Travis, "The Organization of Neglect: Limited Liability Companies and Housing Disinvestment," *American Sociological Review* 84, no. 1 (2019): 142–170.

48. Emily Badger, "Anonymous Owner, L.L.C.: Why It Has Become So Easy to Hide in the Housing Market," *New York Times*, April 30, 2018, https://www.nytimes.com/2018/04/30/upshot/anonymous-owner-llc-why-it-has-become-so-easy-to-hide-in-the-housing-market.html?searchResultPosition=1.

49. Blomquist, "Home Flipping Pyramid."

50. Ben Casselman and Colin Dougherty, "Want a House Like This? Prepare for a Bidding War with Investors," *New York Times*, June 20, 2019, https://www.nytimes.com/interactive/2019/06/20/business/economy/starter-homes-investors.html.

51. Andrea Riquier, "Mom-and-Pop Landlords Push Investor Share of Home Purchases to 19-Year High," *MarketWatch*, June 30, 2019, https://www.marketwatch.com/story/mom-and-pop-landlords-push-investor-share-of-home-purchases-to-19-year-high-2019-06-20; Laura Kusisto, "Investors Are Buying More of the U.S. Housing Market Than Ever Before," *Wall Street Journal*, June 20, 2019, https://www.wsj.com/articles/investors-are-buying-more-of-the-u-s-housing-market-than-ever-before-11561023120.

52. "What's notable about recent activity is that smaller investors, not big financial institutions, are driving the uptick. Large investors' share declined from 24.3% in 2013, the aftermath of the crisis, to 15.8% last year." Riquier, "Mom-and-Pop Landlords."

53. Ibid.

54. Casselman and Dougherty, "Want a House Like This?"

55. Ibid. KKR has invested over $1 billion in companies that deal in short-term bridge loans.

56. Burns, "You Think Your Landlord Is Bad?" See also Abood, "AFR Report."

57. Conlin, "Spiders, Sewage, and a Flurry of Fees."

58. Laurie Goodman and Karan Kaul, "GSE Financing of Single-Family Rentals," Urban Institute, May 10, 2017, https://www.urban.org/research/publication/gse-financing-single-family-rentals.

59. Ibid.

60. Shawn Tully, "Meet the A.I. Landlord That's Building a Single-Family-Home Empire," *Fortune*, June 21, 2019, http://fortune.com/longform/single-family-home-ai-algorithms/.

61. Daniel McCue, "Headlines from the 2019 State of the Nation's Housing Report," *Housing Perspectives*, August 7, 2019, https://www.jchs.harvard.edu/blog/headlines-from-the-2019-state-of-the-nations-housing-report/.

62. Matthew Gardner (chief economist at Windermere Real Estate), quoted in RealtyTrac, "A Flip of the Numbers."

63. Blomquist, "Home Flipping Pyramid."

64. Patrick Sisson, Jeff Andrews, and Alex Bazeley, "The Affordable Housing Crisis, Explained," *Curbed*, March 2, 2020, https://www.curbed.com/2019/5/15/18617763/affordable-housing-policy-rent-real-estate-apartment; Jeremiah Jensen, "ATTOM: Housing Affordability Falls to 10-Year Low," *HousingWire*, June 21, 2018, https://www.housingwire.com/articles/43744-attom-housing-affordability-falls-to-10-year-low.

65. Kate Wagner, "McMansion, USA," *Jacobin*, November 9, 2017, https://jacobinmag.com/2017/11/mcmansions-housing-architecture-rich-people.

66. McLaughlin and Jobe, "A Wild Flipping Ride"; Blomquist, "Home Flipping Pyramid."

67. Goodman and Kaul, "GSE Financing of Single-Family Rentals."

68. Ibid.

69. McLaughlin and Jobe, "A Wild Flipping Ride."

70. Meredith Blake, "HGTV Builds into a Top Cable Network on Foundation of No-Frills Shows," *Los Angeles Times*, July 18, 2014, http://www.latimes.com/entertainment/tv/la-et-hgtv-cable-network-20th-anniversary-20140720-story.html.

71. Jim Sollisch, "Blame Television for the Bubble: The Real Housing Villain Is on Cable," *Wall Street Journal*, January 3, 2009, http://www.wsj.com/articles/SB123094453377450603.

72. Ron Becker, "Horribly Guilty Television: HGTV and the Promotion of America's Ownership Society," *Flow*, April 24, 2008, http://flowtv.org/2008/04/horribly-guilty-television-hgtv-and-the-promotion-of-americas-ownership-society/.

73. Statista, "Share of Americans Who Watched HGTV in the Past Month in 2018, by Age," October 2018, https://www.statista.com/statistics/228962/cable-tv-networks-hgtv-watched-within-the-last-7-days-usa/.

74. Alessandra Stanley, "On HGTV, Fixing Homes and Hearts," *New York Times*, March 18, 2010, http://tv.nytimes.com/2010/03/18/arts/television/18hgtv.html?ref=alessandrastanley.

75. Blake, "HGTV Builds into a Top Cable Network."

76. Liz Hoffman and Peter Rudegeair, "Goldman Sachs to Lend to House-Flippers," *Wall Street Journal*, October 12, 2017, https://www.wsj.com/articles/goldman-sachs-to-buy-house-flipping-lender-1507826252.

77. Patrick Clark, "Long Island Home Flippers Sell to Each Other in Red-Hot Market," *Bloomberg*, August 27, 2019, https://www.bloomberg.com/news/articles/2019-08-27/long-island-home-flippers-sell-to-each-other-in-red-hot-market. Whereas the whole-

salers who operate at local and regional scales outsource their search for real estate leads to the Philippines, the more heavily capitalized fintech companies such as Opendoor and Zillow substitute proprietary technology platforms to step in between buyers and sellers.

78. Hoffman and Rudegeair, "Goldman Sachs to Lend to House-Flippers."
79. Clark, "Long Island Home Flippers."
80. Harsh Chauhan, "A Full-Blown U.S. Housing Market Crisis Is on the Way," *CCN*, December 15, 2019, https://www.ccn.com/full-blown-us-housing-market-crisis-on-the-way/.
81. Prashant Gopal, "Rookie Home-Flippers Get Burned in U.S. Downturn," *Bloomberg*, May 9, 2019, https://www.bloomberg.com/news/videos/2019-05-09/rookie-home-flippers-get-burned-in-u-s-downturn-video.
82. Joy Wiltermuth, "Lending Standards to Slide for Homeowners with Spotty Credit, Moody's Warns in 2020 Outlook," *MarketWatch*, December 10, 2019, https://www.marketwatch.com/story/lending-standards-to-slide-for-homeowners-with-spotty-credit-moodys-warns-in-2020-outlook-2019-12-10.
83. Michael Sasso, "Home-Flipping Trend Weakens as High-Interest Lenders Jump 40%," *Bloomberg*, June 12, 2019, https://www.bloomberg.com/news/articles/2019-06-12/high-interest-lenders-up-40-even-as-home-flipping-trend-weakens.

CHAPTER 4

1. Pedro Nicolaci da Costa, "America's Humongous Wealth Gap Is Widening Further," *Forbes*, May 29, 2019, https://www.forbes.com/sites/pedrodacosta/2019/05/29/americas-humungous-wealth-gap-is-widening-further/.
2. Benjamin Landy, "A Tale of Two Recoveries: Wealth Inequality after the Great Recession," Century Foundation, August 28, 2013, https://www.tcf.org/blog/detail/a-tale-of-two-recoveries.
3. Michael Batty et al., "Introducing the Distributional Financial Accounts of the United States," Board of Governors of the Federal Reserve System, Finance and Economics Discussion Series 2019-017, March 2019, p. 26, https://www.federalreserve.gov/econres/feds/files/2019017pap.pdf.
4. Tom Lamb, quoted in Itay Hod, "The 'Property Brothers' Are Reality Television's Crack Cocaine," *Daily Beast*, July 11, 2017, http://www.thedailybeast.com/articles/2013/09/08/the-property-brothers-are-reality-television-s-crack-cocaine.html.
5. Jean Baudrillard, *The System of Objects*, trans. James Benedict (London: Verso, 1996), 170.
6. Monica Hesse, "Granite: Why Every Homeowner Wants a Piece of the Rock," *Washington Post*, February 6, 2012, https://www.washingtonpost.com/lifestyle/style/granite-why-every-homeowner-wants-a-piece-of-the-rock/2012/02/01/gIQANBN4uQ_story.html.
7. Ibid.
8. Fiona Allon, "Money, Debt and the Business of 'Free Stuff,'" *South Atlantic Quarterly* 114, no. 2 (April 2015): 284.
9. Rakesh Kochhar, "How Americans Compare with the Global Middle Class," Pew Research Center, July 9, 2015, http://www.pewresearch.org/fact-tank/2015/07/09/how-americans-compare-with-the-global-middle-class/.
10. Matthew T. Huber, *Lifeblood: Oil, Freedom and the Forces of Capital* (Minneapolis: University of Minnesota, 2013), xvi.

11. Neil Smith, "Toward a Theory of Gentrification: A Back to the City Movement by Capital, not People," *Journal of the American Planning Association* 45, no. 4 (1979): 545.

12. David Gergen, quoted on dust jacket of Marc Dunkelman, *The Vanishing Neighbor: The Transformation of American Community* (New York: Norton, 2014).

13. Sandy Isenstadt, "The Rise and Fall of the Picture Window," in *Housing and Dwelling: Perspectives on Modern Domestic Architecture*, ed. Barbara Miller Lane (London: Routledge, 2007), 304.

14. Marshall Berman, *All That Is Solid Melts into Air* (New York: Simon and Schuster, 1982), 68.

15. Kathleen Finch, quoted in J. Bryan Lowder, "A Rotten Beam Threatens to Undermine HGTV's Fall Lineup," *Slate*, May 7, 2014, https://slate.com/human-interest/2014/05/hgtvs-flip-it-forward-with-extreme-anti-gay-conservatives-david-and-jason-benham-canceled.html.

16. Michelle Alexander, *The New Jim Crow: Mass Incarceration in the Age of Colorblindness* (New York: New Press, 2010).

17. Scott Brothers, "FAQ," previously available at http://www.thescottbrothers.com/faq/ (accessed October 14, 2017).

18. Henri Lefebvre, *The Production of Space*, trans. Donald Nicholson-Smith (Cambridge, MA: Blackwell, 1991), 342.

19. Anthony Giddens, "The Contours of Modernity," in *Modernity and Self-Identity* (Stanford: Stanford University Press, 1991), 17–19; Berman, "All That Is Solid."

20. Jason Hackworth and Neil Smith, "The Changing State of Gentrification," *Tijdschrift voor economische en sociale geografie* 92, no. 4 (2001): 464–477; Neil Smith, "Gentrification Generalized: From Local Anomaly to Urban 'Regeneration' as Global Urban Strategy," in *Frontiers of Capital: Ethnographic Reflections on the New Economy*, ed. Melissa Fisher and Greg Downey (New York: City University of New York, 2006), 191–208.

21. Neil Smith, "New Globalism, New Urbanism: Gentrification as Global Urban Strategy," *Antipode* 34, no. 3 (2002): 427.

22. Loretta Lees, Tom Slater, and Elvin Wyly, *Gentrification* (London: Routledge, 2008).

23. Manuel B. Aalbers, "Introduction to the Forum: From Third to Fifth-Wave Gentrification," *Tijdschrift voor economische en sociale geografie* 110, no. 1 (2019): 6.

24. N. Smith, "Toward a Theory of Gentrification," 545.

25. Jason Hackworth, "Postrecession Gentrification in New York City," *Urban Affairs Review* 37, no. 6 (2002): 819.

26. When class domination takes the form of racialized domination, as has been the case in other gentrifying districts of Indianapolis, the narrative properly shifts to the "ethnic cleansing of Black Indianapolis." Wildstyle Paschall, "The Ethnic Cleansing of Black Indianapolis," *New America*, February 4, 2020, http://newamerica.org/indianapolis/blog/indiana-avenue-ethnic-cleansing-black-indianapolis/.

27. After 2017, the *Flip or Flop* strategy shifted to compensate for a declining rate of profit in the El Moussas' rent-gap business model by expanding their flips to include customized upscale backyards (bars, barbecue pits, pools, and simulated waterfalls) in their renovations. However, this necessitated moving up to wealthier neighborhoods because buyers are not going to risk paying for upscale yard features in still-contested neighborhoods where an asking price exceeds the comps by a mile. Postfinancial crisis cocooning may be a new consumer preference that the show's hosts are tapping into,

but a more decisive factor motivates their move into the backyard transformation game: there is additional value to be mined in elaborate yard landscape designs.

28. Tom Slater, "Planetary Rent Gaps," *Antipode* 49 (2017): 119.

29. Laura Gottesdiener, "Wall Street's Hot New Financial Product: Your Rent Check," *Mother Jones*, March–April 2014, https://www.motherjones.com/politics/2014/02/blackstone-rental-homes-bundled-derivatives/.

30. Emily T. Molina, "Foreclosures, Investors, and Uneven Development during the Great Recession in the Los Angeles Metropolitan Area," *Journal of Urban Affairs* 38, no. 4 (2016): 571.

31. Alan Mallach, "Meeting the Challenge of Distressed Property Investors in America's Neighborhoods," Local Initiatives Support Corporation, 2010, https://www.lisc.org/media/filer_public/4f/46/4f462994-10b0-4eb0-8855-ddafc6e82d37/08142018_resources_distressed_property_investors.pdf. See also Dan Immergluck, "The Role of Investors in the Single-Family Market in Distressed Neighborhoods: The Case of Atlanta," What Works Collaborative, 2013, https://www.urban.org/sites/default/files/publication/23291/412743-The-Role-of-Investors-in-the-Single-Family-Market-in-Distressed-Neighborhoods-The-Case-of-Atlanta.PDF.

32. Molina, "Foreclosures, Investors, and Uneven Development," 573.

33. Ibid., 574. "Corporate real estate capital found its spatial fix in the oldest housing stock of the region in the city of Los Angeles and its proximate suburbs during the recession, while homebuyers increasingly invested—with significant financing assistance from the private and public sectors—in the newest housing on the region's fringe" (574).

34. Carl Hoover and Kristin Hoppa, "Car Smashes into 'Fixer Upper' House," *Waco Tribune-Herald*, July 8, 2017, http://www.wacotrib.com/news/city_of_waco/car-smashes-into-fixer-upper-house/article_bb418fb0-0e9e-5d5a-80e9-cc659032e3e6.html.

35. See On Data Suite, "Campus: Brook Avenue EL," June 21, 2017, https://www.wacoisd.org/site/handlers/filedownload.ashx?moduleinstanceid=10286&dataid=9409&FileName=bae.pdf.

36. Richard Lawson, "Did a Car Accident Reveal a Darker Side of HGTV's Biggest Hit?" *Vanity Fair*, July 10, 2017, http://www.vanityfair.com/style/2017/07/fixer-upper-hgtv-car-drives-through-house7.

37. J. B. Smith, "Waco Housing Boom Leaves Its Mark on Tax Appraisals," *Waco Tribune-Herald*, May 20, 2017, http://www.wacotrib.com/news/business/waco-housing-boom-leaves-its-mark-on-tax-appraisals/article_9bc6e987-a841-5927-80a3-ca5a5dc8c066.html.

38. Kelly Downs, quoted in Taysha Murtaugh, "What That 'Fixer Upper' Car Crash Says about Waco and Your Favorite HGTV Show," *Country Living*, July 12, 2017, http://www.countryliving.com/life/entertainment/news/a43890/fixer-upper-car-crash-aftermath/. Murtaugh also writes, "The '*Fixer Upper* effect' on property taxes has been a hot topic in Waco. McLennan County homeowners claimed they saw a spike in appraisals (sometimes by more than $100,000) in the year following *Fixer Upper* fame. The Chief County Appraiser replied that houses featured on the show are viewed separately from surrounding properties. 'We have a different neighborhood code for those than other homes in the neighborhood, because they are actually selling for more than regular homes. We don't use them as comparable for other homes renovated by other homeowners.'" See also Kristin Hoppa, "Witness Describes Aftermath of 'Fixer Upper' Crash," *Waco Tribune-Herald*, July 10, 2017, http://www.wacotrib.com/news/city_of

_waco/witness-describes-aftermath-of-fixer-upper-crash/article_3e82d207-be0a-59e7-9e5b-b34b5925326c.html.

39. Waco Convention and Visitors Bureau, "Tourism Research and Statistics," https://wacoheartoftexas.com/tourism-research-and-statistics/ (accessed February 15, 2018).

40. J. B. Smith, "'Fixer Upper' Effect: Waco's Economy Benefits from Chip and Joanna Gaines Lifestyle Empire," *USA Today*, November 21, 2017, https://www.usatoday.com/story/money/economy/2017/11/21/fixer-upper-effect-wacos-economy-benefits-chip-and-joanna-gaines-lifestyle-empire/884830001/.

41. *Fixer Upper*, season 3, episode 4, "A Home Away from Home for the Holidays" (High Noon Entertainment, HGTV, Discovery, 2015). Note that there are discrepancies in episode numbers and titles among listings on the HGTV website, the Magnolia website, and other sources. For the purpose of this book, I have used HGTV's episode titles. However, I have reason to believe, based on my real-time research, that some of HGTV's episode numbers are inaccurate. So for episode numbers, I use the prevailing number among the sources.

42. Vrbo, "Three Little Pigs House as Seen on Fixer Upper!" https://www.vrbo.com/1509274?unitId=2068066&noDates=true (accessed July 21, 2017); Mackenzie Schmidt, "*Fixer Upper* Homeowner Says Chip and Joanna Gaines 'Deceived' Her about 'Not Safe' Neighborhood," *People*, July 10, 2017, https://people.com/home/fixer-upper-homeowner-says-chip-and-joanna-gaines-deceived-her-about-not-safe-neighborhood/.

43. Schmidt, "*Fixer Upper* Homeowner."

44. Selena Barrientos, "These Four *Fixer Upper* Houses Have Been on the Market for Almost a Year," *House Beautiful*, September 24, 2019, https://www.housebeautiful.com/lifestyle/a28722955/fixer-upper-houses-for-sale/. See also *Fixer Upper*, season 3, episode 8, "Tiny House, Big Charm" (High Noon Entertainment, HGTV, Discovery, 2016); *Fixer Upper*, season 3, episode 6, "A Home for Country Living" (High Noon Entertainment, HGTV, Discovery, 2016); and *Fixer Upper*, season 3, episode 7, "Old House, New Memories" (High Noon Entertainment, HGTV, Discovery, 2016).

45. Karl Marx and Frederick Engels, *Manifesto of the Communist Party* (Peking: Foreign Language Press, 1970), 34.

CHAPTER 5

1. Neil Smith, *The New Urban Frontier: Gentrification and the Revanchist City* (London: Routledge, 1996).

2. Daniel José Older, "Gentrification's Insidious Violence: The Truth about American Cities," *Salon*, April 8, 2014, https://www.salon.com/2014/04/08/gentrifications_insidious_violence_the_truth_about_american_cities/.

3. Jamie Peck, Nik Theodore, and Neil Brenner, "Neoliberal Urbanism: Models, Moments, Mutations," *SAIS Review of International Affairs* 29, no. 1 (2009): 52.

4. For a summary of the history of public policy efforts (and failures) to regulate the financialization of housing between 1995 and 2008, see Dan Immergluck, *Foreclosed: High-Risk Lending, Deregulation, and the Undermining of America's Mortgage Market* (Ithaca, NY: Cornell University Press, 2009), 167–196.

5. Megan Goulding, "Rising Rent Burden in Los Angeles," Neighborhood Data for Social Change, October 2017, https://usc.data.socrata.com/stories/s/Rising-Rent-Burden-in-Los-Angeles/4wjy-s7d9; Elijah Chiland, "LA County Median Home Prices Shatter

$600K Mark," *Curbed LA*, June 21, 2018, https://la.curbed.com/2018/6/21/17489270/los-angeles-home-prices-record-how-much-to-buy.

6. Cara Courage, "Why Indianapolis Is a Test Case for a Fairer Form of Gentrification," *The Guardian*, August 21, 2015, https://www.theguardian.com/cities/2015/aug/21/indianapolis-gentrification-arts-big-car-jim-walker-fountain-square-garfield-park; see also Brian D. Smith, "The Artists Are Disappearing from Fountain Square," *Indianapolis Monthly*, February 15, 2017, https://web.archive.org/web/20170215145631/https://www.indianapolismonthly.com/arts-culture/artists-disappearing-fountain-square/.

7. Erica Irish, "Priorities Evolve as 'Good Bones' Stars Begin Filming Fourth Season," *Indianapolis Business Journal*, August 1, 2018, https://www.ibj.com/articles/69927-priorities-evolve-as-good-bones-stars-begin-filming-fourth-season.

8. *Good Bones*, season 1, episode 9, "Duplex Remodel, Double Trouble" (High Noon Entertainment, HGTV, Discovery, 2016).

9. N. Smith, *New Urban Frontier*, 190.

10. *Revitalization*, "Indianapolis Land Trust Is Revitalizing Area by Renovating Vacant Homes for Artists," *Revitalization*, May 1, 2017, https://revitalization.org/article/non-profit-renovates-vacant-houses-artists-revitalize-indianapolis-neighborhood/.

11. Aaron M. Renn, "Parallel Societies," *Aaron Renn* (blog), May 5, 2013, https://www.urbanophile.com/2013/05/05/replay-parallel-societies/.

12. Michael Maciag, "Indianapolis Gentrification Maps and Data," *Governing*, February 1, 2015, https://www.governing.com/gov-data/indianapolis-gentrification-maps-demographic-data.html.

13. Roland Barthes, *Mythologies* (New York: Hill and Wang, 1972), 111–115.

14. Adam Barker and Emma Battell Lowman, "Settler Colonialism," *Global Social Theory*, https://globalsocialtheory.org/concepts/settler-colonialism/ (accessed December 29, 2020).

15. David Harvey, "The 'New' Imperialism: Accumulation by Dispossession," *Socialist Register* 40 (2004): 74.

16. *Barnwood Builders*, season 3, episode 3, "Spring House Revival" (DIY Network, Discovery, 2016).

17. Bowe's company, Antique Cabins and Barns, LLC, turns materials "rescued from pioneer homesteads" into "modern homes of distinction throughout the country. Our designs are nostalgic, creating homes with emotion and character that are rooted in our country's rustic heritage while seamlessly integrating the lifestyles of modern life." Barnwood Living, "Project Gallery," https://barnwoodliving.com/project-gallery/ (accessed March 8, 2021).

18. Dwight Billings and Kathleen M. Blee, *The Road to Poverty: The Making of Wealth and Hardship in Appalachia* (Cambridge: Cambridge University Press, 2000), 11–14.

19. Robert Louis Chianese, "Is Nature Photography Too Beautiful?" *American Scientist* 102, no. 1 (2014): 64.

20. Matthew T. Huber, *Lifeblood: Oil, Freedom and the Forces of Capital* (Minneapolis: University of Minnesota, 2013), 18.

CHAPTER 6

1. Roland Barthes, *The Fashion System* (Berkeley: University of California Press, 1990), 43.

2. Jean Baudrillard, "The Order of Simulacra," in *Symbolic Exchange and Death*, trans. Iain Hamilton Grant (London: Sage, 1993), 50–52.

3. Kieran Healy, "Fuck Nuance," *Sociological Theory* 35, no. 2 (2017): 123.

4. See Arjun Appadurai, "Commodities and the Politics of Value," in *Interpreting Objects and Collections*, ed. Susan Pearce (London: Routledge, 1994), 87.

5. *Beach Flip*, season 1, episode 8, "And the Winner Is . . ." (HGTV, Discovery, 2015).

6. Green and red tags designate that city inspectors have determined that a house is too dilapidated or unsafe to live in. When a housing structure is thus deemed to be out of compliance with city building standards, it may be condemned for teardown if not repaired.

7. City of Waco, "Consolidated Plan for 2009–2013," 2009, www.waco-texas.com/pdf/housing/Consolidated%20Plan%202009-2013.pdf.

8. Neighborhood Scout, "Waco TX: Appreciation Rate Trends and Housing Market Data and Appreciation Trends," https://www.neighborhoodscout.com/tx/waco/real-estate (accessed June 4, 2017).

9. J. B. Smith, "Faith-Motivated Newcomers Take Root in North Waco," *Waco Tribune-Herald*, May 1, 2011, http://www.wacotrib.com/news/faith-motivated-newcomers-take-root-in-north-waco/article_28d8b1d1-02a8-5e3c-b9b5-ccd88e0e5929.html.

10. Katherine Hankins and Andy Walter, "'Gentrification with Justice': An Urban Ministry Collective and the Practice of Place-Making in Atlanta's Inner-City Neighbourhoods," *Urban Studies* 49, no. 7 (2012): 1511, 1522.

11. Blake Tommey, "For This Intentional Christian Community, Seeking the World's Healing Means Battling Gentrification Close at Home," *Baptist News Global*, January 3, 2018, https://baptistnews.com/article/qc-family-tree-gentrification.

12. Austin Meek, "Downtown Depot: Jimmy Dorrell," *Waco Business News*, July 21, 2017, http://www.wacobusinessnews.com/the-latest/downtown-depot-jimmy-dorrell.

13. *Fixer Upper*, season 1, episode 1, "Embracing Revitalization" (High Noon Entertainment, HGTV, Discovery, 2013).

14. Ibid.

15. Ibid.

16. *Fixer Upper*, season 1, episode 6, "Family Craves Urban Feel" (High Noon Entertainment, HGTV, Discovery, 2014).

17. J. B. Smith, "Neglected North Waco Houses Transformed as HGTV Cameras Roll," *Waco Tribune-Herald*, February 16, 2014, http://www.wacotrib.com/news/business/neglected-north-waco-houses-transformed-as-hgtv-cameras-roll/article_dbf75c5e-460e-5ee8-a63c-81e1171c5f8f.html.

18. *Fixer Upper*, season 1, episode 6.

19. Ibid.

20. Karl Marx, *Capital: A Critique of Political Economy*, trans. Ben Fowkes (New York: Vintage Books, 1977), 1:73.

21. David Graeber, *Toward an Anthropological Theory of Value* (New York: Palgrave, 2001), 115.

22. Emily Peck and Charles Maldonado, "How Airbnb Is Pushing Locals Out of New Orleans' Coolest Neighborhoods," *Huffington Post*, October 30, 2017, https://www.huffingtonpost.com/entry/airbnb-new-orleans-housing_us_59f33054e4b03cd20b811699.

23. Kevin Fox Gotham, "Creating Liquidity out of Spatial Fixity: The Secondary Circuit of Capital and the Subprime Mortgage Crisis," *International Journal of Urban and Regional Research* 33, no. 2 (2009): 355–371.

24. *Fixer Upper*, season 3, episode 8, "Tiny House, Big Charm" (High Noon Entertainment, HGTV, Discovery, 2016).

25. Ibid.

26. Taysha Murtaugh, "What Chip and Joanna Really Think of Clients Listing Their 'Fixer Uppers' as Vacation Rentals," *Country Living*, August 15, 2017, http://www.countryliving.com/life/entertainment/news/a44387/fixer-upper-clients-renting-out-homes/.

27. Chris Rogers, "Inside the Multi-million Dollar Waco Development Project," *KCEN-TV*, February 28, 2017, https://www.kcentv.com/article/news/local/inside-the-multi-million-dollar-waco-development-project/500-416097757.

28. Mike Copeland, "Owner Defends Almost $1 Million Asking Price for Seventh Street Shotgun House," *Waco Tribune-Herald*, June 24, 2017, https://wacotrib.com/business/owner-defends-almost-1-million-asking-price-for-seventh-street-shotgun-house/article_a9cee38b-0a02-559c-9b79-4bd905729fff.html.

29. Kate Wagner, "Behind-the-Scenes of Rustic Modernism: Your Complete Guide to Farmhouse and Industrial Chic," *Curbly*, June 22, 2017, https://www.curbly.com/rustic-modernism-guide.

30. Rahel Aima, "Desiring Machines," *New Inquiry*, June 2012, http://digitalcuration.umaine.edu/resources/aima_desiring_machines.pdf.

31. See the Magnolia home page, at https://magnolia.com (which cycles through different parts of the manifesto each time the page is refreshed).

32. Magnolia, "Authenticity Leather Sign," https://shop.magnolia.com/collections/wall-decor/products/authenticity-leather-sign (accessed March 5, 2021).

CHAPTER 7

1. Michael Hardt and Antonio Negri, *Empire* (Cambridge: Harvard University Press, 2000); Maurizio Lazzarato, "Immaterial Labor," in *Radical Thought in Italy: A Potential Politics*, ed. Paolo Virno and Michael Hardt (Minneapolis: University of Minnesota Press, 1996), 133–147.

2. Rob Horning, "On Real and Formal Subsumption," *Pop Matters*, September 15, 2011, https://www.popmatters.com/148650--2495950141.html.

3. Karl Marx, *Capital: A Critique of Political Economy*, trans. Ben Fowkes (New York: Vintage Books, 1977), 1:60.

4. Ibid., 1:44.

5. Rachel Teodoro, "What It's Really Like to Be Cast on Fixer Upper, Part II," *Rachel Teodoro* (blog), September 2017, http://www.rachelteodoro.com/2017/09/what-its-really-like-to-be-cast-on.html.

6. Caitlin Flanagan, "Beware the Open-Plan Kitchen," *Vulture*, September 2017, https://www.vulture.com/2017/09/the-ugliness-behind-hgtv-never-ending-fantasy-loop.html.

7. Marx, *Capital*, 1:131.

8. *Holmes on Homes* is the exception to this representational rule. Mike Holmes credits the skilled subcontractors on whom he relies, instructing viewers to hire licensed subcontractors and not those who take shortcuts because they lack knowledge and skill.

9. Bradford Johnson, James Manyika, and Lareina Yee, "The Next Revolution in Interactions," *McKinsey Quarterly*, November 1, 2005, https://www.mckinsey.com/business-functions/organization/our-insights/the-next-revolution-in-interactions.

10. Brenda Weber, *Makeover TV: Selfhood, Citizenship and Celebrity* (Durham, NC: Duke University Press, 2009).

11. Jean Baudrillard, "Transaesthetics," in *The Transparency of Evil: Essays on Extreme Phenomena*, trans. James Benedict (New York: Verso, 1993), 16.

12. Beverley Skeggs and Helen Wood, "The Labour of Transformation and Circuits of Value 'Around' Reality Television," *Continuum* 22, no. 4 (2008): 560. See also Miranda Joseph, "The Performance of Production and Consumption," *Social Text* 54 (1998): 25–61.

13. See G.W.F. Hegel, *The Phenomenology of Mind*, trans. J. B. Baillie (New York: Harper, 1967).

14. Eva Illouz, *Cold Intimacies: The Making of Emotional Capitalism* (Cambridge, UK: Polity, 2007).

15. Arlie Russell Hochschild, *The Managed Heart: Commercialization of Human Feeling* (Berkeley: University of California Press, 1985).

16. Goetz Bachmann and Andreas Wittel, "Enthusiasm as Affective Labour: On the Productivity of Enthusiasm in the Media Industry," *M/C Journal* 12, no. 2 (2009), https://doi.org/10.5204/mcj.147.

17. HGTV, "Property Virgins," http://www.hgtv.com/shows/property-virgins (accessed December 30, 2020).

18. Erving Goffman, "On Cooling the Mark Out: Some Aspects of Adaptation to Failure," *Psychiatry* 15, no. 4 (1952): 451–463.

19. Jason Glynos, Robin Klimecki, and Hugh Willmott, "Cooling Out the Marks: The Ideology and Politics of the Financial Crisis," *Journal of Cultural Economy* 5, no. 3 (2012): 301.

20. Millie Rothrock, "'Barnwood Builders' Spring into Action in Wytheville," *SWVA Today*, January 14, 2016, http://www.swvatoday.com/news/smyth_county/article_43d8e56a-b966-11e5-8fe5-277c6c3ba13e.html.

21. *Barnwood Builders*, season 3, episode 4, "Cable County Cabin," DIY Network, Discovery, 2016.

22. *Barnwood Builders* represents itself as the inverse of Marx's argument that alienation is experienced as self-estrangement and as separation from others. To overcome alienated labor, the work team makes labor immediately social by joining self with others in the act of labor. *Barnwood Builders* illustrates the strength of Marx's theory while also hinting at the historical limits of Marx's ideas about working-class solidarity. The most important limit, though it need not be, is the perception of race and ethnicity. Marx theorized the power of worker solidarity to transform their total social product, as long as the work group shares a consciousness of their shared position. *Barnwood Builders* features white Appalachian working-class men who share an almost religious faith in the power of hard work to liberate themselves, but there are no men of color and there are no women. Can the *Barnyard Builder* philosophy maintain itself if blacks, Hispanics, and women are included? And what about LGBTQ? Just a question, not an accusation.

23. Greg Johnson, "Catching Up with the Barnwood Builders," *Greenbrier Valley Quarterly*, October 2016, http://www.gvquarterly.com/blog/2016/10/27/catching-up-with-the-barnwood-builders.

24. Ibid.

25. David Montgomery, *Workers' Control in America* (Cambridge: Cambridge University Press, 1980), 13.

26. On the subject of virtuosity and labor, see Paolo Virno, *A Grammar of the Multitude: For an Analysis of Contemporary Forms of Life*, trans. Isabella Bertoletti, James Cascaito, and Andrea Casson (Los Angeles: Semiotext(e); Cambridge, MA: MIT Press, 2004).

27. Claude Lévi-Strauss, *The Savage Mind* (Chicago: University of Chicago, 1962); Dick Hebdige, *Subculture: The Meaning of Style* (London: Methuen, 1979); Celeste Olalquiaga, *Megalopolis: Contemporary Cultural Sensibilities* (Minneapolis: University of Minnesota, 1992).

28. Rachel Louise Ensign, Paul Overberg, and AnnaMaria Andriotis, "Banks' Embrace of Jumbo Mortgages Means Fewer Loans for Blacks, Hispanics," *Wall Street Journal*, June 1, 2016, https://www.wsj.com/articles/banks-embrace-of-jumbo-mortgages-means-fewer-loans-for-blacks-hispanics-1464789752.

29. Ibid.

30. See Sarah Burd-Sharps and Rebecca Rasch, "Impact of the US Housing Crisis on the Racial Wealth Gap across Generations," Social Science Research Council, June 2015, https://www.ssrc.org/publications/view/impact-of-the-us-housing-crisis-on-the-racial-wealth-gap-across-generations/; and Aaron Glantz and Emmanuel Martinez, "For People of Color, Banks Are Shutting the Door to Homeownership," *Reveal*, February 15, 2018, https://www.revealnews.org/article/for-people-of-color-banks-are-shutting-the-door-to-homeownership/.

31. Slavoj Žižek, *The Sublime Object of Ideology* (London: Verso, 1989), 30.

32. Drew DeSilver and Kristen Bialik, "Blacks and Hispanics Face Extra Challenges in Getting Home Loans," Pew Research Center, January 10, 2017, http://www.pewresearch.org/fact-tank/2017/01/10/blacks-and-hispanics-face-extra-challenges-in-getting-home-loans/.

33. Glantz and Martinez, "For People of Color."

34. Ibid.

35. Marion Fourcade and Kieran Healy, "Classification Situations: Life-Chances in the Neoliberal Era," *Accounting, Organizations and Society* 38, no. 8 (2013): 566, 570. Keeanga-Yamahtta Taylor shows how histories of racial discrimination and stacked decks seep back into ostensibly "color neutral" credit scores in a manner that reproduces patterns of "predatory financial arrangements." Keeanga-Yamahtta Taylor, "Back Story to the Neoliberal Moment: Race Taxes and the Political Economy of Black Urban Housing in the 1960s," *Souls* 14, no. 3–4 (2012): 202.

36. Michelle Buckley, "Between House and Home: Renovations Labor and the Production of Residential Value," *Economic Geography* 95, no. 3 (2019): 209–230; Marc Doussard, *Degraded Work: The Struggle at the Bottom of the Labor Market* (Minneapolis: University of Minnesota Press, 2013).

37. Buckley, "Between House and Home," 221.

38. Ibid., 209.

39. Diane Elson, "The Value Theory of Labor," in *Value: The Representation of Labour in Capitalism* (Atlantic Highlands, NJ: Humanities Press, 1979), 115–180. More recently, David Harvey has advanced a comparable critique. See David Harvey, "Marx's Refusal of the Labour Theory of Value," *Reading Marx's Capital with David Harvey* (blog), March 14, 2018, http://davidharvey.org/2018/03/marxs-refusal-of-the-labour-theory-of-value-by-david-harvey/.

40. Geoff Mann, "Value after Lehman," *Historical Materialism* 18, no. 4 (2010): 176.

CHAPTER 8

1. Lauren Berlant, *Cruel Optimism* (Durham, NC: Duke University Press, 2011), 1.

2. David Graeber, *Debt: The First 5,000 Years* (Brooklyn, NY: Melville House, 2011).

3. FRED Economic Research, "Household Debt to GDP for United States," November 20, 2020, https://fred.stlouisfed.org/series/HDTGPDUSQ163N.

4. Louis Moreno, "The Urban Process under Financialised Capitalism," *City* 18, no. 3 (2014): 250.

5. John Brenkman, "Mass Media: From Collective Experience to the Culture of Privatization," *Social Text*, no. 1 (1979): 99.

6. See Noelle Stout, *Dispossessed: How Predatory Bureaucracy Foreclosed on the American Middle Class* (Oakland: University of California Press, 2019).

7. Dick Bryan, Michael Rafferty, and Chris Jefferis, "Risk and Value: Finance, Labor, and Production," *South Atlantic Quarterly* 114, no. 2 (2015): 323.

8. Ivan Ascher, *Portfolio Society: On the Capitalist Mode of Prediction* (New York: Zone Books, 2016), 71–73.

9. Maurizio Lazzarato, *The Making of the Indebted Man*, trans. Joshua David Jordan (Los Angeles, CA: Semiotext(e), 2012), 30–31. For a lengthy discussion of the morality of debt, see also Graeber, *Debt*.

10. Mark Kear, "Playing the Credit Score Game: Algorithms, 'Positive' Data and the Personification of Financial Objects," *Economy and Society* 46, no. 3–4 (2017): 346–368.

11. Marion Fourcade and Kieran Healy, "Classification Situations: Life-Chances in the Neoliberal Era," *Accounting, Organizations and Society* 38 (2013): 564.

12. James Hay, "Too Good to Fail: Managing Financial Crisis through the Moral Economy of Realty TV," *Journal of Communication Inquiry* 34, no. 4 (2010): 388.

13. Maurizio Lazzarato, "From Capital-Labour to Capital-Life," *Ephemera* 4, no. 3 (2004): 187.

14. David Harvey, "Marx's Refusal of the Labour Theory of Value," *Reading Marx's Capital with David Harvey* (blog), March 14, 2018, http://davidharvey.org/2018/03/marxs-refusal-of-the-labour-theory-of-value-by-david-harvey/.

15. Geoff Mann, "Value after Lehman," *Historical Materialism* 18, no. 4 (2010): 175.

16. My writing here implies a theoretical consensus about whether finance capitalism has really changed its stripes from its industrial predecessor. This perspective remains open to debate. See Beverley Best's critique of the position outlined in "Political Economy through the Looking Glass: Imagining Six Impossible Things about Finance before Breakfast," *Historical Materialism* 25, no. 3 (2017): 76–100.

17. Ascher, *Portfolio Society*, 26.

18. Bryan, Rafferty, and Jefferis, "Risk and Value," 320.

19. Karl Marx, *Capital: A Critique of Political Economy*, trans. Ben Fowkes (New York: Vintage Books, 1977), 1:1034–1038.

20. Bryan and Rafferty use the analogy of sports betting to explain derivatives. You don't have to own a horse to bet on it; similarly, one does not have to be exposed to the risks of owning mortgages to bet on the derivatives. Dick Bryan and Mike Rafferty, *Risking Together* (Sydney: Sydney University Press, 2018), 46–47.

21. Marion Fourcade and Kieran Healy, "Seeing Like a Market," *Socio-economic Review* 15, no. 1 (2017): 9–29; Ascher, *Portfolio Society*, 71–75.

22. Costas Lapavitsas, "Financialisation, or the Search for Profits in the Sphere of Circulation," *Research on Money and Finance*, Discussion Paper no. 10, May 2009, p. 3.

23. Dick Bryan, Randy Martin, and Mike Rafferty, "Financialization and Marx: Giving Labor and Capital a Financial Makeover," *Review of Radical Political Economics* 41, no. 4 (2009): 464.

24. Dick Bryan, "The Duality of Labour and the Financial Crisis," *Economic and Labour Relations Review* 20, no. 2 (2010): 52.

25. Edward LiPuma and Benjamin Lee, "Financial Derivatives and the Rise of Circulation," *Economy and Society* 34, no. 3 (2005): 408.

26. André Orléan and Rainer Diaz-Bone, "Questioning Economists' Notion of Value: André Orléan Interviewed by Rainer Diaz-Bone," *Economic Sociology, the European Electronic Newsletter* 14, no. 3 (2013): 42.

27. Dick Bryan and Michael Rafferty, "Financial Derivatives as Social Policy beyond Crisis," *Sociology* 48, no. 5 (2014): 892; Bryan and Rafferty, *Risking Together*, 43.

28. Émile Durkheim, *The Division of Labor in Society* (New York: Free Press, 1984).

29. Zygmunt Bauman, *Liquid Life* (Cambridge, UK: Polity 2005), 36.

30. Ascher, *Portfolio Society*, 61.

31. Ibid., 24.

32. Michael Lewis, *The Big Short* (New York: Norton, 2010), 130.

33. Jean Baudrillard, "The End of Production," in *Symbolic Exchange and Death*, trans. Iain Hamilton Grant (London: Sage, 1993), 6.

34. Jean Baudrillard, *Simulacra and Simulation*, trans. Sheila Glaser (Ann Arbor: University of Michigan Press, 1994), 6.

35. Bethany McLean and Joe Nocera, *All the Devils Are Here: The Hidden History of the Financial Crisis* (New York: Penguin, 2011), 54.

36. Gillian Tett, *Fool's Gold* (New York: Free Press, 2010).

37. Lewis, *The Big Short*, 131.

38. Ibid., 77.

39. Bill Maurer, "Repressed Futures: Financial Derivatives' Theological Unconscious," *Economy and Society* 31, no. 1 (2002): 18.

40. Nevertheless, in both its spectacular and financial forms, the hyperreal is a vehicle for exercising hegemony.

41. David Hawkes, "Against Financial Derivatives: Towards an Ethics of Representation," *Journal of Interdisciplinary Economics* 31, no. 2 (2019): 166.

42. Jean Baudrillard, "After the Orgy," in *The Transparency of Evil: Essays on Extreme Phenomena*, trans. James Benedict (London: Verso, 1993), 5. Even measures of value become subject to the rules of the hyperreal amid this epidemic: in 2012, the notional value of the global derivatives market reportedly stood at a fantastical (and inconceivable) $1.2 quadrillion.

43. Jean Baudrillard, *Jean Baudrillard: Selected Writings*, ed. Mark Poster, trans. Jacques Mourrain (Stanford: Stanford University Press, 2001), 125.

44. Baudrillard, "End of Production," 7; Baudrillard, "After the Orgy," 5.

45. CDOs are like ground beef. You never know which cow you're eating; you could be eating from a hundred when you eat a single burger.

46. David Harvey, *The Enigma of Capital and the Crises of Capitalism* (New York: Oxford University Press, 2010).

47. Best, "Political Economy through the Looking Glass," 98.

48. Maurer, "Repressed Futures," 17.

49. See Donald MacKenzie, "Physics and Finance: S-Terms and Modern Finance as a Topic for Science Studies," *Science, Technology, and Human Values* 26, no. 2 (2001): 115–144.

50. Baudrillard, "End of Production," 10.

51. Ibid., 30.

52. Manuel B. Aalbers, "The Financialization of Home and the Mortgage Market Crisis," *Competition and Change* 12, no. 2 (2008): 148–166.

53. Baudrillard, *Jean Baudrillard: Selected Writings*, 121.

EPILOGUE

1. Daniel McCue, "Headlines from the 2019 State of the Nation's Housing Report," *Housing Perspectives*, August 7, 2019, https://www.jchs.harvard.edu/blog/headlines-from-the-2019-state-of-the-nations-housing-report/. In addition to those 18 million households that are "severely" cost burdened, another 38 million households, or nearly a third of all U.S. households, are cost burdened because they spend more than 30 percent of their incomes on housing. The longer historical trajectory of the secular descent of the poor into a chronic crisis of rent affordability is presented in Matthew Desmond, "Heavy Is the House: Rent Burden among the American Urban Poor," *International Journal of Urban and Regional Research* 42, no. 1 (2018): 160–170.

2. Niema Jordan, "Moms 4 Housing Is Fighting to Make Sure Everyone Has a Home," *Shondaland*, May 18, 2020, https://www.shondaland.com/act/news-politics/a32501691/moms-4-housing-homeless-activism/.

3. Wedgewood, "About Us," https://www.wedgewood-inc.com/about/ (accessed January 17, 2020).

4. Marisa Endicott, "The Rent in the Bay Area Is Too Damn High: So These Moms Occupied a Vacant House," *Mother Jones*, December 23, 2019, https://www.motherjones.com/politics/2019/12/bay-area-moms-homeless-squatters/.

5. Rebecca Burns, "Oakland's Moms 4 Housing Were Evicted by a Giant Corporation That Runs National Home-Flipping Operation," *The Intercept*, January 17, 2020, https://theintercept.com/2020/01/17/moms-4-housing-eviction-wedgewood/. As discussed in Chapter 3, firms like Wedgewood amass houses anonymously by doing "business nationwide through an alphabet-soup of companies such as HMC Assets LLC and FI-337 LLC." Burns, "Oakland's Moms 4 Housing."

6. Marisa Kendall, "Moms 4 Housing Victory: Property Owner Gives Squatters Chance to Reclaim House," *Mercury News*, January 20, 2020, https://www.mercurynews.com/2020/01/20/moms-4-housing-victory-group-gets-chance-to-buy-house-through-nonprofit/.

Bibliography

Aalbers, Manuel B. "The Financialization of Home and the Mortgage Market Crisis." *Competition and Change* 12, no. 2 (2008): 148–166.

———. "Introduction to the Forum: From Third to Fifth-Wave Gentrification." *Tijdschrift voor economische en sociale geografie* 110, no. 1 (2019): 1–11.

Abood, Maya. "AFR Report: Wall Street and Single-Family Rentals." *Americans for Financial Reform*, January 17, 2018. http://ourfinancialsecurity.org/2018/01/afr-report-wall-street-and-single-family-rentals/.

Agamben, Giorgio. "The Endless Crisis as an Instrument of Power: In Conversation with Giorgio Agamben." *Verso* (blog), June 2013. https://www.versobooks.com/blogs/1318-the-endless-crisis-as-an-instrument-of-power-in-conversation-with-giorgio-agamben.

Aima, Rahel. "Desiring Machines." *New Inquiry*, June 2012. http://digitalcuration.umaine.edu/resources/aima_desiring_machines.pdf.

Albanesi, Stefania, Giacomo DiForgio, and Jaromir Nosal. "Credit Growth and the Financial Crisis: A New Narrative." NBER Working Paper No. 23740, August 2017. https://www.nber.org/papers/w23740.

Alexander, Michelle. *The New Jim Crow: Mass Incarceration in the Age of Colorblindness*. New York: New Press, 2010.

Allen, Marcus, Jessica Rutherford, Ronald Rutherford, and Abdullah Yavas. "Impact of Investors in Distressed Housing Markets." *Journal of Real Estate Finance and Economics* 56, no. 4 (2018): 622–652.

Allon, Fiona. "Money, Debt, and the Business of 'Free Stuff.'" *South Atlantic Quarterly* 114, no. 2 (April 2015): 283–305.

———. "Speculating on Everyday Life: The Cultural Economy of the Quotidian." *Journal of Communication Inquiry* 34, no. 4 (2010): 366–381.

Allon, Fiona, and Guy Redden. "The Global Financial Crisis and the Culture of Continual Growth." *Journal of Cultural Economy* 5, no. 4 (2012): 375–390.

Althusser, Louis. "Ideology and Ideological State Apparatuses." In *Lenin and Philosophy, and Other Essays*, 127–188. New York: Monthly Review Press, 1971.
Amherst Capital Management. "U.S. Single-Family Rental—an Emerging Institutional Asset Class." November 2016. https://www.amherstcapital.com/documents/20649/22737/US+SFR+Emerging+Asset+Class/9d84e0da-4a9f-4665-9880-88a4515d9d2b.
Andrews, Edmund. "Treasury Chief Aims to Steady Credit Markets." *New York Times*, October 16, 2007. https://www.nytimes.com/2007/10/16/business/16rescue.html.
Andrews, Jeff. "How Wall Street, Silicon Valley Institutionalized Home Flipping." *Curbed*, May 9, 2018. https://www.curbed.com/2018/5/9/17319958/house-flipping-lenders-roc-capital-lendinghome.
———. "10 Years after the Financial Crisis, Is the Housing Market Still at Risk?" *Curbed*, August 29, 2018. https://www.curbed.com/2018/8/29/17788844/financial-crisis-2008-cause-housing-mortgage-lending.
Appadurai, Arjun. "Commodities and the Politics of Value." In *Interpreting Objects and Collections*, edited by Susan Pearce, 76–91. London: Routledge, 1994.
Arellano, Megan. "In Booming Denver, the Role of Flipped Houses Is Changing." *Denverite*, June 9, 2016. https://denverite.com/2016/06/09/booming-denver-role-flipped-houses-changing/.
Ascher, Ivan. *Portfolio Society: On the Capitalist Mode of Prediction*. New York: Zone Books, 2016.
ATTOM Data Solutions. "U.S. Foreclosure Activity Drops to 12-Year Low in 2017." January 16, 2018. https://www.attomdata.com/news/foreclosure-trends/2017-year-end-u-s-foreclosure-market-report.
———. "U.S. Home Flipping Increases to 11-Year High in 2017 with More Than 200,000 Homes Flipped for Second Straight Year." March 7, 2018. https://www.attomdata.com/news/home-flipping/2017-u-s-home-flipping-report/.
———. "U.S. Home Flipping Returns Drop to Seven-Year Low in 2018." February 26, 2019. https://www.attomdata.com/news/most-recent/2018-year-end-u-s-home-flipping-report/.
Auerbach, David. "Georg Simmel's Philosophy of Money, Part 1: Value and Money." *Waggish* (blog), August 16, 2014. https://www.waggish.org/2014/georg-simmels-philosophy-of-money-1-value-and-money/.
Bachmann, Goetz, and Andreas Wittel. "Enthusiasm as Affective Labour: On the Productivity of Enthusiasm in the Media Industry." *M/C Journal* 12, no. 2 (2009). https://doi.org/10.5204/mcj.147.
Badger, Emily. "Anonymous Owner, L.L.C.: Why It Has Become So Easy to Hide in the Housing Market." *New York Times*, April 30, 2018. https://www.nytimes.com/2018/04/30/upshot/anonymous-owner-llc-why-it-has-become-so-easy-to-hide-in-the-housing-market.html?searchResultPosition=1.
Baldauf, Annette. "Betting the House." *Rethinking Marxism* 22, no. 2 (2010): 219–230.
Barker, Adam, and Emma Battell Lowman. "Settler Colonialism." *Global Social Theory*. https://globalsocialtheory.org/concepts/settler-colonialism/ (accessed December 29, 2020).
Barnwood Builders. Season 3, episode 3, "Spring House Revival." DIY Network, Discovery, 2016.
———. Season 3, episode 4, "Cable County Cabin." DIY Network, Discovery, 2016.
Barnwood Living. "Project Gallery." https://barnwoodliving.com/project-gallery/ (accessed March 8, 2021).

Barrientos, Selena. "These Four Fixer Upper Houses Have Been on the Market for Almost a Year." *House Beautiful*, September 24, 2019. https://www.housebeautiful.com/lifestyle/a28722955/fixer-upper-houses-for-sale/.
Barthes, Roland. *The Fashion System*. Berkeley: University of California Press, 1990.
———. *Mythologies*. New York: Hill and Wang, 1972.
Batty, Michael, Jesse Bricker, Joseph Briggs, Elizabeth Holmquist, Susan McIntosh, Kevin Moore, Eric Nielsen, Sarah Reber, Molly Shatto, Kamila Sommer, et al. "Introducing the Distributional Financial Accounts of the United States." Board of Governors of the Federal Reserve System, Finance and Economics Discussion Series 2019-017, March 2019. https://www.federalreserve.gov/econres/feds/files/2019017pap.pdf.
Baudrillard, Jean. "After the Orgy." In *The Transparency of Evil: Essays on Extreme Phenomena*, translated by James Benedict, 3–14. New York: Verso, 1993.
———. "The Destiny of Value." In *Paroxysm: Interviews with Philippe Petit*, translated by Chris Turner, 1–4. London: Verso, 1998.
———. "The End of Production." In *Symbolic Exchange and Death*, translated by Iain Hamilton Grant, 6–49. London: Sage, 1993.
———. *Jean Baudrillard: Selected Writings*. Edited by Mark Poster. Translated by Jacques Mourrain. Stanford: Stanford University Press, 2001.
———. "The Order of Simulacra." In *Symbolic Exchange and Death*, translated by Iain Hamilton Grant, 50–86. London: Sage, 1993.
———. *Paroxysm: Interviews with Philippe Petit*. Translated by Chris Turner. London: Verso, 1998
———. *Simulacra and Simulation*. Translated by Sheila Glaser. Ann Arbor: University of Michigan Press, 1994.
———. *The System of Objects*. Translated by James Benedict. London: Verso, 1996.
———. "Transaesthetics." In *The Transparency of Evil: Essays on Extreme Phenomena*, translated by James Benedict, 14–19. New York: Verso, 1993.
Bauman, Zygmunt. *Liquid Life*. Cambridge, UK: Polity, 2005.
———. *Liquid Modernity*. Cambridge, UK: Polity, 2000.
Bayer, Patrick, Christopher Geissler, Kyle Mangum, and James W. Roberts. "Speculators and Middlemen: The Strategy and Performance of Investors in the Housing Market." NBER Working Paper 16784, February 2011. https://doi.org/10.3386/w16784.
Beach Flip. Season 1, episode 8, "And the Winner Is . . . ." HGTV, Discovery, 2015.
Becker, Ron. "Horribly Guilty Television: HGTV and the Promotion of America's Ownership Society." *Flow*, April 24, 2008. http://flowtv.org/2008/04/horribly-guilty-television-hgtv-and-the-promotion-of-americas-ownership-society/.
Berger, John. *Ways of Seeing*. New York: Viking, 1973.
Berlant, Lauren. *Cruel Optimism*. Durham, NC: Duke University Press, 2011.
Berman, Marshall. *All That Is Solid Melts into Air*. New York: Simon and Schuster, 1982.
Best, Beverley. "Political Economy through the Looking Glass: Imagining Six Impossible Things about Finance before Breakfast." *Historical Materialism* 25, no. 3 (2017): 76–100.
Billings, Dwight B., and Kathleen M. Blee. *The Road to Poverty: The Making of Wealth and Hardship in Appalachia*. Cambridge: Cambridge University Press, 2000.
Blake, Meredith. "HGTV Builds into a Top Cable Network on Foundation of No-Frills Shows." *Los Angeles Times*, July 18, 2014. http://www.latimes.com/entertainment/tv/la-et-hgtv-cable-network-20th-anniversary-20140720-story.html.

Blomquist, Daren. "The Home Flipping Pyramid." RealtyTrac, June 9, 2017. https://www.realtytrac.com/news/the-home-flipping-pyramid/.

Bradford, Harry. "Foreclosure Vandals Threaten Prospective Homeowners: 'Only Going to Get Worse.'" *Huffington Post*, May 2, 2012. http://www.huffingtonpost.com/2012/05/02/foreclosure-vandals-threaten-homeowners-take-my-house_n_1471472.html.

Brenkman, John. "Mass Media: From Collective Experience to the Culture of Privatization." *Social Text*, no. 1 (1979): 94–109.

Brenner, Robert. *The Economics of Global Turbulence*. New York: Verso, 2006.

Bryan, Dick. "The Duality of Labour and the Financial Crisis." *Economic and Labour Relations Review* 20, no. 2 (2010): 49–60.

Bryan, Dick, Randy Martin, and Mike Rafferty. "Financialization and Marx: Giving Labor and Capital a Financial Makeover." *Review of Radical Political Economics* 41, no. 4 (2009): 458–472.

Bryan, Dick, and Michael Rafferty. "Financial Derivatives as Social Policy beyond Crisis." *Sociology* 48, no. 5 (2014): 887–903.

———. "Political Economy and Housing in the Twenty-First Century—from Mobile Homes to Liquid Housing?" *Housing, Theory and Society* 31, no. 4 (2014): 404–412.

———. *Risking Together*. Sydney: Sydney University Press, 2018.

Bryan, Dick, Michael Rafferty, and Chris Jefferis. "Risk and Value: Finance, Labor, and Production." *South Atlantic Quarterly* 114, no. 2 (2015): 307–329.

Bryan, Dick, Michael Rafferty, and Bruno Tinel. "Households at the Frontiers of Monetary Development." *Behemoth—a Journal on Civilisation* 9, no. 2 (2016): 46–58.

Buckley, Michelle. "Between House and Home: Renovations Labor and the Production of Residential Value." *Economic Geography* 95, no. 3 (2019): 209–230.

Burd-Sharps, Sarah, and Rebecca Rasch. "Impact of the US Housing Crisis on the Racial Wealth Gap across Generations." Social Science Research Council, June 2015. https://www.ssrc.org/publications/view/impact-of-the-us-housing-crisis-on-the-racial-wealth-gap-across-generations/.

Burns, Rebecca. "Oakland's Moms 4 Housing Were Evicted by a Giant Corporation That Runs National Home-Flipping Operation." *The Intercept*, January 17, 2020. https://theintercept.com/2020/01/17/moms-4-housing-eviction-wedgewood/.

———. "You Think Your Landlord Is Bad? Try Renting from Wall Street." *The Intercept*, January 20, 2018. https://theintercept.com/2018/01/20/you-think-your-landlord-is-bad-try-renting-from-wall-street/.

Camus, Albert. *The Myth of Sisyphus and Other Essays*. Translated by Justin O'Brien. New York: Vintage Books, 1991.

Carruthers, Bruce, and Arthur Stinchcombe. "The Social Structure of Liquidity: Flexibility, Markets, and States." *Theory and Society* 28, no. 3 (1999): 353–382.

Casselman, Ben, and Colin Dougherty. "Want a House Like This? Prepare for a Bidding War with Investors." *New York Times*, June 20, 2019. https://www.nytimes.com/interactive/2019/06/20/business/economy/starter-homes-investors.html.

Chauhan, Harsh. "A Full-Blown U.S. Housing Market Crisis Is on the Way." *CCN*, December 15, 2019. https://www.ccn.com/full-blown-us-housing-market-crisis-on-the-way/.

Chianese, Robert Louis. "Is Nature Photography Too Beautiful?" *American Scientist* 102, no. 1 (2014): 64–67.

Chiland, Elijah. "LA County Median Home Prices Shatter $600K Mark." *Curbed LA*, June 21, 2018. https://la.curbed.com/2018/6/21/17489270/los-angeles-home-prices-record-how-much-to-buy.
Christie, Les. "Foreclosures up a Record 81% in 2008." *CNN*, January 15, 2019. https://money.cnn.com/2009/01/15/real_estate/millions_in_foreclosure/.
City of Waco. "Consolidated Plan for 2009–2013." 2009. www.waco-texas.com/pdf/housing/Consolidated%20Plan%202009-2013.pdf.
Clark, Patrick. "Long Island Home Flippers Sell to Each Other in Red-Hot Market." *Bloomberg*, August 27, 2019. https://www.bloomberg.com/news/articles/2019-08-27/long-island-home-flippers-sell-to-each-other-in-red-hot-market.
Conlin, Michelle. "Spiders, Sewage and a Flurry of Fees—the Other Side of Renting a House from Wall Street." *Reuters*, July 27, 2018. https://www.reuters.com/investigates/special-report/usa-housing-invitation/.
Copeland, Mike. "Owner Defends Almost $1 Million Asking Price for Seventh Street Shotgun House." *Waco Herald-Tribune*, June 24, 2017. https://wacotrib.com/business/owner-defends-almost-1-million-asking-price-for-seventh-street-shotgun-house/article_a9cee38b-0a02-559c-9b79-4bd905729fff.html.
Courage, Cara. "Why Indianapolis Is a Test Case for a Fairer Form of Gentrification." *The Guardian*, August 21, 2015. https://www.theguardian.com/cities/2015/aug/21/indianapolis-gentrification-arts-big-car-jim-walker-fountain-square-garfield-park.
da Costa, Pedro Nicolaci. "America's Humongous Wealth Gap Is Widening Further." *Forbes*, May 29, 2019. https://www.forbes.com/sites/pedrodacosta/2019/05/29/americas-humungous-wealth-gap-is-widening-further/.
Debord, Guy. *Society of the Spectacle*. Detroit: Red and Black, 1971.
Deleuze, Gilles. "Postscript on the Societies of Control." *October* 59 (Winter 1992): 3–7.
Deleuze, Gilles, and Felix Guattari. *A Thousand Plateaus: Capitalism and Schizophrenia*. Minneapolis: University of Minnesota Press, 2007.
DeSilver, Drew, and Kristen Bialik, "Blacks and Hispanics Face Extra Challenges in Getting Home Loans." Pew Research Center, January 10, 2017. http://www.pewresearch.org/fact-tank/2017/01/10/blacks-and-hispanics-face-extra-challenges-in-getting-home-loans/.
Desmond, Matthew. *Evicted: Poverty and Profit in the American City*. New York: Broadway Books, 2017.
———. "Heavy Is the House: Rent Burden among the American Urban Poor." *International Journal of Urban and Regional Research* 42, no. 1 (2018): 160–170.
Dezember, Ryan, and Peter Rudegeair. "The Future of Housing Rises in Phoenix: High-Tech Flippers Such as Zillow Are Using Algorithms to Reshape the Housing Market." *Wall Street Journal*, June 19, 2019. https://www.wsj.com/articles/the-future-of-housing-rises-in-phoenix-11560957036.
Douglas, Mary. *Purity and Danger*. London: Routledge, 1966.
Doussard, Marc. *Degraded Work: The Struggle at the Bottom of the Labor Market*. Minneapolis: University of Minnesota Press, 2013.
Du Bois, W.E.B. *W.E.B. Du Bois's Data Portraits: Visualizing Black America*. Hudson, NY: Princeton Architectural Press, 2018.
Dunkelman, Marc. *The Vanishing Neighbor: The Transformation of American Community*. New York: Norton, 2014.
Durkheim, Émile. *The Division of Labor in Society*. New York: Free Press, 1984.

Dwyer, Dustin, and Kaye LaFond. "Pushed Out: A Documentary on Housing in Grand Rapids." *All Things Considered*, April 26, 2017. https://stateofopportunity.michiganradio.org/post/pushed-out-documentary-housing-grand-rapids.

Dwyer, Rachel, and Lois Lassus. "The Great Risk Shift and Precarity in the U.S. Housing Market." *Annals AAPSS* 660 (July 2015): 199–216.

Elson, Diane. "The Value Theory of Labour." In *Value: The Representation of Labour in Capitalism*, 115–180. Atlantic Highlands, NJ: Humanities Press, 1979.

Endicott, Marisa. "The Rent in the Bay Area Is Too Damn High: So These Moms Occupied a Vacant House." *Mother Jones*, December 23, 2019. https://www.motherjones.com/politics/2019/12/bay-area-moms-homeless-squatters/.

Ensign, Rachel Louise, Paul Overberg, and AnnaMaria Andriotis. "Banks' Embrace of Jumbo Mortgages Means Fewer Loans for Blacks, Hispanics." *Wall Street Journal*, June 1, 2016. https://www.wsj.com/articles/banks-embrace-of-jumbo-mortgages-means-fewer-loans-for-blacks-hispanics-1464789752.

Falcon, Julia. "Foreclosure Filings Fell to a Record Low in 2019." *HousingWire*, January 16, 2020. https://www.housingwire.com/articles/foreclosure-filings-fell-to-a-record-low-in-2019/.

Federal Reserve Bank of New York. "Total Household Debt Climbs for 20th Straight Quarter as Mortgage Debt and Originations Rise." August 13, 2019. https://www.newyorkfed.org/newsevents/news/research/2019/20190813.

Fixer Upper. Season 1, episode 1, "Embracing Revitalization." High Noon Entertainment, HGTV, Discovery, 2013.

———. Season 1, episode 6, "Family Craves Urban Feel." High Noon Entertainment, HGTV, Discovery, 2014.

———. Season 2, episode 3, "Homebuilder's Dream Home." High Noon Entertainment, HGTV, Discovery, 2015.

———. Season 3, episode 4, "A Home Away from Home for the Holidays." High Noon Entertainment, HGTV, Discovery, 2015.

———. Season 3, episode 6, "A Home for Country Living." High Noon Entertainment, HGTV, Discovery, 2016.

———. Season 3, episode 7, "Old House, New Memories." High Noon Entertainment, HGTV, Discovery, 2016.

———. Season 3, episode 8, "Tiny House, Big Charm." High Noon Entertainment, HGTV, Discovery, 2016.

Flanagan, Caitlin. "Beware the Open-Plan Kitchen." *Vulture*, September 2017. https://www.vulture.com/2017/09/the-ugliness-behind-hgtv-never-ending-fantasy-loop.html.

Flip or Flop. Season 2, episode 1, "Foreclosure Shock." Pie Town Productions, HGTV, Discovery, 2014.

Foner, Eric. *Free Soil, Free Labor, Free Men: The Ideology of the Republican Party before the Civil War*. Oxford: Oxford University Press, 1995.

Fourcade, Marion, and Kieran Healy. "Classification Situations: Life-Chances in the Neoliberal Era." *Accounting, Organizations and Society* 38 (2013): 559–572.

———. "Seeing Like a Market." *Socio-economic Review* 15, no. 1 (2017): 9–29.

FRED Economic Research. "Household Debt to GDP for United States." November 20, 2020. https://fred.stlouisfed.org/series/HDTGPDUSQ163N.

Frohlich, Thomas C., and Michael B. Sauter. "6 Best States to Flip a House." *USA Today*, February 2, 2014. http://www.usatoday.com/story/money/business/2014/02/02/6-best-states-to-flip-a-house/5115321/.

Garboden, Philip, and Eva Rosen. "Serial Filing: How Landlords Use the Threat of Eviction." *City and Community* 18, no. 2 (2019): 638–661.

Gelain, Paolo, Kevin J. Lansing, and Gisle J. Natvik. "Explaining the Boom-Bust Cycle in the U.S. Housing Market: A Reverse-Engineering Approach." Federal Reserve Bank of San Francisco Working Paper 2015-02, February 2018. http://www.frbsf.org/economic-research/publications/working-papers/2015/02/.

Giddens, Anthony. "The Contours of Modernity." In *Modernity and Self-Identity*, 10–34. Stanford: Stanford University Press, 1991.

Glantz, Aaron. *Homewreckers: How a Gang of Wall Street Kingpins, Hedge Fund Magnates, Crooked Banks, and Vulture Capitalists Suckered Millions out of Their Homes and Demolished the American Dream*. New York: HarperCollins, 2019.

Glantz, Aaron, and Emmanuel Martinez. "For People of Color, Banks Are Shutting the Door to Homeownership." *Reveal*, February 15, 2018. https://www.revealnews.org/article/for-people-of-color-banks-are-shutting-the-door-to-homeownership/.

Glynos, Jason, Robin Klimecki, and Hugh Willmott. "Cooling Out the Marks: The Ideology and Politics of the Financial Crisis." *Journal of Cultural Economy* 5, no. 3 (2012): 297–319.

Goffman, Erving. "On Cooling the Mark Out: Some Aspects of Adaptation to Failure." *Psychiatry* 15, no. 4 (1952): 451–463.

Gold, Kerry. "The Property Brothers Are Back Home—and on the Hunt for Bargains." *Globe and Mail*, March 18, 2013. http://www.theglobeandmail.com/life/home-and-garden/real-estate/the-property-brothers-are-back-home-and-on-the-hunt-for-bargains/article9870798/.

Goldman, Robert, and Stephen Papson. *Landscapes of Capital*. Cambridge, UK: Polity, 2011.

———. *Sign Wars*. New York: Guilford, 1996.

Good Bones. Season 1, episode 9, "Duplex Remodel, Double Trouble." High Noon Entertainment, HGTV, Discovery, 2016.

Goodman, Laurie, and Karan Kaul. "GSE Financing of Single-Family Rentals." Urban Institute, May 10, 2017. https://www.urban.org/research/publication/gse-financing-single-family-rentals.

Gopal, Prashant. "Rookie Home-Flippers Get Burned in U.S. Downturn." *Bloomberg*, May 9, 2019. https://www.bloomberg.com/news/videos/2019-05-09/rookie-home-flippers-get-burned-in-u-s-downturn-video.

Gordon, Avery. *Ghostly Matters*. Minneapolis: University of Minnesota Press, 1997.

Gotham, Kevin Fox. "Creating Liquidity out of Spatial Fixity: The Secondary Circuit of Capital and the Subprime Mortgage Crisis." *International Journal of Urban and Regional Research* 33, no. 2 (2009): 355–371.

Gottesdiener, Laura. *A Dream Foreclosed: Black America and the Fight for a Place to Call Home*. Westfield, NJ: Zuccotti Park Press, 2013.

———. "How Wall Street Has Turned Housing into a Dangerous Get-Rich-Quick Scheme—Again." *Mother Jones*, November 29, 2013. https://www.motherjones.com/politics/2013/11/wall-street-buying-foreclosed-homes/.

———. "Wall Street's Hot New Financial Product: Your Rent Check." *Mother Jones*, March–April 2014. https://www.motherjones.com/politics/2014/02/blackstone-rental-homes-bundled-derivatives/.

Goulding, Megan. "Rising Rent Burden in Los Angeles." Neighborhood Data for Social Change, October 2017. https://usc.data.socrata.com/stories/s/Rising-Rent-Burden-in-Los-Angeles/4wjy-s7d9.

Graeber, David. *Debt: The First 5,000 Years*. Brooklyn, NY: Melville House, 2011.
———. *Toward an Anthropological Theory of Value*. New York: Palgrave, 2001.
Granju, Kate Allison. "Quartz: The New Countertop Contender." HGTV. https://www.hgtv.com/design/rooms/kitchens/quartz-the-new-countertop-contender (accessed December 28, 2020).
Greenfieldboyce, Nell. "Workers Are Falling Ill, Even Dying, after Making Kitchen Countertops." *NPR*, October 2, 2019. https://www.npr.org/sections/health-shots/2019/10/02/766028237/workers-are-falling-ill-even-dying-after-making-kitchen-countertops.
Grossberg, Lawrence, Carolyn Hardin, and Michael Palm. "Contributions to a Conjunctural Theory of Valuation." *Rethinking Marxism* 26, no. 3 (2014): 306–335.
Guilford, Gwynn. "House Flippers Triggered the US Housing Market Crash, not Poor Subprime Borrowers." *Quartz*, August 29, 2017. https://qz.com/1064061/house-flippers-triggered-the-us-housing-market-crash-not-poor-subprime-borrowers-a-new-study-shows.
Guthman, Julie. *Weighing In: Obesity, Food Justice, and the Limits of Capitalism*. Berkeley: University of California Press, 2011.
Hackworth, Jason. "Postrecession Gentrification in New York City." *Urban Affairs Review* 37, no. 6 (2002): 815–843.
Hackworth, Jason, and Neil Smith. "The Changing State of Gentrification." *Tijdschrift voor economische en sociale geografie* 92, no. 4 (2001): 464–477.
Hall, Stuart, and Doreen Massey. "Interpreting the Crisis." *Soundings: A Journal of Politics and Culture* 44 (Spring 2010): 57–71.
Hankins, Katherine, and Andy Walter. "'Gentrification with Justice': An Urban Ministry Collective and the Practice of Place-Making in Atlanta's Inner-City Neighbourhoods." *Urban Studies* 49, no. 7 (2012): 1507–1526.
Hardt, Michael, and Antonio Negri. *Empire*. Cambridge: Harvard University Press, 2000.
Harvey, David. *The Condition of Postmodernity*. Cambridge, MA: Basil Blackwell, 1989.
———. *The Enigma of Capital and the Crises of Capitalism*. New York: Oxford University Press, 2010.
———. "From Managerialism to Entrepreneurialism: The Transformation in Urban Governance in Late Capitalism." *Geografiska Annaler: Series B, Human Geography* 71, no. 1 (1989): 3–17.
———. *Marx, Capital and the Madness of Economic Reason*. Oxford: Oxford University Press, 2018.
———. "Marx's Refusal of the Labour Theory of Value." *Reading Marx's Capital with David Harvey* (blog), March 14, 2018. http://davidharvey.org/2018/03/marxs-refusal-of-the-labour-theory-of-value-by-david-harvey/.
———. "The 'New' Imperialism: Accumulation by Dispossession." *Socialist Register* 40 (2004): 63–87.
Haughwout, Andrew, Donghoon Lee, Joseph Tracy, and Wilbert van der Klaauw. "Real Estate Investors, the Leverage Cycle, and the Housing Market Crisis." Federal Reserve Bank of New York Staff Report 514, September 2011. https://www.newyorkfed.org/medialibrary/media/research/staff_reports/sr514.pdf.
Hawkes, David. "Against Financial Derivatives: Towards an Ethics of Representation." *Journal of Interdisciplinary Economics* 31, no. 2 (2019): 165–182.
Hay, James. "Too Good to Fail: Managing Financial Crisis through the Moral Economy of Realty TV." *Journal of Communication Inquiry* 34, no. 4 (2010): 382–402.

Healy, Kieran. "Fuck Nuance." *Sociological Theory* 35, no. 2 (2017): 118–127.

Hebdige, Dick. *Subculture: The Meaning of Style*. London: Methuen, 1979.

Hegel, G.W.F. *The Phenomenology of Mind*. Translated by J. B. Baillie. New York: Harper, 1967.

Hesse, Monica. "Granite: Why Every Homeowner Wants a Piece of the Rock." *Washington Post*, February 6, 2012. https://www.washingtonpost.com/lifestyle/style/granite-why-every-homeowner-wants-a-piece-of-the-rock/2012/02/01/gIQANBN4uQ_story.html.

HGTV. "Joanna's Take on Modern Design." *YouTube*, August 10, 2018. https://www.youtube.com/watch?v=LupnuDz2k0M&list=PL3ciaInkqyXDbsiR3ehFDbHSRoKiM2XtI.

———. "Property Virgins." http://www.hgtv.com/shows/property-virgins (accessed December 30, 2020).

Hochschild, Arlie Russell. *The Managed Heart: Commercialization of Human Feeling*. Berkeley: University of California Press, 1985.

Hod, Itay. "The 'Property Brothers' Are Reality Television's Crack Cocaine." *Daily Beast*, July 11, 2017. http://www.thedailybeast.com/articles/2013/09/08/the-property-brothers-are-reality-television-s-crack-cocaine.html.

Hoffman, Liz, and Peter Rudegeair. "Goldman Sachs to Lend to House-Flippers." *Wall Street Journal*, October 12, 2017. https://www.wsj.com/articles/goldman-sachs-to-buy-house-flipping-lender-1507826252.

Hoover, Carl, and Kristin Hoppa. "Car Smashes into 'Fixer Upper' House." *Waco Tribune-Herald*, July 8, 2017. http://www.wacotrib.com/news/city_of_waco/car-smashes-into-fixer-upper-house/article_bb418fb0-0e9e-5d5a-80e9-cc659032e3e6.html.

Hoppa, Kristin. "Witness Describes Aftermath of 'Fixer Upper' Crash." *Waco Tribune-Herald*, July 10, 2017. http://www.wacotrib.com/news/city_of_waco/witness-describes-aftermath-of-fixer-upper-crash/article_3e82d207-be0a-59e7-9e5b-b34b5925326c.html.

Horkheimer, Max, and Theodor Adorno. *Dialectic of Enlightenment: Philosophical Fragments*. Edited by Gunzelin Schmid Noerr. Translated by Edmund Jephcott. Stanford: Stanford University Press, 2002.

Horning, Rob. "On Real and Formal Subsumption." *Pop Matters*, September 15, 2011. https://www.popmatters.com/148650--2495950141.html.

Huber, Matthew T. *Lifeblood: Oil, Freedom and the Forces of Capital*. Minneapolis: University of Minnesota, 2013.

Illouz, Eva. *Cold Intimacies: The Making of Emotional Capitalism*. Cambridge, UK: Polity, 2007.

Immergluck, Dan. *Foreclosed: High-Risk Lending, Deregulation, and the Undermining of America's Mortgage Market*. Ithaca, NY: Cornell University Press, 2009.

———. "The Role of Investors in the Single-Family Market in Distressed Neighborhoods: The Case of Atlanta." What Works Collaborative, 2013. https://www.urban.org/sites/default/files/publication/23291/412743-The-Role-of-Investors-in-the-Single-Family-Market-in-Distressed-Neighborhoods-The-Case-of-Atlanta.PDF.

Immergluck, Dan, Jeff Ernsthausen, Stephanie Earl, and Allison Powell. "Evictions, Large Owners, and Serial Filings: Findings from Atlanta." *Housing Studies* 35, no. 5 (2019): 903–924.

Irish, Erica. "Priorities Evolve as 'Good Bones' Stars Begin Filming Fourth Season." *Indianapolis Business Journal*, August 1, 2018. https://www.ibj.com/articles/69927-priorities-evolve-as-good-bones-stars-begin-filming-fourth-season.

Isenstadt, Sandy. "The Rise and Fall of the Picture Window." In *Housing and Dwelling: Perspectives on Modern Domestic Architecture*, edited by Barbara Miller Lane, 298–306. London: Routledge, 2007.

Jensen, Jeremiah. "ATTOM: Housing Affordability Falls to 10-Year Low." *HousingWire*, June 21, 2018. https://www.housingwire.com/articles/43744-attom-housing-affordability-falls-to-10-year-low.

John. "Do the People on Property Brothers Get to Keep the Furnishings?" *Starcasm*, April 11, 2016. http://starcasm.net/archives/346920.

Johnson, Bradford, James Manyika, and Lareina Yee. "The Next Revolution in Interactions." *McKinsey Quarterly*, November 1, 2005. https://www.mckinsey.com/business-functions/organization/our-insights/the-next-revolution-in-interactions.

Johnson, Greg. "Catching Up with the Barnwood Builders." *Greenbrier Valley Quarterly*, October 2016. http://www.gvquarterly.com/blog/2016/10/27/catching-up-with-the-barnwood-builders.

Jordan, Niema. "Moms 4 Housing Is Fighting to Make Sure Everyone Has a Home." *Shondaland*, May 18, 2020. https://www.shondaland.com/act/news-politics/a32501691/moms-4-housing-homeless-activism/.

Joseph, Miranda. "The Performance of Production and Consumption." *Social Text* 54 (1998): 25–61.

Kear, Mark. "Playing the Credit Score Game: Algorithms, 'Positive' Data and the Personification of Financial Objects." *Economy and Society* 46, no. 3–4 (2017): 346–368.

Kendall, Marisa. "Moms 4 Housing Victory: Property Owner Gives Squatters Chance to Reclaim House." *Mercury News*, January 20, 2020. https://www.mercurynews.com/2020/01/20/moms-4-housing-victory-group-gets-chance-to-buy-house-through-nonprofit/.

Kim, Susanna. "Here's the Keys, and Some Cement down the Drains." *ABC News*, January 18, 2011. http://abcnews.go.com/Business/million-dollar-foreclosed-home-vandalized/story?id=12638936.

Kochhar, Rakesh. "How Americans Compare with the Global Middle Class." Pew Research Center, July 9, 2015. http://www.pewresearch.org/fact-tank/2015/07/09/how-americans-compare-with-the-global-middle-class/.

Kurutz, Stephen. "The Housing Bubble Burst All Over HGTV." *New York Times*, September 12, 2018. https://www.nytimes.com/interactive/2018/09/12/business/media/hgtv-housing-mortgage-crisis.html.

Kusisto, Laura. "Investors Are Buying More of the U.S. Housing Market Than Ever Before." *Wall Street Journal*, June 20, 2019. https://www.wsj.com/articles/investors-are-buying-more-of-the-u-s-housing-market-than-ever-before-11561023120.

Landy, Benjamin. "A Tale of Two Recoveries: Wealth Inequality after the Great Recession." Century Foundation, August 28, 2013. https://www.tcf.org/blog/detail/a-tale-of-two-recoveries.

Langhorne, Daniel. "Local Couple Star in HGTV Reality Show on Flipping Houses." *Orange County Register*, April 4, 2013. http://www.ocregister.com/articles/moussa-502466-tarek-houses.html.

Lapavitsas, Costas. "Financialisation, or the Search for Profits in the Sphere of Circulation." *Research on Money and Finance*, Discussion Paper no. 10, May 2009, pp. 1–26.

———. "Theorizing Financialization." *Work, Employment and Society* 25, no. 4 (2011): 611–626.

Lawson, Richard. "Did a Car Accident Reveal a Darker Side of HGTV's Biggest Hit?" *Vanity Fair*, July 10, 2017. https://www.vanityfair.com/style/2017/07/fixer-upper-hgtv-car-drives-through-house.

Lazzarato, Maurizio. "From Capital-Labour to Capital-Life." *Ephemera* 4, no. 3 (2004): 187–208.

———. "Immaterial Labor." In *Radical Thought in Italy: A Potential Politics*, edited by Paolo Virno and Michael Hardt, 133–147. Minneapolis: University of Minnesota Press, 1996.

———. *The Making of the Indebted Man*. Translated by Joshua David Jordan. Los Angeles, CA: Semiotext(e), 2012.

Lee, Hyojung. "Who Owns Rental Properties, and Is It Changing?" *Housing Perspectives*, August 18, 2017. https://www.jchs.harvard.edu/blog/who-owns-rental-properties-and-is-it-changing/.

Lees, Loretta, Tom Slater, and Elvin Wyly. *Gentrification*. London: Routledge, 2008.

Lefebvre, Henri. *The Production of Space*. Translated by Donald Nicholson-Smith. Cambridge, MA: Blackwell, 1991.

Lévi-Strauss, Claude. *The Savage Mind*. Chicago: University of Chicago, 1962.

Lewis, Michael. *The Big Short*. New York: Norton, 2010.

Li, Wenli. "Smart Money or Dumb Money: Investors' Role in the Housing Bubble." *Federal Reserve Bank of Philadelphia Business Review* Q1 (2015). https://citeseerx.ist.psu.edu/viewdoc/download?doi=10.1.1.679.9560&rep=rep1&type=pdf.

LiPuma, Edward, and Benjamin Lee. "Financial Derivatives and the Rise of Circulation." *Economy and Society* 34, no. 3 (2005): 404–427.

Lopez, Steve. "As Renters Struggle to Pay the Bills, Landlords and Speculators Cash In." *Los Angeles Times*, November 4, 2017. https://www.latimes.com/local/california/la-me-lopez-housing-profiteers-20171104-story.html.

Lowder, J. Bryan. "A Rotten Beam Threatens to Undermine HGTV's Fall Lineup." *Slate*, May 7, 2014. https://slate.com/human-interest/2014/05/hgtvs-flip-it-forward-with-extreme-anti-gay-conservatives-david-and-jason-benham-canceled.html.

Maciag, Michael. "Indianapolis Gentrification Maps and Data." *Governing*, February 1, 2015. https://www.governing.com/gov-data/indianapolis-gentrification-maps-demographic-data.html.

MacKenzie, Donald. "Physics and Finance: S-Terms and Modern Finance as a Topic for Science Studies." *Science, Technology, and Human Values* 26, no. 2 (2001): 115–144.

Macpherson, C. B. *The Political Theory of Possessive Individualism*. Oxford: Oxford University Press, 1962.

Madormo, Carrie. "The Untold Truth of Rehab Addict." *The List*, December 17, 2016. http://www.thelist.com/32115/untold-truth-rehab-addict/?utm_campaign=clip.

Magdoff, Fred. "The Jobs Disaster in the United States." *Monthly Review*, June 1, 2011. https://monthlyreview.org/2011/06/01/the-jobs-disaster-in-the-united-states/.

Magnolia. "Authenticity Leather Sign." https://shop.magnolia.com/collections/wall-decor/products/authenticity-leather-sign (accessed March 5, 2021).

———. "Premium Interior Paint." https://shop.magnolia.com/collections/premium-colors/color-beige (accessed February 25, 2021).

Mallach, Alan. "Meeting the Challenge of Distressed Property Investors in America's Neighborhoods." Local Initiatives Support Corporation, 2010. https://www.lisc.org/media/filer_public/4f/46/4f462994-10b0-4eb0-8855-ddafc6e82d37/08142018_resources_distressed_property_investors.pdf.

Mann, Geoff. "Value after Lehman." *Historical Materialism* 18, no. 4 (2010): 172–188.
Marx, Karl. *Capital: A Critique of Political Economy*, vol. 1, translated by Ben Fowkes. New York: Vintage Books, 1977.
———. *Grundrisse*. Harmondsworth, UK: Penguin, 1973.
Marx, Karl, and Frederick Engels. *Manifesto of the Communist Party*. Peking: Foreign Language Press, 1970.
Maurer, Bill. "Repressed Futures: Financial Derivatives' Theological Unconscious." *Economy and Society* 31, no. 1 (2002): 15–36.
McClanahan, Annie. *Dead Pledges: Debt, Crisis, and Twenty-First-Century Culture*. Stanford: Stanford University Press, 2017.
McCue, Daniel. "Headlines from the 2019 State of the Nation's Housing Report." *Housing Perspectives*, August 7, 2019. https://www.jchs.harvard.edu/blog/headlines-from-the-2019-state-of-the-nations-housing-report/.
McLaughlin, Ralph. "Special Report: House Flipping and Profits." *CoreLogic Insights Blog*, April 9, 2019. https://www.corelogic.com/blog/2019/04/special-report-house-flipping-and-profits.aspx.
McLaughlin, Ralph, and Arthur Jobe. "A Wild Flipping Ride: Economic Returns to U.S. House Flipping, 2002–2018." Paper presented at 47th American Real Estate and Urban Economics Association National Conference, Washington, DC, May 31, 2019.
McLean, Bethany, and Joe Nocera. *All the Devils Are Here: The Hidden History of the Financial Crisis*. New York: Penguin, 2011.
Meek, Austin. "Downtown Depot: Jimmy Dorrell." *Waco Business News*, July 21, 2017. http://www.wacobusinessnews.com/the-latest/downtown-depot-jimmy-dorrell.
Miller, Daniel. "The Uses of Value." *Geoforum* 39 (2008): 1122–1132.
Mishel, Lawrence. "The Wedges between Productivity and Median Compensation Growth." *Economic Policy Institute* (blog), April 26, 2012. https://www.epi.org/publication/ib330-productivity-vs-compensation/.
Molina, Emily, T. "Foreclosures, Investors, and Uneven Development during the Great Recession in the Los Angeles Metropolitan Area." *Journal of Urban Affairs* 38, no. 4 (2016): 564–580.
Montgomery, David. *Workers' Control in America*. Cambridge: Cambridge University Press, 1980.
Moreno, Louis. "The Urban Process under Financialised Capitalism." *City* 18, no. 3 (2014): 244–268.
Moskowitz, Peter. *How to Kill a City: Gentrification, Inequality, and the Fight for the Neighborhood*. New York: Bold Type Books, 2017.
Mrozowski, Daniel. "From Hoarders to Pickers: Salvage Aesthetics and Reality Television in the Great Recession." In *The Great Recession in Fiction, Film, and Television: Twenty-First-Century Bust Culture*, edited by Kirk Boyle and Daniel Mrozowski, 189–208. Lanham, MD: Lexington Books, 2013.
Murtaugh, Taysha. "What Chip and Joanna Really Think of Clients Listing Their 'Fixer Uppers' as Vacation Rentals." *Country Living*, August 15, 2017. http://www.countryliving.com/life/entertainment/news/a44387/fixer-upper-clients-renting-out-homes/.
———. "What That 'Fixer Upper' Car Crash Says about Waco and Your Favorite HGTV Show." *Country Living*, July 12, 2017. http://www.countryliving.com/life/entertainment/news/a43890/fixer-upper-car-crash-aftermath/.
Neighborhood Scout. "Waco TX: Appreciation Rate Trends and Housing Market Data," https://www.neighborhoodscout.com/tx/waco/real-estate (accessed June 4, 2017).

Olalquiaga, Celeste. *Megalopolis: Contemporary Cultural Sensibilities*. Minneapolis: University of Minnesota, 1992.

Older, Daniel José. "Gentrification's Insidious Violence: The Truth about American Cities." *Salon*, April 8, 2014. https://www.salon.com/2014/04/08/gentrifications_insidious_violence_the_truth_about_american_cities/.

Olick, Diana. "Home Flippers Are Fleeing the Market as Their Profits Shrink." *CNBC*, November 1, 2018. https://www.cnbc.com/2018/11/01/home-flippers-are-fleeing-the-market-as-their-profits-shrink.html.

On Data Suite. "Campus: Brook Avenue EL." June 21, 2017. https://www.wacoisd.org/site/handlers/filedownload.ashx?moduleinstanceid=10286&dataid=9409&FileName=bae.pdf.

Orléan, André, and Rainer Diaz-Bone. "Questioning Economists' Notion of Value: André Orléan Interviewed by Rainer Diaz-Bone." *Economic Sociology, the European Electronic Newsletter* 14, no. 3 (2013): 41–47.

Ossa, Felipe. "Why 'Build to Rent' Is Having Its Moment." *Asset Securitization Report*, February 14, 2018. https://asreport.americanbanker.com/news/why-build-to-rent-is-having-its-moment.

Ott, Julia, and Louis Hyman. "The Politics of Debt: How Labor Should Think about the Debt Question." *New Labor Forum* 22, no. 2 (2013): 29–38.

Paschall, Wildstyle. "The Ethnic Cleansing of Black Indianapolis." *New America*, February 4, 2020. http://newamerica.org/indianapolis/blog/indiana-avenue-ethnic-cleansing-black-indianapolis/.

Peck, Emily, and Charles Maldonado. "How Airbnb Is Pushing Locals Out of New Orleans' Coolest Neighborhoods." *Huffington Post*, October 30, 2017. https://www.huffingtonpost.com/entry/airbnb-new-orleans-housing_us_59f33054e4b03cd20b811699.

Peck, Jamie, Nik Theodore, and Neil Brenner. "Neoliberal Urbanism: Models, Moments, Mutations." *SAIS Review of International Affairs* 29, no. 1 (2009): 49–66.

Raymond, Elora Lee, Richard Duckworth, Benjamin Miller, Michael Lucas, and Shiraj Pokharel. "From Foreclosure to Eviction: Housing Insecurity in Corporate-Owned Single-Family Rentals." *Cityscape 20*, no. 3 (2018): 159–188.

RealtyTrac. "A Flip of the Numbers." *Think Realty*, April 21, 2016. https://thinkrealty.com/a-flip-of-the-numbers/.

Renn, Aaron M. "Parallel Societies." *Aaron Renn* (blog), May 5, 2013. https://www.urbanophile.com/2013/05/05/replay-parallel-societies/.

Revitalization. "Indianapolis Land Trust Is Revitalizing Area by Renovating Vacant Homes for Artists." *Revitalization*, May 1, 2017. https://revitalization.org/article/non-profit-renovates-vacant-houses-artists-revitalize-indianapolis-neighborhood/.

Rifkin, Jeremy. *The Zero Marginal-Cost Society*. New York: St. Martin's, 2014.

Riquier, Andrea. "Mom-and-Pop Landlords Push Investor Share of Home Purchases to 19-Year High." *MarketWatch*, June 30, 2019. https://www.marketwatch.com/story/mom-and-pop-landlords-push-investor-share-of-home-purchases-to-19-year-high-2019-06-20.

Roberts, Michael, and David Harvey. "Marx's Law of Value: A Debate between David Harvey and Michael Roberts." *Michael Roberts Blog*, April 2, 2018. https://thenextrecession.wordpress.com/2018/04/02/marxs-law-of-value-a-debate-between-david-harvey-and-michael-roberts/.

Rogers, Chris. "Inside the Multi-million Dollar Waco Development Project." *KCEN-TV*, February 28, 2017. https://www.kcentv.com/article/news/local/inside-the-multi-million-dollar-waco-development-project/500-416097757.

Rosenfield, Kat, and Todd Jacobs. "Why Property Brothers Is Totally Fake." *Nicki Swift*, November 3, 2016. https://www.nickiswift.com/27699/property-brothers-totally-fake/.

Rothrock, Millie. "'Barnwood Builders' Spring into Action in Wytheville." *SWVA Today*, January 14, 2016. http://www.swvatoday.com/news/smyth_county/article_43d8e56a-b966-11e5-8fe5-277c6c3ba13e.html.

Rubenstein, Diane. "The Mirror of Reproduction: Baudrillard and Reagan's America." *Political Theory* 17, no. 4 (1989): 582–606.

Rugh, Jacob, Len Albright, and Douglas Massey. "Race, Space, and Cumulative Disadvantage: A Case Study of the Subprime Lending Collapse." *Social Problems* 62, no. 2 (2015): 186–218.

Ruyer, Raymond. *La philosophie de la valeur*. Paris: Armand Collin, 1952.

Ryckaert, Vic. "Two Chicks and a Hammer Nail HGTV Deal." *USA Today*, May 26, 2015. http://www.usatoday.com/story/life/tv/2015/05/26/two-chicks-and-a-hammer-nail-hgtv-deal/27988425/.

Sasso, Michael. "Home-Flipping Trend Weakens as High-Interest Lenders Jump 40%." *Bloomberg*, June 12, 2019. https://www.bloomberg.com/news/articles/2019-06-12/high-interest-lenders-up-40-even-as-home-flipping-trend-weakens.

Saussure, Ferdinand de. *Course in General Linguistics*. Translated by Wade Baskin. Edited by Perry Meisel and Haun Saussy. New York: Columbia University Press, 2011.

Schmidt, Mackenzie. "*Fixer Upper* Homeowner Says Chip and Joanna Gaines 'Deceived' Her about 'Not Safe' Neighborhood." *People*, July 10, 2017. https://people.com/home/fixer-upper-homeowner-says-chip-and-joanna-gaines-deceived-her-about-not-safe-neighborhood/.

Schumpeter, Joseph. *Capitalism, Socialism, and Democracy*. London: Routledge, 1994.

Scott, Robert. "We Can Reshore Manufacturing Jobs, but Trump Hasn't Done It." Economic Policy Institute, August 10, 2020. https://www.epi.org/publication/reshoring-manufacturing-jobs/.

Scott Brothers. "FAQ." Previously available at http://www.thescottbrothers.com/faq/ (accessed October 14, 2017).

Shapiro, Ari. "A Decade after the Bubble Burst, House Flipping Is on the Rise." *NPR*, April 17, 2018. https://www.npr.org/2018/04/17/601925433/a-decade-after-the-bubble-burst-house-flipping-is-on-the-rise.

Sharf, Samantha. "Forbes Fintech 50 2018: The Future of Lending." *Forbes*, February 13, 2018. https://www.forbes.com/sites/samanthasharf/2018/02/13/forbes-fintech-50-2018-the-future-of-lending/#37a037051329.

———. "Wall Street Firms Build a Single-Family Rental Giant, but It's Still a Minnow in Housing Market." *Forbes*, August 10, 2017. https://www.forbes.com/sites/samanthasharf/2017/08/10/single-family-rental-leaders-invitation-homes-starwood-waypoint-homes-to-combine/.

Shimpach, Shawn. "Realty Reality: HGTV and the Subprime Crisis." *American Quarterly* 64, no. 3 (2012): 515–542.

Simmel, Georg. *The Philosophy of Money*. London: Routledge, 2004.

Sisson, Patrick. "Millennials, Priced out of Homes Locally, Shop for Investment Properties Online." *Curbed*, September 10, 2019. https://www.curbed.com/2019/9/10/20852849/millennial-buy-a-home-homeownership-remote.

Sisson, Patrick, Jeff Andrews, and Alex Bazeley. "The Affordable Housing Crisis, Explained." *Curbed*, March 2, 2020. https://www.curbed.com/2019/5/15/18617763/affordable-housing-policy-rent-real-estate-apartment.

Skeggs, Beverly, and Helen Woods. "The Labour of Transformation and Circuits of Value 'Around' Reality Television." *Continuum* 22, no. 4 (2008): 559–572.

Slater, Tom. "Planetary Rent Gaps." *Antipode* 49 (2017): 114–137.

Smith, Brian D. "The Artists Are Disappearing from Fountain Square." *Indianapolis Monthly*, February 15, 2017. https://web.archive.org/web/20170215145631/https://www.indianapolismonthly.com/arts-culture/artists-disappearing-fountain-square/.

Smith, J. B. "Faith-Motivated Newcomers Take Root in North Waco." *Waco Tribune-Herald*, May 1, 2011. http://www.wacotrib.com/news/faith-motivated-newcomers-take-root-in-north-waco/article_28d8b1d1-02a8-5e3c-b9b5-ccd88e0e5929.html.

———. "'Fixer Upper' Effect: Waco's Economy Benefits from Chip and Joanna Gaines Lifestyle Empire." *USA Today*, November 21, 2017. https://www.usatoday.com/story/money/economy/2017/11/21/fixer-upper-effect-wacos-economy-benefits-chip-and-joanna-gaines-lifestyle-empire/884830001/.

———. "Neglected North Waco Houses Transformed as HGTV Cameras Roll." *Waco Tribune-Herald*, February 16, 2014. http://www.wacotrib.com/news/business/neglected-north-waco-houses-transformed-as-hgtv-cameras-roll/article_dbf75c5e-460e-5ee8-a63c-81e1171c5f8f.html.

———. "Waco Housing Boom Leaves Its Mark on Tax Appraisals." *Waco Tribune-Herald*, May 20, 2017. http://www.wacotrib.com/news/business/waco-housing-boom-leaves-its-mark-on-tax-appraisals/article_9bc6e987-a841-5927-80a3-ca5a5dc8c066.html.

Smith, Neil. "Gentrification Generalized: From Local Anomaly to Urban 'Regeneration' as Global Urban Strategy." In *Frontiers of Capital: Ethnographic Reflections on the New Economy*, edited by Melissa Fisher and Greg Downey, 191–208. New York: City University of New York, 2006.

———. "New Globalism, New Urbanism: Gentrification as Global Urban Strategy." *Antipode* 34, no. 3 (2002): 427–450.

———. *The New Urban Frontier: Gentrification and the Revanchist City*. London: Routledge, 1996.

———. "Toward a Theory of Gentrification: A Back to the City Movement by Capital, not People." *Journal of the American Planning Association* 45, no. 4 (1979): 538–548.

Sollisch, Jim. "Blame Television for the Bubble: The Real Housing Villain Is on Cable." *Wall Street Journal*, January 3, 2009. http://www.wsj.com/articles/SB123094453377450603.

Stanley, Alessandra. "On HGTV, Fixing Homes and Hearts." *New York Times*, March 18, 2010. http://tv.nytimes.com/2010/03/18/arts/television/18hgtv.html?ref=alessandrastanley.

Statista. "Share of Americans Who Watched HGTV in the Past Month in 2018, by Age." October 2018. https://www.statista.com/statistics/228962/cable-tv-networks-hgtv-watched-within-the-last-7-days-usa/.

Steil, Justin, Len Albright, Jacob Rugh, and Douglas Massey. "The Social Structure of Mortgage Discrimination." *Housing Studies* 33, no. 5 (2018): 759–776.

Stout, Noelle. *Dispossessed: How Predatory Bureaucracy Foreclosed on the American Middle Class*. Oakland: University of California Press, 2019.

Sullivan, Paul. "Investors Push into a Resurging Market: House Flipping." *New York Times*, October 20, 2017. https://www.nytimes.com/2017/10/20/your-money/house-flipping-loans.html.

Taylor, Keeanga-Yamahtta. "Back Story to the Neoliberal Moment: Race Taxes and the Political Economy of Black Urban Housing in the 1960s." *Souls* 14, no. 3–4 (2012): 185–206.

———. *Race for Profit: How Banks and the Real Estate Industry Undermined Black Homeownership*. Chapel Hill: University of North Carolina Press, 2019.

Teodoro, Rachel. "What It's Really Like to Be Cast on Fixer Upper, Part II." *Rachel Teodoro* (blog), September 2017. http://www.rachelteodoro.com/2017/09/what-its-really-like-to-be-cast-on.html.

Tett, Gillian. *Fool's Gold*. New York: Free Press, 2010.

Tommey, Blake. "For This Intentional Christian Community, Seeking the World's Healing Means Battling Gentrification Close at Home." *Baptist News Global*, January 3, 2018. https://baptistnews.com/article/qc-family-tree-gentrification.

Travis, Adam. "The Organization of Neglect: Limited Liability Companies and Housing Disinvestment." *American Sociological Review* 84, no. 1 (2019): 142–170.

Tsing, Anna Lowenhaupt. *The Mushroom at the End of the World: On the Possibility of Life in Capitalist Ruins*. Princeton, NJ: Princeton University Press, 2017.

Tully, Shawn. "Meet the A.I. Landlord That's Building a Single-Family-Home Empire." *Fortune*, June 21, 2019. http://fortune.com/longform/single-family-home-ai-algorithms/.

Velasco, Schuyler. "'House Hunters' TV Show Is Fake: Does It Matter?" *Christian Science Monitor*, June 15, 2012. http://www.csmonitor.com/Business/2012/0615/House-Hunters-TV-show-is-fake.-Does-it-matter.

Virno, Paolo. *A Grammar of the Multitude: For an Analysis of Contemporary Forms of Life*. Translated by Isabella Bertoletti, James Cascaito, and Andrea Casson. Los Angeles: Semiotext(e); Cambridge, MA: MIT Press, 2004.

Vrbo. "Three Little Pigs House as Seen on Fixer Upper!" https://www.vrbo.com/1509274?unitId=2068066&noDates=true (accessed July 21, 2017).

Waco Convention and Visitors Bureau. "Tourism Research and Statistics." https://wacoheartoftexas.com/tourism-research-and-statistics/ (accessed February 15, 2018).

Wagner, Kate. "Behind-the-Scenes of Rustic Modernism: Your Complete Guide to Farmhouse and Industrial Chic." *Curbly*, June 22, 2017. https://www.curbly.com/rustic-modernism-guide.

———. "How Beige Took Over American Homes." *Atlas Obscura*, September 26, 2016. http://www.atlasobscura.com/articles/how-beige-took-over-american-homes.

———. "McMansion, USA." *Jacobin*, November 9, 2017. https://jacobinmag.com/2017/11/mcmansions-housing-architecture-rich-people.

Weber, Brenda. *Makeover TV: Selfhood, Citizenship and Celebrity*. Durham, NC: Duke University Press, 2009.

Wedgewood. "About Us." https://www.wedgewood-inc.com/about/ (accessed December 30, 2020).

Wiggin, Teke. "Fix-and-Flip Mortgage Bonds: Wall Street's New Housing Bet to Boost Home Flippers." *Inman*, February 15, 2017. https://www.inman.com/2017/02/15/fix-flip-mortgage-bonds-wall-streets-new-housing-bet-boost-home-flippers/.

Williamson, Judith. *Decoding Advertisements: Ideology and Meaning in Advertising.* London: Marion Boyars, 1978.

Wiltermuth, Joy. "Blackstone Pays Up but Wins Big on New SFR Bond." *Yahoo! Life*, May 23, 2014. https://www.yahoo.com/lifestyle/tagged/health/blackstone-pays-wins-big-sfr-151926023.html.

———. "Lending Standards to Slide for Homeowners with Spotty Credit, Moody's Warns in 2020 Outlook." *MarketWatch*, December 10, 2019. https://www.marketwatch.com/story/lending-standards-to-slide-for-homeowners-with-spotty-credit-moodys-warns-in-2020-outlook-2019-12-10.

Wolfe, Edward, Lindsey A. Owens, and Esra Burak. "How Much Wealth Was Destroyed?" In *The Great Recession*, edited by David B.Grusky, Bruce Western, and Christopher Wimer, 127–157. New York: Russell Sage Foundation, 2011.

Zaloom, Caitlin. "How to Read the Future: The Yield Curve, Affect, and Financial Prediction." *Public Culture* 21, no. 2 (2009): 245–268.

Žižek, Slavoj. *The Sublime Object of Ideology.* London: Verso, 1989.

Index

Aalbers, Manuel, 93, 187, 194, 204
Abood, Maya, 65, 189
Accumulation by dispossession, 97, 105, 111, 113, 131, 156, 177
Aesthetic modernism, 133; and affect, 76–77, 137, 145; codes and design value, 32, 53–54, 83, 113, 118, 135; commodity, 86, 113, 114, 117, 120, 132, 135, 151, 153; desire and gratification, 32, 46, 47; and feminine sensibilities, 143, 152; of industrial, rustic, and shabby chic, 8, 30, 42, 102, 113, 119, 133–134, 136, 149, 152–153; self-identity, 31, 47, 83, 119–120; signifiers, 83, 119; surplus value of the sign, 143; stylized, 112, 116, 135–136, 143; tastes and judgments, 4, 46, 119, 120, 133, 134, 142; value effect, 32, 47, 105, 117, 118, 128, 131–132, 135, 142–143, 146
Affordability of housing, 17, 59, 61, 70, 73–75, 79, 90, 96, 159; cost burdened housing, 74, 166, 178, 204; housing wage, 179
African American (Black) households, cultural appropriation of vernacular architecture, 130–131; and disinvestment, 155–156; on Good Bones, 96; and HGTV's colorblind representations, 156, 159; HGTV images of diversity, 47, 89; legacies of segregated housing, 122–123; loan discrimination, 37, 57, 155–156, 157–158; Moms 4 Housing, 179–180; subprime mortgages and foreclosures, 14, 65; transfers of wealth, 16, 65–66
Airbnb, celebrity rentals, 32; fix to rent, 46, 71; and gentrification, 93, 102, 117, 130; and premium rent gaps, 102, 128, 131
Albanesi, Stefania, Giacomo DiForgio, and Jaromir Nosal, 15, 183
Alexander, Michelle, 90
Allon, Fiona, 8, 19, 83, 182, 183, 185, 209
Alreadyness, 31, 128, 136
Althusser, Louis, 31
Anomie, 6, 172–173, 177
Appadurai, Arjun, 32, 119, 185, 198
Ascher, Ivan, 38, 62, 169, 173, 185, 187, 202, 203
ABS, Asset-backed securities, 5, 170
Auerbach, David, 20
Authenticity, 29; as anti-commodity meaning, 34; and artisanship, 153; historical, 43, 104; inauthenticity, 133; as moral code, 150; signification of, 135, 136

224 / Index

Banks, 2007–2008 financial crisis, 5, 13, 14, 15, 106; bank auctions, 97; bank foreclosures, 44, 58, 68, 110; Chase Bank ads customizing home renovation loans, 157; discriminatory banking practices, 156, 158; and fix-and-flip loans, 77; investment bankers trading in home loan derivatives, 37, 165, 172, 173–174; loan origination, 36; and structural violence, 97, 107, 160, 179
Barnwood Builders, 42, 113–114, 148–151
Barthes, Roland, 111–112, 118, 197
Baudrillard, Jean, 1, 24, 25, 30, 49, 118, 143, 171, 174–175, 177, 184, 185, 186
Bauman, Zygmunt, 41, 173, 186, 203
Berlant, Lauren, 18, 162, 183, 203
Best, Beverley, 176, 202, 203
Big reveal (the), 32, 39, 46, 49, 50, 54–56, 120–121, 146, 163, 175
Bricolage, 7, 42, 133, 143; reordering of signifiers and signifieds, 153
Bryan, Dick and Michael Rafferty, 14, 22, 169, 171, 183, 184, 185, 202, 203
Buckley, Michelle, 160–161, 201
Budgets, 5, 16, 17, 46–48, 49, 50, 82, 120, 126, 157; connotation, 160; managing the budget, 52, 53, 118; calculation, 126, 160, 163
Burd-Sharps, Sarah and Rebecca Rasch, 156, 189, 201

Circulation, 22, 24; arrested, 40; and commodity afterlife, 41, 42, 51; of houses, 63; cultural, 93; and finance capital, 169–170, 172, 174; recirculation of commodities, 40, 51, 127; of risk, 173; of sign values, 30–31, 119, 172; and salvage economy, 40, 42; velocity, 51, 169–174; speed of circulation, 37, 41, 51
Commodification, 86, 166; of affect, 33; of authenticity, 136; customized, 153; home as master commodity, 4; of lifestyle, 103; overcommodification, 34
Commodity culture, 1, 2, 24–25, 27; alienated, 34, 76–77; and Wayfair appropriation, 153; and the structural law of value, 174
Commodity fetishism, 4, 11, 46, 54, 111, 117, 127–128, 145, 150; commodity sign fetishism, 142; fetishism of value, 172; fetishized signifiers, 47; slow motion, 54; interior design porn, 85; real-estate porn, 47, 76
Commodity form, 25, 28–29, 127, 161, 162, 165, 169; hegemony of, 29; and semiotics, 30; law of equivalence exchange, 28, 31, 139, 171. *See also* Money form; Value form
Commodity signs, 136, 143; as brand values, 174; fetishism, 142; structural law of value, 30–31, 174, 175, 176
CDOs, Collateralized debt obligations, 6, 164, 173–175, 203
Comps, 33–34, 93–94, 96, 129, 132, 194
Consumption, alienated, 34; built environment for gentrified consumption, 86; consumer capitalism, 3, 11; debt-fueled, 19; hyperreal commodity culture, 175; overconsumption, 165; and second mortgages, 2, 63, 164; as signification practices, 30; as site for value articulation, 22, 25; sublimating anxieties, 162; consumer oriented speculative economy, 178
Consumers, debt and credit, 38, 156–157, 164–166; desire, 7, 46, 48, 54, 76, 79, 116, 128, 146; HGTV's consumer-oriented models, 9, 178; as investors, 127, 168; as performers of affective labor, 146; as spectators performing interpretive labor, 31, 33; and theories of value, 27–28
Contradictions, of financialization and housing, 7; of commodity fetishism, 128; of cultural economies, 19; of derivatives and liquidity, 17; of finance capitalism and consumer indebtedness, 18; of flipping economy, 58, 61; and affordability, 74; of sign value, 24, 136; of urban inequality, 85, 119; of value and value form, 22, 25, 161, 169; between political economy and cultural economy, 25; between wages and asset accumulation, 83, 164; between wages and automation, 11; between wages and consumer "freedom," 18, 29, 83, 164
Creative destruction, 12–13, 35–36, 43, 46, 51–52, 105
Creative erasure, defined, 105; as narrative strategy, 9; as ideology, 12–13, 35, 51, 104–109, 115
Credit scores, 15; discrimination, 159, 201; FICO, 79, 166–167, 171; classification and sorting, 158–159, 167, 160; self-policing

tool, 167; surveillance device, 167; and securitization, 166–167
CDSs, Credit default swaps, 5, 6, 14, 173–174, 175
Crisis, 3, 182; of affordability, 74, 79, 94, 96, 159; anomic crisis of value, 6, 17, 172–173, 177; conjunctural crisis, 61, 169; credit default crisis, 3, 4, 15, 58, 147, 164–166, 178; derivatives, 3, 65, 67; of faith, 5, 165, 176; 2007–2008 financial, 3–6, 10, 17, 36, 38, 64, 87, 93, 108, 155, 158; foreclosure and eviction, 1, 58, 60, 65, 97, 179, 189; of hyperreal finance, 3, 172, 174–177; of legibility, 176–177; legitimation, 6; 2007–2008 mortgage crisis, 6, 7, 9, 12, 14–19, 65, 73, 76, 85, 93, 110, 160, 165, 168; of neoliberalism, 17; of referentiality, 176–177; of spiraling wealth inequality, 38, 82, 158, 165; subprime crisis narrative, 14–17, 65; of value, 3, 5, 6, 17, 19, 173. *See also* Narratives of crisis
Cruel optimism, 162, 177
Cultural economy of value, 12, 19, 153, 174
Curation; commodity accents, 104, 135–136; cultural capital, 76; culture industry, 108; feminized labor, 135; memorabilia and signifiers of history, 112; self-identity, 33, 121; staging, 53; style choices, 47, 135

Debord, Guy, 22, 184
Debt, as risk asset, the debt question, 7; 14, 19, 36–38, 59, 80, 161, 165, 169–171, 173; household debt, 4, 7, 14, 18, 38, 62, 163–165, 170; indebtedness, 5, 14, 18, 83, 162, 163–164; overleveraged debt, 15, 38, 76, 106, 164; as moral defect, 163, 167; mortgage, 15–16, 38, 63, 172; as obligation, 5, 7, 36–37; repayment, 38; trading debt obligations, 36; securitizing debt, 37; 83
Defaults, credit default, 166; subprime mortgage defaults, 15; real-estate flippers defaults, 15–16; mortgage default, 1, 15–17, 37, 58, 64–65, 75, 97; risks of default, 163–164, 172, 173
Deleuze, Gilles and Felix Guattari, 21, 184
Demolition, ritual, 39, 46; purging the past, 51–52, 111; symbolic violence, 51, 105; dumpster debris, 115; low-wage labor, 160. *See also* Creative destruction

Derivatives, 5, 11, 13, 38, 41, 65, 67, 142, 168, 169, 171–172, 174, 175, 176, 202, 203. *See also* CDOs; CDSs; MBSs
Deterritorialization, 28, 81, 93
Devaluation, decay, 85; 104, 156; HGTV dialectic of devaluation and valuation, 36; due to crises, 9, 87, 97; due to disinvestment, 9, 108, 110, 129, 156; due to oversaturation, 24, 30; loss of differentiation, 24, 41; semiotics of, 104, 126; and uneven development, 61
Discounts on houses, abstracted, 11–12; bloodless, 16; foreclosure discounts, 67, 85; suburban, 35; distressed properties, 44, 64, 68, 107; granite, 48; speculative, 63, 64; and profit margins, 66–67; competition advantages for discounted properties, 68, 71, 73; shrinking, 97; deep-discount HGTV renovations, 92, 99, 107; rent-gap discounts, 81, 104; adding value, 130; discount exploitation, 156; informal labor market discounts, 160
Discourses about value, 18; discursive contests and volatility, 22; discursive economy of value, 168; discursive power of derivatives, 176; HGTV as discursive site, 24; HGTV and discursive labor, 32; value as discursive construct, 21–22; spectacle and discursive circulation, 22–23
Disinvestment, central city, 96, 108; discount opportunity, 126, 156; and gentrification frontier, 109–110; LLC's, 70; racially motivated, 43, 84, 94, 97, 106, 127, 129. *See also* Devaluation
Displacement, 2, 95–97, 105, 109; flipping as displacement machine, 179
Dispossession, 82, 96, 106, 109, 155–156, 160–161
Douglas, Mary, 40, 52, 186, 187
Durkheim, Emile, 163, 172–173
Dwyer, Rachel and Lois Lassus, 65, 189

Elson, Diane, 161, 183, 201
Entitlement, 39, 48; on a budget, 82; commodity look, 83; 100, 168
Entrepreneur, entrepreneurial consumer, 10, 61, 168; entrepreneurial innovator, 35; entrepreneurial investors, 15; entrepreneurial labor, 7, 10, 137–138, 151; HGTV ideology of entrepreneurial labor, 7;

Entrepreneur (*continued*)
HGTV as spirit of entrepreneurial capital, 8, 138, 171; and moral economy, 5, 34; and neoliberalism, 8, 167; renovators and flippers as heroes, 44, 45, 77, 89, 90; representations of moral entrepreneurs, 5, 8, 90, 167–168; and venturous risk, 39, 109, 167

Erasure, 51, 105; of bankers, brokers and lenders, 105, 107, 154–157; of capitalism, 2; of debt and the mortgage economy, 16, 105, 155, 160, 165; of defaults, 11, 16, 105; of discrimination, 57; of disinvestment, 106; of displacement, 96, 105, 112; of dispossession, 106; of evictions, 11, 58, 106; of financialization and securitization, 36, 105, 107; of foreclosures, 11–12, 57–58, 105–107, 163; of housing geographies, 11, 91; of history, 12, 85, 104, 108, 111–112, 114; of loans, 57, 197, 154–155; of low wage racialized labor, 160; of nature and climate change, 115–116; of neighbors and neighborhoods, 87, 93–94, 104, 105; of neoliberal politics, 58, 106; of poverty, 11, 82, 96, 110–111, 126–127; of racial discrimination, 9, 11, 57, 82, 105, 111, 155–159; of subprime loans, predatory lending and mortgage crisis, 12, 46, 58, 82, 105, 160, 163; of urban geography and real-estate markets, 9–11, 93, 106, 107–108, 109; utopia of erasure, 105; as violence, 105; visual frames and visual effects, 10, 29, 39, 56, 57, 83, 85, 105, 129, 168

Evictions, evict to flip, 180; rates, 65, 72; serial evictions, 68, 190; as structural violence, 58, 97, 106. *See also* Foreclosures

Finance Capital, increasing reliance on circulation, 18, 22, 169–172; bypassing production, 13–14; circuits of value extraction, 24, 39, 106, 167–169; 173, 176; contradictions, 17, 18, 161, 169; flows of global investment, 72; global crisis, 1, 6, 41; global investment firms, 78; hyperreal, 13, 174; leveraged debt, 14, 16, 59, 159, 163–164, 170–171, 172; leveraging enhanced profitability, 73; new paradigm of value, 173; neoliberal, 5, 6, 138; political economy, 14, 161; and restructuring of real estate, 62, 65; and real subsumption, 170; and rental housing investing, 68; and securitization, 36–39, 93; risk as prime asset, 5, 169; speculative bets, 5, 9, 169; and wage labor, 141–142, 169; Wall Street, 14, 66, 72, 79, 80, 174. *See also* Names of specific finance capital firms

Financial speculation, as crisis trigger, 5, 13, 17; betting on risk, 169; flipping pre-crisis and generalized price speculation, 60, 63, 67; institutional speculators corning foreclosure market, 66; and investors in REO market, 98; real-estate speculators, 15–16, 64; wagers on future prices, 63, 172

Financialization, and 2007 leverage crisis, 93, 106; of homeowners, housing and precarity, 7, 36, 76, 161, 177, 196; of housing as object of leveraged investment, 19, 164; and flipping industry, 60; and changing value form, 161, 168; expropriation of household debt, 14, 32, 170; hyperreal, 175; leveraged risk and debt, 5, 16; methodology of extracting wealth, 18; politics of, 106–107; and sphere of circulation, 170–171

Fintech, financial technology, 66, 79; algorithms, 68, 190, 191; artificial intelligence, 68, 69; speed and efficiency in investment circuits, 69; big data, 69, 190, 193

Fixer Upper (Joanna and Chip Gaines), 2, 11; celebrity labor, 140–141; celebrity value, 33; demo day, 51; design style leader, 30, 32; embourgeoisement fantasy, 86, 88; as entrepreneurial heroes, 44; family life, 88, 152; and gendered labor, 144–145; home decorating philosophy, 111, 117, 119–136; instant equity, 56, 117; and local artisans, 151–153; most popular renovation show, 77; open concept, 92; orgasms of value, 54; staging, 53, 55; therapeutic performance, 147; TV ad, 107; upscaling, 91, 95

Fixer-Upper effect (aka Magnolia effect in Waco), 101–103, 124; economic multiplier effect, 99, 128, 131, 195

Flip or Flop (Tarek and Christina El Moussa), 2; auctions, 46; bubble pushers chasing risk, 96–97, 98, 107–108; calculus of interior design, 119; declining rate

of profit and strategy, 194; distressed housing and predatory flipping, 58–59; flipper show, 43, 77; flipping as rolling investments, 45; gendered flipping roles, 144; generic flips, 50; speed, 51; ghostly labor, 139; houses as fungible commodities, 88; philosophy of flipping, 93–94, 107; staging, 53; top dollar, 43–44, 75; transaction formula, 154; use of comps, 132; vandalism, 57–58
Flea Market Flip, 42, 153
Flippers, cash versus loans, 64; fix-and-flippers, 71; HGTV as motivator, 78–80; investor-driven, 59, 64–65, 67, 68, 70; predatory flippers, 46, 58–59, 98, 161; professionalization, 69, 70, 77; real estate investors as flippers, 15, 77–78. *See also* Investor Strategies
Foreclosures, bank foreclosures (REOs) and foreclosure markets, 9, 17, 44, 58, 68, 70, 94; crisis of, 1, 7, 9, 179; and discounts, 67, 71, 85; and fix-and-flip markets, 77; foreclosure crisis and flipping, 46, 50, 60, 61–62, 65, 75, 77, 85; and geographies of flipping and gentrification, 64, 97–98, 179; turned into empires of rent, 65; structural violence and value added flipping, 12, 57–58, 77, 98, 160; subprime foreclosures, 14, 16–17, 65; and vandalism, 58
Fourcade, Marion and Kieran Healy, 159, 167

Gentrification, consumer-oriented, 9; interior centric; 10, 94; aestheticized on TV, 9; and Airbnb, 93, 102, 117, 124, 128, 130, 131; class politics, 81; 98–101, 107; collateral, 85; diffused, 93; distributed gentrification and flipping, 92–93; frontier, 105; faith-based, 124; and flipping, 67, 85, 94; generalized, 9, 35, 92, 102; geography free, 35, 93–94, 97; HGTV's rent-gap sales pitch, 48, 81, 85, 88, 91, 124; leveraging ground rent, 102; and mortgage crisis, 93; without neighborhoods, 10; neoliberal, 8–9, 122; renovation gentrification, 48; rent-gap gentrification, 9, 35, 48, 94–95; and settler colonialism, 123; and structural racism, 59; suburban, 19, 30, 35, 46, 84, 92, 95; television simulation, 85–86, 112

Geography, abstracted, 35, 69, 93, 88, 109; in abstracto, 91
Glantz, Aaron and Emmanuel Martinez, 156, 158, 187, 189, 201
Glynos, Jason, Robin Klimecki, and Hugh Willmott, 147, 200
Good Bones (Mina Starsiak and Karen Laine), 45, 95–96, 108–111, 144, 153
Goodman, Laurie and Karan Paul, 192
Gottesdiener, Laura, 12, 65, 66, 97, 183, 189, 190, 195
Guthman, Julie, 8, 182

Hackworth, Jason and Neil Smith, 92–93, 194
Hall, Stuart and Doreen Massey, 61
Harvey, David, 8, 17, 20, 22, 35, 113, 169
Hawkes, David, 175, 203
Hay, James, 8, 168, 182, 202
HGTV narrative formula, 1, 33, 39; flipping and renovation formula, 46–56; and ideological bias, 163; narrative absences, 57–58; time compression, 51; visual formula, 141
HGTV narratives, of aesthetic modernism, 11, 132–133, 136; color-blind gentrification, 82; of color-blind multiculturalism, 12–13, 57, 82, 89–90, 124, 156, 159, 194; creative erasure, 9; of diversity and inclusion, 12, 47, 89, 90; of entrepreneurial moral economy, 5, 88; entrepreneurial risk management, 39, 53, 161; of family sanctuary, hearth and home, 4, 11, 44, 47, 56, 81, 86–87, 88–89, 103, 131, 144, 152; forever dream home, 13, 82, 103, 117, 127, 130–131, 152, 172, 177; of gentrification, 9, 10, 85, 86, 106, 124; geography of nowhere, 91, 93; of home ownership and wealth building, 6, 7, 17–18, 57, 87, 156, 159; of instant equity and wealth effect, 116, 117, 120, 127, 130; of interior space, 92; of labor, 7–8, 29, 59, 137–161; of moral re-centering of family home, 11, 42, 56; of neoliberal entitlement, 82, 168; of neoliberal ideology, 4, 59; nostalgia, 18, 162; of salvage capitalism, 39, 43; home renovation narratives, 5, 8; restoration of value, 6, 7, 11, 42; of time compression, 50–51, 53, 127, 138; of value added, 12, 16, 46, 85, 119, 128, 132, 145, 159, 161, 163

High tech, algorithms and nonhuman actors, 7, 68, 167, 177, 191; automation and job loss, 3, 10; computerized modeling, securities and real-estate, 14, 68, 74, 191; and finance capital, 161; and fintech, 190, 191, 193; high-tech devaluing labor, 11, 29; innovation and creative destruction, 35, 52; internet fever, 62; online technology, 66; digital finance technologies, 169, 170, 175; versus hand tool technology, 148

Hispanic (households), HGTV images of diversity, 47, 156; loan discrimination, 37, 155; subprime exploitative lending, 12, 14; transfer of wealth, 16, 65–66; in Waco, 99, 122

History as signified; as curated commodity accents and patina of use, 104, 112; as erasure and curation, 112; and semiotic codes, 153; saving material artifacts, 114; signifiers of charm and character, 104, 112; simulating the look of history, 152–153; visual signifier, 111

Hoarders, 40–41, 186

Hochschild, Arlie, 145

Homelessness, 8, 58, 178–179

Home Town, 133, 153

Horning, Rob, 138, 199

Housing asset bubble, 44, 62; burst, 64; contradictions of financialized housing, 107; crisis, 174; flippers and bubble tendencies, 74; bubble pushers, 96–97; HGTV and housing bubble, 75–77, 82; HGTV's utopian space, 177; mortgage indebtedness, 164; rapidly inflated asset values, 63, 83; return to the bubble, 147; and subprime loans, 67

House flipping, as master narrative of value, 2, 27; and class struggle, 107, 179–180; and housing affordability, 67, 75; fixer uppers, path to wealth and security, 12, 16–17, 63; flipping as political economy, 2008-2018, 60–80; flipping as gentrification, 9; HGTV and the flipping economy, 75–80

Huber, Matthew, 84, 193, 116, 197

Hyperreal, finance capital, 6, 13, 172, 174–175, 178; and hegemony, 203; HGTV's spectacular flipping model, 61, 83, 120, 132, 172, 175, 177, 178, 203; models and simulations, 49, 175; securities and derivatives, 174–176; and structural law of value, 174

Immergluck, Dan, 196

Income Property (Scott McGillivray), 45, 56, 91, 120

Individual investors, citizen-speculator, 19; homeowners as consumers and investors, 6, 45, 63, 85, 127, 128, 164, 168; and fix-and-flip loans, 71, 72, 80; hard money loans, 64, 71; competitive disadvantages, 68, 69–70; and online resources, 69; and uneven markets, 60, 62. *See also* Mom and pop investors

Individualism, 10, 18–19, 21, 28, 39, 161 (neoliberal), 165, 184

Instant equity, 29, 56, 116–117, 120–122, 127–130, 132, 163, 171

Institutional real-estate investors, and MBSs, 37; acquisition of REO foreclosures, 65, 68, 71, 78; bulk purchases, 74, 179; and cap rates, 71–72; SFR flipping to rent economy, 60, 67–70, 74; siphoning wealth, 65, 97; surplus cash and lines of credit, 64, 72, 78

Interior spaces, 2, 10; blank slate, 35, 92; as curated sanctuary, 53, 83; insulated, 82; open-concept, 89–90; as petit-bourgeois utopias, 48–49; privatized landscapes, 13, 59, 105; and TV gentrification, 85–87, 128; and visual ontology, 85

Investing strategies pre-crisis, 63, 77, 98; arbitrage, 63; buy-to-rent, 98; flipping McMansions, 74; milkers, 98; predatory flippers, 59, 98

Investing strategies post-crisis, 64, 77; flipping smaller houses, 74; global cash infusion, 72; REO to rental and securitization, 65, 67–68; renovate to sell, 75; flip to rent, 69–70, 74, 80; professional flippers, 69, 70; professional investors, 6, 64

Labor, labor's relation to value, 10–11, 13–14, 21, 28–29; labor and debt, 38; abstract, 139–141, 159; aesthetic labor, 135, 142–145, 159; artisanal, 28, 29, 125, 137, 141, 151–153; bricoleur, 153; as capital, 171; celebrity, 28, 32, 140–141; as commodity, 28–29, 139–140; construction

labor, 140; creative imagination, 34, 42, 142, 144, 153; decorating as curation, 31, 111, 135, 144; design, designers, 32–34, 43, 49, 53, 54, 76, 83; 56, 76, 142–143; discursive, 32; emotional and affective, 33–34, 137, 138, 145–147, 200; entrepreneurial, 7, 137–138, 151, 171; feminized, 142–145; ghostly, 138–141, 142, 159; heroization, 7, 144, 148, 161; independent, honest, hard work, 6, 8, 149–150; immaterial, 137, 138, 142, 145, 154, 161, 199; interior design, 2, 47, 53, 76, 83, 85, 135, 143–144; interpretive, 31, 33, 145, 146; renovation, 50; material versus unproductive, 149; migrant, 132, 160–161; remoralizing value, 11; sign labor, 145; staging, 53; sweat equity, 11, 28, 29; and time-compressed representations of labor (slow motion and speed-ups), 139–141; virtuoso, 53, 145, 151. See also Value
Labor power, 139–141
Labor theory of value, 10, 21, 29, 161. See also Value theory of labor
Labor time, 28, 51, 140–141
Landy, Benjamin, 63, 188
Lapavitsas, Costas, 24, 183, 202
Lawson, Richard, 101, 186
Lazzarato, Maurizio, 167, 168, 199, 202
Legibility, rules of value, 6, 11, 172–173, 176–177
Lewis, Michael, 173, 174
Lévi-Strauss, Claude, 153
LLC, limited liability corporations, 70–71, 179, 191, 204
Liquidity, 17, 36–37, 41, 68, 169, 170, 171–172, 185, 198
Loans, bridge loans, 191; bundled, 37–38; crowd sourcing, 69; 107; fintech lending, 66, 69, 190, 191; fix-and-flip loans, 38, 51, 64, 66–68, 71, 77–80, 188, 190; hard money loans, 64, 71, 77, 79, 107; online lenders, 66, 69; originate-and-distribute model, 36; pre-crisis and post-crisis home loans, 63–64, 66, 73; renovation, 50. See also Subprime loans
Locke, John, 10, 21, 105

Macpherson, C.B., possessive individualism, 21
Mann, Geoff, 161, 169, 201, 202

Marx, Karl, 10, 17, 20, 21, 22, 27, 28, 103, 139–141, 161, 200; and Frederick Engels, 35, 185, 186
Maurer, Bill, 174, 176, 203
McClanahan, Annie, 19, 183
McLaughlin, Ralph, 66–67, 187, 188, 190, 191, 192
Miller, Daniel, 21, 184
Modernism, and aesthetic appearances, 11, 30, 132–136, 152, 153; and creative destruction, 52, 92; farmhouse, 8, 11, 30, 44, 117, 133–135; midcentury nostalgia, 3, 47, 84, 116, 153, 162; salvage, 102, 135
Molina, Emily, 97–98
Mom and pop flippers/investors, 60, 68; populist imagery, 59, 71; entrepreneurs, 78; flip to rent, 69, 79; and LLCs, 70; fix-and-flip loans, 71, 78, 79, 98; inexperienced rookies, 64, 78, 79; foot soldiers for securitization, 59, 60, 80; and HGTV motivations, 78–79, 88, 98; as landlords, 65, 71, 79. See also Investors
Money, circuits of capital, 69; currency as universal equivalence, 26, 28, 171; digital, 41; expression, representation of value, 20–22, 24, 26, 142; making money, 9, 42–44; price appreciation, 63, 108, 172; and price tags of value, 4, 26, 29, 34, 47, 49, 62, 75, 131, 171; and time (speed), 51, 69, 140
Money form, and abstraction of value, 28, 174; deterritorialized, 28, 41; derivatives realized in, 11; flipper's metric, 43–44, 76, 119; Locke, 10; value's measure, 14
Moral economy versus money economy, 5, 6, 34, 148–149, 155, 168, 182
Morality of value; amoral system of financial abstractions, 11, 168, 177; Barnwood Builders restoration of moral order, 42, 148, 150; commodity morality, 56; Hoarders as value parable, 40; remoralizing the home, 177; remoralizing markets; 155; remoralizing neoliberal real estate, 168, 172–173, 177; remoralizing value, 5–6, 8, 11, 133, 154; salvaging the morality of housing markets, 17, 148, 163, 177
MBS, mortgage-backed securities, 5, 14, 15, 17, 25, 36–38, 67, 68, 164, 166, 170, 173–174

Mrozowski, Daniel, 40
Must haves and wish lists, 46–47; cultural homogeneity, 101; entitlement, 48; fetishized, 16; a roof and four walls, 179; versus budgets, 47
Myth of Sisyphus, 23–24

Names of specific finance capital firms, American Homes for Rent, 65; Amherst Holdings, 68; Bank of America, 8, 98; Blackstone, 65, 67–68, 72–73, 79, 189–190; BNY Mellon, 68; Colony Homes, 65; Deutsche Bank, 66, 189; Fannie Mae, 74; Goldman Sachs, 77, 78, 79, 169, 189; Genesis Capital, 77, 78; JP Morgan, 78, 189; KKR, 78, 79; Lehman Brothers, 13; Morgan Stanley, 189; Nomura Holdings, 78; Opendoor, 68, 191, 193; Softbank, 68, 78, 79; Starwood Waypoint Residential Trust, 67; Wedgewood Property Management, 179–180; Wells Fargo, 78; Zillow, 68, 75, 157, 190, 191, 193. *See also* Fintech
Narratives of the 2007-2008 crisis, 13–17
Neighbors, avoidance of, 83, 86, 78, 98, 101, 105
Neighborhoods, and valuation, 26, 29, 35, 81, 84, 91, 94, 110, 126–128, 132; and discriminatory disinvestment, 155–156; flippers in poor neighborhoods, 66, 94, 98–99; flipping, gentrification and class conflict, 98–101, 160–161, 179; and foreclosures, 64; gentrifying, 57, 85, 92, 95–96, 97, 122–125; invisibility on HGTV, 35, 85–86, 98, 104–106; central city and geography of poverty, 108–110; and tourist districts, 128
Neoliberalism, defined, 8; capitalism, 5, 61, 162, 165; globalization, 3, 169, 173; housing market, 106, 132, 162, 168; ideology, 9, 12, 39, 59, 86, 161, 167; individual freedom and entitlement, 59, 82, 161; lessons of risk reward, 53; politics of risk shifting and state policy, 4, 76, 167–169, 171; neoliberal society, 4, 5; 17, 167; and salvage capitalism, 7, 42, 169; and securitization, 165; and suburbanism, 85, 107; and urbanism, 8–9, 104
Nostalgia, 6, 25, 113, 147, 162, 165

Open concept, and aesthetic desire, 48; architecture of interior space, 47, 51, 92; blank slate, 92, 105; color-blind, 82, 89; and conceptions of family life, 89; customized, 85; and entertaining, 56; and erasure, 51; and freedom, 12, 89, 90, 105; and gilded cage, 143; unfettered space; 163; and unfreedom, 179
Orléan, André, 172

Poverty, disinvestment and poverty, 122; signifiers of poverty and disinvestment, 96, 125–126; suburban, 85, 95, 98; urban, 96, 109, 123, 124, 127, 178–179; working-class, 11, 96, 97–98, 99–100, 110, 122–123, 127, 131, 160. *See also* Disinvestment
Precarity, 1; of debt, 5; of homeownership, 7, 177; of housing, 38, 65, 107, 163, 178–179; of labor, 160–161; of value, 17
Property Brothers (Jonathon and Drew Scott), 2, 16, 77; approachability, 83; client-focused, 44; exemplar of HGTV narrative formula, 48–56; generic narrative curve, 46; hiding geography, 34, 85, 91–92, 93; invisibility of TV realtors, 154; selling commodity lifestyles, 117, 135; spectacle of entitlement, 168; performing therapeutically, 146–147; in Toronto, 160; tournament of value, 116; visualizing open-concept rent gap strategies, 84, 85, 88; the value of appearances, 132, 135

Racial discrimination, and 2008 crisis, 37, 65; and disinvestment, 94, 97, 156; 96; use of credit scores, 157–158, 168; critique of color blindness, 89–90; mortgage and lending discrimination, 12, 57, 155–159, 160, 166; predatory inclusion, 12, 201; predatory lending and subprime loans, 12, 14, 37–38, 82, 97, 106; and racial wealth gap, 65, 98, 158, 189, 201; racialized urban geographies, 11, 106, 122, 128–129; and disinvestment, 90, 123, 124, 127, 156, 179; redlining, 82, 87, 97, 106, 158; reverse redlining, 106; structural racism, 12, 13, 59, 84, 129. *See also* Erasure; Predatory lending
Real subsumption, 138, 166, 170, 177
Referentiality, crisis and hyperreal finance, 13, 172, 174–177; derivatives and fictional referents, 174; derivatives in self-referential loop, exchanged against themselves, 174; loss of referentiality, 13,

132; referentiality crisis and 2007–2008, 177; referential slippage, 111; referents, estranged from valuations, 12, 132; self-referential signs of value, 25; self-referential value measured against price, 172; valuations unchained from referents, 12, 30, 171, 174

Rehab Addict (Nicole Curtis), 43, 77, 88, 95, 119, 144, 153

Regimes of value, 6, 24–25

Renters, 67–68, 96, 99, 138, 189; and compressed cap rates, 73; corporate rent empires, 61, 65, 67, 68, 71; cost burdened rentership, 74, 166; rent hikes, 17, 65, 68, 72, 97; rent insecurity, 17, 65; rent stream payments, 8, 45, 59, 67, 70, 71, 97; rentier class, 45, 161

Rent gap and gentrification, 9, 35, 81–82; as consumer lifestyle choice; 84–85; declining rates of profit, 194; HGTV and rent gap formula, 9–10, 85, 95; rent-gap discount, 81, 104; suburban rent gap, 84, 87, 93–95, 96, 97, 99, 104, 122, 124

REO, Real-estate owned, aka Bank owned, 58, 65, 70, 74, 97–98, 110. *See also* Foreclosures

ROI, Return on investment, 42, 93, 117, 120, 127, 132, 138, 145, 170

Rifkin, Jeremy, 184

Risk, as an asset, 38, 165, 169; hedging risk and defaults, 173, 176; high risk lending, 37, 79, 106; leveraging debt risk, 5, 38, 170, 173; and liquidity, 171–172; managing risk on HGTV, 48, 52–53, 116, 147; risk economy, 5, 52–53, 169–172, 174; risk investing, 4, 37–38, 44; representations of risk on HGTV, 39, 43, 46, 58, 97, 110; shifting risk, 8, 38, 169–170; as tradable commodity, 173; tranches of risk, 38, 163–164, 174

Rubenstein, Diane, mirror of reproduction, 22, 184

Sacrifice, and value realization, 27, 33, 54

Salvage Dawgs, 42, 153

Salvage capitalism, salvage economies, salvage accumulation, 1, 2, 9, 19, 42–43, 149, 153, 169; and bricolage, 7, 42, 133, 153; and gentrification, 129; HGTV's translation of, 9, 17, 18, 19, 39; and labor forms, 137; and neoliberalism, 7, 9, 19, 39, 42; 161, 169, 172; salvage modernism, 102, 133; as secondary circuit of capital, 129

Salvage television narratives, 7, 39, 40–43, 145, 153; flipping, 27, 43–44, 161; formula, 27; renovation, 7, 11, 16, 44–45, 91, 145; rehabilitation, 43, 94; salvage contests, 41–42

Securitization, 8, 36–39, 41, 59, 67, 69; and deterritorialized mortgages, 93; housing precarity and rent insecurity, 65; leverage, 72–73; 80, 93, 142, 167, 168–171, 189; leveraged financial instruments, 142, 173

Securities, fix-and-flip loan backed securities, 38, 68, 71, 77–78, 80; mortgage backed securities, 5, 14–15, 18, 36–39, 67, 164, 170; rent check backed securities, 38, 68, 72–73, 189

Semiotics, commodity semiotics and political economy, 19, 168; bricolage as applied semiotics, 42; codes, 30–31; commodity aesthetics, 83, 117, 119; and commodity form, 30; of consumer desire, 46, 79, 83; erasing histories, 112, 152; HGTV as a semiotic factory, 19, 30, 39; of interior design, 83; predetermined binaries, 46; pump-priming, 79; recombining disconnected signifiers, 42, 87; of renovation value, 39, 48, 118–119; reproduction of work of art, 54

Settler colonialism, 111, 112–114, 123, 148

Shimpach, Shawn, 8, 15, 53–54

Schumpeter, Joseph, 35, 43

Signifiers, aesthetic modernism, 133–134; of cultural capital, 76; demolition of the past, 51; family life, 152; farmhouse modernism, 135; floating signifiers, 28, 175; hyperactive labor, 139; of lifestyle envy, 18; neutral, 50; nostalgia, 151; organized by the code, 118; rustic, 30; second-order, 111, 126; unhinged and reordered to produce sign values, 5, 9, 30, 31, 43, 153

Sign value, 30–32; aesthetic surplus value, 143; appropriation of hot signs, 13; brand value, 30, 174; celebrity as motivator, 33; circulation, 30–31, 91, 119; contradictions, 24; currency of, 83; differentiation, 31; emotional management, 137; fetishism, 117; HGTV as a system of visual signs, 19, 39, 53; HGTV's renovation code, 118; labor as sign, 140–141; modernism in a sign economy,

Sign value (*continued*) 132–133; reproducing sign value, 48; self-referential, 24–25, 30–32, 119, 143; sign economy, 12, 132; sign economy and political economy, 169; signification of value, 118; staging, 143

Simmel, Georg, 27, 48, 184, 186

Simulacrum, 39, 61, 83

Simulation, 11, 3D modeling, 46, 49; of bourgeois appearances, 48, 56, 58, 124; of class and lifestyle status, 53, 87, 118; and redefining the real, 49; simulating history, 151–152; theory of, 175

SFRs. Single-family residential rentals, 67–69, 72–73, 74, 189–190, 191; single-family rental backed securities, 67, 72, 166

Slater, Tom, 93, 97, 194, 195

Smith, Neil, 9, 81, 84, 85, 109, 182, 194, 196

Society of the spectacle, 22–25, 32, 50 (and time), 75; influencing valuations, 117, 119, 142, 159 (and representation) 162, 168, 174, 184

Staging, 32, 39, 46, 53–54, 143, 186

Steil, Justin, Len Albright, Jacob Rugh, and Douglas Massey, 38, 185

Suburbs; and abstracted geography, 35; inner and middle rings, 84–85, 87, 92, 95–98, 116; and oil privatism, 116; spatial fix, 19, 195; suburban teardowns, 45–46. *See also* Gentrification

Subprime mortgage loans, and crisis, 4, 15, 65, 67; and default, 64, 65, 106; as demographic category, 12; foreclosures, 14, 16–17, 46, 58, 65, 67, 97, 105. *See also* Predatory lending; Racial discrimination

Taylor, Keeanga-Yamahtta, 12, 183, 201

Texas Flip N Move, working-class flippers, 45–46, 154

Tourism, 101–102; and Airbnb and gentrified housing, 117, 128; Magnolia effect, 128, 131; tourist gaze and real-estate gaze, 115, 128; and vacation homes, 113

Tournaments of value, 116, 119

Tsing, Anna, 5

Value, 1–8, 10–11; Capital, as value in motion, 17, 21, 25, 37; everyday meanings, 20–22; abstraction, 4, 6, 25, 28, 171, 176; aesthetics, 32, 47, 76; as appearances, 82; artisanship, 152–153; celebrity, 32–33, 102, 117, 131; and consumer preferences, 28; crisis of, 3, 6, 19; decoupling from labor, 11, 29, 142; design, 32, 54, 56, 142–143; and desire and pricing, 46–47, 48, 77; differentiation, 24, 31, 43; emotional/affect, 33, 46, 49, 54, 76–77; equivalence exchange, 171; exchange value, 10, 11, 21–22, 26–29, 30–32, 40, 56, 119, 131, 132, 171–172; as flows versus fixed assets, 25; fixer uppers, as remedy to crisis of value, 19; fractal value, 24, 175; immaterial, 23, 161; negation of value, 40; as a negotiated construct, 21; non-value, 35; perception, 27–28, 142; performative, 33, 146, 161; prestige, 26, 31, 32; as a relationship, 21; reproduction of, 22–24; reputational, 26, 32–33, 98; real estate, 34–35; risk and value, 169; scarcity/oversaturation, 29–30, 73, 130; social construction of, 22; speculative value, 176; surplus, 32, 106, 120, 143, 146, 169, 171, 172; symbolic interaction, 21, 23, 175; as a system of signs, 19; use, 27, 31, 40, 56, 127; via circulation, 42, 112, 113, 169; zombie, 35

Value added, the goal, 2; accounting, 132; before and after binaries, 55, 92; creative labor in interior spaces, 85, 159, 161; eco-chic vibe, 116; feminized labor, 145; flipping REO properties, 98; HGTV arithmetic, 120; HGTV flipping shows, 12, 16, 120, 128, 140, 146; HGTV narrative, 46; HGTV programming shift to, 77; Locke, 21; reputational, 32; via discounts, 130, 132, 140. *See also* HGTV narratives

Value form, in transition, 25; and aesthetics, 32; anti-commodity, 34; code governed, 31; derivatives, 36; historical changes, 168–169; interest payments, 170; Marx, 27; past and present, 161; and reference models, 175; securitization, 39. *See also* Commodity form

Value theory of labor, 10–11, 28, 51, 143, 145, 161, 172. *See also* Labor theory of value

Wages, 1950s wages, 3; and debt repayments, 38, 62, 74, 142; flat, and second mortgages, 2, 3, 4; and limits on consumption and on housing affordability, 11, 78, 176; wage exploitation, 159–160, 164

Wage labor, as cogs, 8; in era of finance capitalism, 142; and commodity form, 28–29; exploitation and profit in informal labor markets; 159–160, 169; crumbling wage system, 177; and financialization, 170–171; generic, 137–138; and measures of value, 11; representation of, 141–142; versus unalienated labor, 149–150; subsumption, 165–166
Wagner, Kate, 8, 74, 182, 186, 192, 199

Wealth gap and wealth inequality, 3, 62, 82, 83, 135, 158
Wealth transfer, crisis driven, 9, 16, 65–66, 97, 98, 107, 155, 160, 165, 170, 178
Wealth building via home ownership, 14, 160–161, 164, 170; and wealth loss, 16, 65
Williamson, Judith, 31

Žižek, Slavoj, 156, 201

Robert Goldman is a Professor Emeritus of Sociology at Lewis & Clark College. He is the author of *Reading Ads Socially*, and the coauthor, with Stephen Papson, of *Sign Wars: The Cluttered Landscape of Advertising*; *Nike Culture: The Sign of the Swoosh*; and *Landscapes of Capital: Representing Time, Space, and Globalization in Corporate Advertising*.

www.ingramcontent.com/pod-product-compliance
Lightning Source LLC
Chambersburg PA
CBHW020648230426
43665CB00008B/355